P9-CAT-481

WALKING CALIFORNIA'S STATE PARKS

Other books in the *Walking the West* series:

Walking the East Mojave

Walking Los Angeles

Walking Santa Barbara

Walking the California Coast

Walking Southern California

Walking California's State Parks

John McKinney

HarperCollins *West*
A Division of HarperCollins*Publishers*

HarperCollins*West* and the author, in association with the Rainforest Action Network, will facilitate the planting of two trees for every one tree used in the manufacture of this book.

WALKING CALIFORNIA'S STATE PARKS

Portions of this book have appeared in the author's hiking column in the *Los Angeles Times*.

FIRST HARPERCOLLINS EDITION

LIBRARY OF CONGRESS CATALOGING-IN-PUBLICATION DATA
McKinney, John
  Walking California's state parks: guide to over 100 historic
parks, preserves and wilderness areas / John McKinney —1st ed.
   p. cm.
  Includes index.
  ISBN (invalid) 0-06-258525-5
  1. Hiking—California—Guidebooks. 2. Parks—California—
Guidebooks. 3. Wilderness areas—California—Guidebooks.
4. California—Guidebooks. I. Title.
GV199.42.C2M36 1994
796.5'1'0974—dc20
          93-41518
          CIP

94 95 96 97 98 CWI 10 9 8 7 6 5 4 3 2 1

Book design and typography by Jim Cook
Maps designed by Susan Kuromiya
Illustrated by Deja Hsu

This edition is printed on acid-free paper that meets the American National Standards Institute Z39.48 Standard.

ACKNOWLEDGEMENTS

The author would like to express his sincere appreciation for the enthusiasm and guidance offered during the preparation of this guide by California Department of Parks and Recreation field personnel. A special thanks goes to all the rangers, district superintendents, and the many park employees who were unfailingly courteous and helpful to me during my visits to the more than 150 parks mentioned in this book. Another thank you goes to the California Park Rangers and the interpretive association members who field- and fact-checked the information in this guide.

  My most heartfelt thank you goes to Cheri Rae for her encouragement and deft editorial hand.

Contents

CENTRAL CALIFORNIA

Introduction

All of us own this land—more than a million acres of it. This land has names like Anza-Borrego, Castle Rock, Grizzly Creek and Richardson Grove.

This land with the colorful names is the California State Park system, widely regarded as the nation's finest.

Other states have high mountains, vast deserts, and scenic shorelines, but only California contains all of these natural features, and preserves examples of them in its park system.

The multitude of intriguing state park environments, and the many fine paths that explore them, add up to some world-class walking adventures—certainly some of the best walks in the West.

It's been my pleasure, as *Los Angeles Times* hiking columnist, to send my readers tripping afoot all over the West, all over the world. Time and time again, readers report that among the walks I've chronicled, the most pleasurable and popular walks they've taken are those in California's state parks.

Ancient redwoods grow along the mist-covered edge of the continent. The alpine beauty of the Sierra Nevada towers above Emerald Bay and Sugar Pine Point state parks on the shores of world-famous Lake Tahoe. Warm, sandy state beaches from San Clemente to Refugio beckon visitors to Southern California. The state's unique history comes alive at the Franciscan mission at La Purísima, the old Customs House in Monterey, the Russian chapel at Fort Ross.

State parks preserve a cross-section of California ecology from the bottom of the Central Valley at Caswell Memorial State Park to the top of alpine peaks at Mt. San Jacinto State Park; from uncommonly dry desert lands, where Joshua trees thrive, such as Saddleback Butte State Park to the near-rain forest environment of Del Norte Coast Redwoods State Park.

State parks showcase a fabulous array of Nature's handiwork: giant Sequoias in Calaveras Big Trees State Park; the rare Torrey pines making a last stand in a reserve near San Diego; palm oases in Anza-

Borrego Desert; some of the tallest trees on earth at Humboldt Red-woods.

State parks highlight California's history—and offer visitors the opportunity to follow the trails of the forty-niners, Spanish missionaries and Native Americans. Hike into history where the Gold Rush began (Marshall Gold State Historic Park), where a famed writer found inspiration (Jack London State Historic Park), where a lonely lighthouse-keeper lived and worked (Pt. Sur State Historic Park).

Park pathways are as varied as the parks themselves. Some trails are easy—a "walk in the park." Leg-stretchers along the Sacramento River at Woodson Bridge and Colusa state recreation areas allow motorists a break from Interstate 5; beach walks from Border Field State Park to MacKerricher State Beach provide a similar break from Coast Highway 1. Take short walks into history, past the Immigration Station on Angel Island, up Fremont Peak, named for the famed pathfinder.

Many state park walks are suitable for the whole family—slow-paced adventures with much to see on a short hike. These family hikes, by using described options, can usually be extended to half-day or even all-day outings.

The avid hiker will find challenges aplenty in the parks, too—long day hikes that offer grand tours and great workouts.

This guide is your invitation to adventure. You'll learn about the

history and natural attractions of California's state parks, as you walk some of California's best trails.

"The Best of California Forever" is the slogan of the California Department of Parks and Recreation. State parks preserve many stunning examples of California's varied landscape; they are yours to protect and enjoy.

California's State Parks

The California Department of Parks and Recreation administers some 275 state park "units," as park officials call them. Don't be surprised if you see or hear a number greater or lesser than 275 ("nearly 300" and "more than 250" are popular descriptions) because there's debate even within the Department about what to count where. When counting parks, does one count state parks administered and operated by a city or county parks department? Should parks acquired by the Department, but not yet open to the public, be counted?

In 1993, the Department began to introduce some "user-friendly" terms to describe itself. The "California Park System" is now often used instead of the redundant "California State Park System." And the Department of Parks and Recreation (or DPR as it's often known) has slowly been introducing the term "California Park Service" to the public.

We usually refer to the state's 200-something units as state parks, but they actually go by a half-dozen different descriptions:

State Parks, by definition, are major areas with outstanding scenic, scientific, natural, or cultural values. They are managed for both recreation and preservation.

State Historic Parks preserve structures and lands of historic interest. These parks may also commemorate a person or historic event.

State Wilderness is an area managed to best preserve the primeval character of the land. No permanent structures are permitted.

In a **State Reserve**, too, ecology comes first. They protect flora, fauna and geology adjudged to be of statewide significance.

State Recreation Areas, often centering around a lake or river, provide large-scale outdoor recreation opportunities and usually host a large number of visitors.

State Beaches have the most popular campgrounds and day-use areas.

California State Parks: A Brief History

Truly, with 275 state parks, there are 275 stories to tell. Each "unit" has a unique story. Each park contributes a page to the whole story—a story-in-the-making, really, because new parks, preserves, recreation areas and historic sites are added to the system every year.

While walking the parks, you'll learn some of these stories. Maybe you'll saunter Colusa-Sacramento River State Recreation Area and learn the "rags-to-riches" story of a stretch of river that was transformed from a dump site to a park site. Or maybe you'll hike through the heart of Humboldt Redwoods State Park and learn how the economically and politically powerful Rockefeller family saved a magnificent redwood forest for the state and nation.

The tale of the park system as a whole is fascinating as well—a saga that includes politics, conservation battles, both noisy and quiet, some Californians with great vision and some with very little, and a public that has consistently supported the parks with its enthusiasm, votes and funding.

As a matter of historical record, the first state park was Yosemite, given to California by President Lincoln's proclamation in 1864. Early in this century, California returned Yosemite to the federal government and began creating its own parks.

In 1902, the California state park system was born with the establishment of California Redwood Park in the Big Basin area of the Santa Cruz Mountains. Perhaps it is only fitting that one of the state's proudest possessions—the magnificent redwoods—provided the inspiration for the creation of the Golden State's park system.

California's first state park—and the establishment of a state park system a quarter-century later—were aided by two strong social movements in America: the conservation movement and the historic preservation movement. While conservationists acted to preserve the natural scene from Mt. San Jacinto in Southern California to Mt. Diablo in Northern California, historical preservationists championed the chapel at Fort Ross, and the Old Customs House in Monterey.

With the founding of the national park service in 1916 and its blossoming in the 1920s to become something Americans pointed to with great pride, California had a working model from which to fashion its own park service and park system.

"California is growing in population more rapidly than any other state," early parks advocate Duncan McDuffie pointed out in 1925. "Unless a comprehensive plan for the preservation of recreational and scenic areas is set in motion, our children and our children's children will want for the opportunity of out of door life that makes for sound bodies, clear brains and good citizenship."

Not everybody agreed. Ultra-conservative Governor William Friend Richardson (who somewhat ironically would one day have a state park named for him) was hostile to the state park movement and vetoed park legislation. "Plain stupid and entirely void of vision," fumed conservationist and Republican Congressman William Kent in response to Richardson's veto. "A blind porcupine could write just as good commentary on the question."

Pro-park forces prevailed, and in 1927 a state park system was established. The following year was really a landmark year for California's parks. Pamphlets were circulated, window stickers stuck in Model A's, a motion picture short released to movie houses—all in support of the park and recreation bond act of 1928. The public voted overwhelmingly to approve the bond and finance a state park system.

Not much of a park service or park system at first, though. It consisted of little more than the original California Redwood Park, a couple of north coast redwood parks, Mt. Diablo, and some historic sites and structures. The entire field staff numbered fifteen.

The other major event of 1928 was the commission of distinguished landscape architect Frederick Law Olmsted, Jr., son of the famed Central Park designer, to conduct a survey of the state to locate and describe possible parks. Olmsted and his staff evaluated 330 sites, and found 125 of them sufficiently worthy for consideration as state parks. Olmsted turned in his lengthy survey report on the last day of 1928 and promptly collapsed from exhaustion. Olmsted's survey was not only a practical plan, but a heartfelt expression of the value of state parks to the physical and mental well-being of Californians.

It was the job of the new state park staff, Olmsted believed, to teach the populace how to enjoy the great outdoors while at the same time preserving it for future generations. A second important mission was to defend the parks against all forms of commercial exploitation.

While the Great Depression of the 1930s caused many Californians untold economic hardship, it did not suppress the rapidly growing state park system. Land prices sharply declined, thus enabling the state to make a number of purchases at bargain prices—particularly in the north woods and along Southern California's beaches. Pfeiffer Big Sur State Park, Castle Crags State Park and San Clemente and Santa Monica Beaches, were among the many acquisitions of the 1930s.

During the hard economic times, the federal Civilian Conservation Corps contributed enormously to the nation's parks and forests. The CCC worked an estimated 10,000 "man-years" in California's state parks. Heavy, infrastructure-type projects such as bridges, roads, and campgrounds were the CCC's specialty. The Corps also built some spectacular structures that are much admired today, including the summit building atop Mt. Diablo and Mountain Theater atop Mt. Tamalpais.

World War II, accompanied by gas and tire rationing and park personnel shortages meant fewer visitors to the state parks. Some parks, such as Anza-Borrego, were closed during the war. Other parks, including Calaveras Big Trees and Pfeiffer Big Sur, were used to house and train troops.

After the war came a travel boom and the beginning of a long period of prosperity. The legislature rushed to approve funding for more parks and more park facilities. Robert Louis Stevenson State Park, Samuel P. Taylor State Park, and San Buenaventura State Beach were some of the units added to the park system in the late 1940s.

In 1951, Governor Earl Warren persuaded Californian Newton Drury, just completing a stint as national park director, to assume the post of state park director. The Drury years (1951-1959) were characterized by much park acquisition, fueled in part by offshore-oil royalties to the state.

Drury figured the Department should fund as many land purchases as possible; modest facilities could always be developed later. Drury reasoned: "People have a right to use the parks, of course. But no generation has a right to use them up."

Emerald Bay on Lake Tahoe, Leo Carrillo and El Capitan State Beaches, and Caswell Memorial State Park in the Central Valley were among the many acquisitions of the 1950s.

Governor Edmund G. Brown (1959-1967) will always and forever be known as the booster and builder of California's gargantuan State Water Project. All that water routed and stored for agriculture and the state's big cities might as well be used for recreation, too, Brown believed. The big "reservoir parks" were given to the park system to develop.

By the early 1960s, some 30 million visitors flocked to state parks. California's rapidly growing population needed more parks and more facilities. A 1964 state parks and recreation bond act earmarked $150 million for the system. Thanks in part to Walt Disney, who served as a parks spokesman, and his production of a short color film that dramatized the need for parks, voters overwhelmingly approved the bond measure.

Sugarloaf Ridge, Point Mugu, Malakoff Diggins and Montana de Oro were some of the parks acquired during the 1960s.

Governor Ronald Reagan (1967-1975) was no park booster, but he appointed a park director who certainly was—William Penn Mott, Jr. Mott defended the parks from the budget axe and expanded the system; he also professionalized the department. He established a training center at Asilomar to educate park staff as naturalists. Modern times, he believed, called for modern law-enforcement methods, and park rangers were required to become peace officers.

The year 1969 was a banner year for the spirit of voluntarism that has contributed so much for so long to California's state parks. The first "Trails Day" turned out hundreds of volunteers to work on the Skyline-to-the-Sea Trail in Big Basin Redwoods and Castle Rock state parks. This effort became the inspiration for California's annual statewide "Trails Day," which enlists the aid of thousands of volunteers to work on park trails.

The California State Parks Foundation was founded in 1969. This nonprofit organization has raised and donated millions of dollars to fund state park land acquisitions, facilities and programs.

Mott pioneered modern fund-raising methods. Under his direction, the Department negotiated improved concessionaire agreements, and in 1970 launched the first computerized campsite-reservation system.

Fueled by off-road vehicle licensing fees, the state park system continued its expansion in the 1970s: Huntington Beach, Empire Mine,

Wilder Ranch. In 1974, California voters once again approved another park bond act, Proposition 1, for $250 million.

As the 1970s progressed, the park's post-war expansion began to slow and the parks were increasingly beset by overcrowding, vandalism, and environmental problems. In a 1978 speech commemorating the park system's fiftieth anniversary, then-director Russell Cahill warned: "I look around today and see a people out of touch: out of touch with nature, out of touch with their history, out of touch with each other."

During the 1980s, the parks began to face the first of ever-increasing budget cuts. The Department was required to earn some of the revenue needed for its ongoing operations—a reasonable requirement that most everyone supported.

However, this mandated fundraising accelerated over the years to amounts the state park system cannot possibly collect. The Department was/is placed in an untenable situation: If the Department fails to meet its revenue goals, it will be penalized by cuts in personnel and programs. If it does meet its goals, state government will require DPR to raise even more revenue.

In the 1990s the Department faces several problems, including a financial situation that is becoming a true crisis in proportion, and deferred maintenance that is mounting. Because of the more-than-usual need for revenue, commercialization of the state park system from those who misinterpret the mission and purpose of state parks is a definite threat these days.

The Department's challenge in the 1990s, and in the next century, is to provide for the recreation needs of a growing population that is increasingly ethnically and culturally diverse, while at the same time preserving and protecting the lands in its charge. Quite a challenge!

Fortunately, California state park visitors have a much better grasp of the value of parks than California state politicians, and understand that their value is more than the yearly revenue they generate. From the beginning of the parks movement early in the twentieth century, California's citizens have supported their parks: preserving priceless lands for future generations and supporting the parks with their votes and volunteer hours, admission fees and tax dollars. And while the state's economy has slowed in recent years, enthusiasm for, and visitation to, state parks has not.

Optimists hope that the present generation of Californians is as forward-looking as an earlier generation who took to heart the words of early parks advocate/ state parks director Newton Drury as he argued (successfully) for the state parks bond act of 1928: "The benefit to Californians will be many times the cost. State Parks will pay not only in increased revenue . . . but, what is more important, will pay rich dividends in the health and happiness of our people by assuring for them and for their successors, enjoyment of the scenic beauty and outdoor recreation which Californians have always looked upon as their heritage."

State of the State's Trails

By some estimates, the state park trail system includes more than 2,000 miles of trail. About a hundred parks have at least one compelling walk or hike, and are thus included in this guide.

For the most part, park trails are in pretty good shape, particularly in comparison to paths in national forests or those of other land-use agencies. While trails are all too often a low-priority maintenance item at the parks, they have stayed in hike-able shape thanks to the hard work of many dedicated volunteers from trails and conservation organizations.

Keeping a watchful eye on the state's trails (including, but not limited to state park trails) are the seven members of the California Recreational Trails Committee. Members, representing various locales around the state and various trail constituencies (cyclists, equestrians, hikers, river-runners, etc.), advise the state parks director on trail matters.

The CRT Committee, formed in 1969, broadened its responsibilities during the 1970s and assumed an advisory and coordination role for trail development in city, county and regional park departments.

In 1977-78, the Committee spearheaded the development of the

California Recreational Trails Plan, which examined the needs of hikers, cyclists, boaters and off-road vehicle users.

Ever since, the Committee has met quarterly in locales around the state. Each meeting gives trails enthusiasts a chance to discuss issues of both regional and statewide importance. While the Committee's power is strictly limited to a sometimes frustrating advisory role, it does serve as a valuable source of trails information.

The Committee hosts a trails conference each spring, usually at the state's Asilomar Conference Center. Trails advocates from all over the state gather to share information about trail projects, get briefed on the latest land-use policy and legal developments, and learn new trail-building and trail-publicizing techniques.

A very important Committee task, assumed in recent years, is the coordination of statewide Trails Days. This annual springtime event enlists volunteers to work on trail projects from the Southern California deserts to the northern redwoods.

Using This Guide

Walking opportunities in more than 100 state parks are detailed in this guide. Add the suggested options and you can design about 200 different walks.

The parks are grouped by geography into chapters, and further organized in rough south-to-north order. Most of the parks clearly belong in their respective categories, but a couple of parks straddle geographical areas and I've made a judgment call as to which chapter to place these parks. For example: San Clemente State Beach clearly belongs to the Southern California Coast chapter. But what about Clear Lake State Park, located in that "other wine country" north of the Napa-Sonoma wine country?

Beneath the name of the state park is the name of the trail. After a brief mention of **Terrain** and **Highlights**, **Distance**, expressed in round-trip mileage figures, follows each destination. The hikes in this guide range from 1 to 15 miles, with the majority in the 5- to 8-mile range. Gain or loss in elevation follows the mileage.

In matching a walk to your ability, **Degree of Difficulty**, you'll want to consider both mileage and elevation as well as condition of the trail, terrain, and season. Hot, exposed chaparral or miles of boulder-hopping can make a short walk seem long.

Hikers vary a great deal in relative physical condition, but you may want to consider the following: An easy walk suitable for beginners and children would be less than five miles with an elevation gain of less than 700 to 800 feet. A moderate walk is considered a walk in the 5- to 10-mile range, with under 2,000 feet of elevation gain. You should be reasonably fit for these. Preteens sometimes find the going difficult. Hikes of more than 10 miles and those with more than a 2,000-foot gain are for experienced hikers in top form.

Season is the next item to consider. California is one of the few places in the country that offers four-season hiking. You can hike some of the trails in this guide all of the time, all of the trails some of the time, but not all of the trails all of the time.

Precautions: A few trails in this guide may be impassable in winter and spring due to high water. Relevant fire and flood information has been noted below the season recommendation.

An introduction to each walk describes what you'll see in a particular state park and what you'll observe along the trail: plants, animals, panoramic views. You'll also learn about the geologic and human history of the region.

Directions to trailhead take you from the nearest major highway to trailhead parking. Alternative transportation, via bus or train where practical, has been suggested. For trails having two desirable trailheads, directions to each are given. A few trails can be walked one way, with the possibility of a car shuttle. Suggested car shuttle points are noted.

After the directions to the trailhead, you'll read a description of The walk. Important junctions and major sights are pointed out, but I've left you to discover the multitude of little things that make a hike an adventure.

Foot notes suggest other walks, either within park boundaries or in nearby areas.

On The Trail

Choose the pace that's best for you. Rest once an hour for a few minutes. To keep your momentum and to avoid stiffness, several shorter rest periods are better than one long one. Set a steady pace, one you can keep up all day. Wear a watch, not because you have an appointment with a waterfall and you have to be punctual, but because a watch gives you some idea of pace and helps you get back to the trailhead before dark.

Walking uphill takes energy. Walking two miles an hour up a 10 percent grade requires as much energy as hiking four miles an hour on level trail. Climbing can be especially difficult in high altitude.

Altitude sickness affects some hikers at about 8,000 feet. Only a few hikes in this guide are above this elevation. Altitude can cause discomfort—shortness of breath, headache and nausea above 5,000 feet.

Walking solo is the preference of many, but having two or three in your party is an advantage if something goes wrong; someone can go for help. Hiking with a group is a good idea for first-time walkers.

Alas, backcountry travelers are not always immune from urban attitudes, stresses, and crimes. While most of our state parks are far safer than our urban environment, walkers—particularly women walkers—must be aware that unsavory characters are not unknown on the trail.

Your "street smarts" coupled with your trail sense are two keys to avoiding trouble.

Sometimes, after a few hikes, a craving for solitude develops—by which time you should be able to take care of yourself on the trail. There's a lot to be said for solitary hiking, as the writings of Thoreau, Whitman and Muir would seem to indicate.

Camping in State Parks

Most state park campsites, including family, group, and environmental sites, can be reserved through the MISTIX computerized reservation system; all others are available on a first-come, first-served basis.

Reservations are particularly important to consider for holiday periods, the busy summer months, and for Southern California's beach campgrounds year-round. Reservations for campsites are placed on sale eight weeks (56 days) in advance. To reserve a campsite, call MISTIX at 1-800-444-PARK (1-800-444-7275).

Developed campgrounds in state parks typically feature improved roads, restrooms (often with hot showers), piped drinking water and campsites with table, stove or fire ring.

Trailer and RV hookups are only available at a few state parks. The maximum RV length park campsites can accommodate varies from park to park.

Primitive campgrounds have few (chemical or pit toilets, central water supply) or even no facilities.

Environmental campsites, very much in keeping with the adventuresome spirit of this guide, are usually situated in especially scenic and quiet areas away from the regular campground. No vehicles may be parked at an environmental site, so to reach the campsites, a short walk is necessary. Each site usually includes a table, stove, primitive toilet. Some have drinking water.

Most state parks charge day-use fees ($2–$6 per vehicle). Due to the severe budget problems the parks have been experiencing in recent years, DPR staff is more aggressive than ever in the collection of these fees.

Sometimes park fees are collected only at the main entrance of the park and not at more remote entrances or trailheads. Some parks have uniformed staff collecting fees at a substantial-looking entry kiosk; other parks make do with "iron rangers"—slotted metal posts into which you deposit an envelope with the required fee.

If you're a frequent park visitor, you may want to take advantage of an Annual Day-Use Pass that permits you take your vehicle into any state park. Seniors 62 years of age or older may obtain a Golden Bear Pass. The Department also offers a Disabled Veteran's Pass and a Disabled Discount Pass.

For additional information about the prices and use conditions of these special passes, contact the Department of Parks and Recreation, Office of Public Relations, P.O. Box 942896, Sacramento, CA 94296, or call (916) 653-6995.

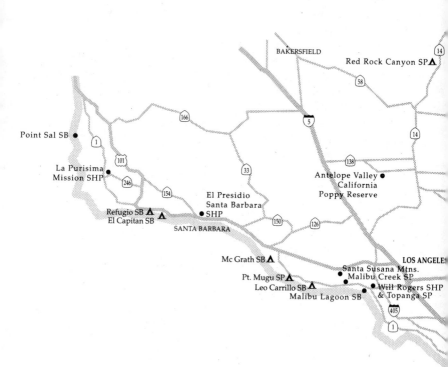

Point Sal SB ●

La Purisima
Mission SHP ●

Refugio SB ▲
El Capitan SB ▲

BAKERSFIELD

Red Rock Canyon SP ▲

14

58

5

14

166

138

33

Antelope Valley ●
California
Poppy Reserve

El Presidio
Santa Barbara
● SHP

150

126

SANTA BARBARA

McGrath SB ▲

Pt. Mugu SP ▲
Leo Carrillo SB ▲
Malibu Lagoon SB

LOS ANGELES

Santa Susana Mtns. ●
Malibu Creek SP ●
● Will Rogers SHP
& Topanga SP

405

1

101

246

154

1

Southern California

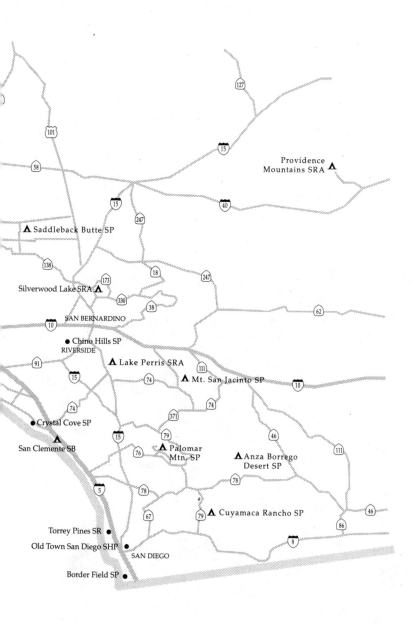

Southern California Desert

Californians who have an affinity for the desert, are fortunate to have portions of two vast deserts preserved in state parks: the Mojave (the high desert) and the Colorado (the low desert). The designations refer to altitude and latitude. There is (relatively) more rainfall in the high desert, and the hot season isn't as hot and severe as it is in the lower desert.

In the Mojave Desert, the walker can explore the Joshua tree forest in Saddleback Butte State Park and the awesome cliffs of Red Rock Canyon State Park. Not to be missed is the state's ultimate spring flower show—the blankets of gold covering the slopes of Antelope Valley California Poppy Reserve. Way out in the East Mojave is an underground attraction—Mitchell Caverns in Providence Mountains State Recreation Area.

More than 600,000 acres of the Colorado Desert are protected by Anza-Borrego Desert State Park. California's largest state park includes virtually every feature visitors associate with a desert—washes, badlands, mesas, palm oases, and a thousand more. It offers a remoteness, a desolation, a special beauty that brings visitors back year after year.

Anza-Borrego Desert State Park
Borrego Palm Canyon Trail

Terrain: Rocky, V-shaped gorge
Highlights: One of California's largest palm oases, seasonal waterfall
Distance: Borrego Campground to Falls is 3 miles round trip with 600-foot elevation gain; to South Fork is 6½ miles round trip with 1,400-foot gain
Degree of difficulty: Moderate to strenuous
Precautions: Usual desert hiking conditions

Anza-Borrego Desert State Park includes virtually every feature visitors associate with a desert: washes, badlands, mesas, palm oases and much more. This diverse desert park boasts more than 20 palm groves and year-round creeks, great stands of cholla and elephant trees, slot canyons and badland formations.

Anza-Borrego is diverse, and it is immense—it covers an area more than three times the size of Zion National Park. The 600,000-acre park stretches almost the whole length of San Diego County's eastern border between Riverside County and Mexico. Its elevation ranges from 100 feet below sea level near the Salton Sea to 6,000 feet above sea level atop San Ysidro Mountain.

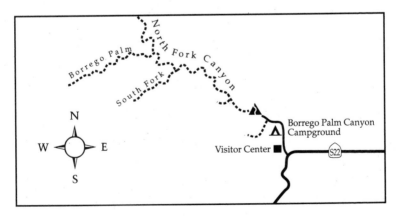

Travelers are welcomed to Anza-Borrego with what is probably the best visitor center in the state park system. Numerous self-guided nature trails and automobile tours allow visitors to set their own pace. An active natural history association and foundation sponsors many regularly scheduled ranger- and naturalist-led activities.

Borrego Palm Canyon is the third-largest palm oasis in California, and was the first site sought for a desert state park back in the 1920s. It's a beautiful, well-watered oasis, tucked away in a rocky V-shaped gorge.

The trail visits the first palm grove and a waterfall. A longer option takes you exploring farther up-canyon. In winter, the trail to the falls is one of the most popular in the park. In summer, you'll have the oasis all to yourself. Watch for bighorn sheep, which frequently visit the canyon.

Directions to trailhead: The trail begins at Borrego Palm Canyon Campground, located one mile north of Anza-Borrego State Park Headquarters. Trailhead parking is available at the west end of the campground near the campfire circle.

The walk: Beginning at the pupfish pond, you walk up-canyon past many desert plants used by Native Americans for food and shelter.

The broad alluvial fan at the mouth of the canyon narrows and the sheer rock walls of the canyon soon enclose you as the trail continues along the healthy but seasonal stream. Already surprised to learn how an apparently lifeless canyon could provide all the necessary survival ingredients to support a Native American population, you're surprised once more when Borrego Palm Oasis comes into view. Just beyond the first group of palms is a damp grotto, where a waterfall cascades over huge boulders. The grotto is a popular picnic area and rest stop.

From the falls, you may take an alternate trail back to the campground. This trail takes you along the south side of the creek, past some magnificent ocotillos, and gives you a different perspective on this unique desert environment. By following the optional route, you can continue hiking up the canyon. Hiking is more difficult up-canyon after the falls, with lots of dense undergrowth and boulders to surmount.

To South Fork: From the "tourist turnaround" continue up the canyon. The creek is a fairly dependable water supply and is usually running late in the fall. The canyon is wet, so watch your footing on the slippery, fallen palm fronds. The canyon narrows even further and the trail dwindles to nothing. Parallel the streambed and boulder-hop

back and forth across the water. The canyon zigs and zags quite a bit, so you can never see much more than a few hundred yards ahead. The hike is well-worth the effort though, because most of the 800 or so palms in the canyon are found in its upper reaches.

The canyon splits 1¾ miles from the falls. Straight ahead, to the southwest, is South Fork. The rocky gorge of South Fork, smothered with bamboo, holds all the canyon's water. It's quite difficult to negotiate. South Fork ascends to the upper slopes of San Ysidro Mountain (6,417 feet). The Middle Fork (the way you came) of Borrego Palm Canyon is dry and more passable. It's possible to hike quite a distance first up Middle Fork, then North Fork of Borrego Palm Canyon, but check with rangers first. It's extremely rugged terrain.

Foot notes: A few more fine day hikes include Rockhouse Canyon Trail (7 miles round trip), which explores two canyons—Bow Willow and Rockhouse; Calcite Canyon Trail (4 miles round trip), a tour of steep sandstone formations; Elephant Trees Discovery Trail (1½ miles round trip) winds through a herd of 500 of the unusual elephant trees.

Providence Mountains
State Recreation Area/
Mitchell Caverns State Reserve

Mitchell Caverns Trail

Terrain: Limestone cave
Highlights: Guided hike of the caverns
Distance: 1½ miles round trip
Degree of difficulty: Easy

Trail trivia question: Where in Southern California can you explore some stunning scenery, be assured that it won't rain, and know that the temperature for your hike will always be a comfortable 65 degrees?

Hint: One of the overlooked gems of the state park system.

If you're in the dark, then you're on the right path—the trail through Mitchell Caverns State Reserve, part of Providence Mountains State Recreation Area. Ranger-led walks through the dramatic limestone caves offer a fascinating geology lesson, one the whole family can enjoy.

In 1932, Jack Mitchell abandoned his Depression-shattered business in Los Angeles and moved to the desert. For a time he prospected for silver, but his real fascination was with what he called the "Providence" or "Crystal Caves" and their potential as a tourist attraction. He constructed several stone buildings to use for lodging. (Today's park visitors center is one of these buildings.) Mitchell and his wife, Ida, provided food, lodging, and guided tours of the caverns until 1954. By all accounts, Jack Mitchell was quite a yarn-spinner. Oldtimers still remember his tall tales of ghosts, lost treasure, and bottomless pits.

Now that the caverns are part of the state park system, rangers lead the tours. They're an enthusiastic lot and quite informative. Visitors walk through the two main caves, which Mitchell named El Pakiva (The Devil's House) and Tecopa (after a Shoshonean chieftain). You'll get a close-up view of stalactites and stalagmites, cave ribbon, cave spaghetti, and flow stone. And you'll learn about some of the caverns' former inhabitants—the Chemehuevi Indians and a Pleistocene ground sloth that stumbled into the darkness some 15,000 years ago.

During Jack Mitchell's day, visitors had to be nimble rock-climbers who waited for their tour leader to toss flares into the darkness. Nowadays, the caverns are equipped with stairs and special lighting.

Guided tours are conducted Monday through Friday at 1:30 p.m. On Saturday and Sunday, tours begin at 10 a.m., 1:30 p.m. and 3 p.m. A tour takes 1½ to 2 hours depending on your group's enthusiasm and collective curiosity, and a fee is charged.

Directions to trailhead: From Interstate Highway 40, about 80 miles east of Barstow, exit on Essex Road and drive 16 miles to road's end at the Providence Mountains State Recreation Area parking lot. Sign up at the visitor center for tours.

Because you can tour the caverns only with a park ranger, and because you wouldn't want me to spoil the many surprises of the cave walk with a step-by-step description, I won't further detail the Mitchell Caverns Trail. However, after exploring "the great indoors" allow some time to explore the park's outdoor pathways.

Pick up an interpretive booklet from the park visitor center and walk the half-mile long Mary Beal Nature Trail, which offers a great introduction to high desert flora. Cliff rose and blue sage share the hillsides with cholla, catsclaw, and creosote.

The trail honors Mary Beal, a Riverside librarian who at the turn of the century was "exiled" to the desert by her doctor for health reasons. For a half-century this remarkable woman wandered through the Providence Mountains and other remote Mojave Desert locales in order to gather and classify hundreds of varieties of plants and wildflowers. The trail was dedicated in 1952 on Beal's seventy-fifth birthday.

The short Overlook Trail leads from the park's tiny campground to a viewpoint that offers vistas of Clipper Valley, the Marble Mountains, and hundreds of square miles of basin and range topography.

The one-mile long Crystal Springs Trail leads into the pinyon pine- and juniper-dotted Providence Mountains by way of Crystal Canyon. Bighorn sheep often travel through this canyon.

Saddleback Butte State Park
Saddleback Butte Trail

> **Terrain:** Granite mountain above Antelope Valley
> **Highlights:** Joshua tree woodland, desert vistas
> **Distance:** Campground to Saddleback Peak is 4 miles round trip
>   with 1,000-foot elevation gain
> **Degree of difficulty:** Moderate

Rarely visited Saddleback Butte State Park, located on the eastern fringe of Antelope Valley, offers an easily reached but out-of-the-way destination for a day hike.

This is high-desert country, a land of creosote bush and Joshua trees. The park, located 75 miles north of Los Angeles, takes the name of its more prominent feature—3,651-foot Saddleback Butte, a granite mountaintop that stands head and shoulders above Antelope Valley.

The spartan country around the butte once supported thousands of pronghorn antelope—hence the name Antelope Valley—and the numerous Native American tribes who hunted them. The antelope are all gone now, victims to hunting and encroaching civilization. By interrupting the antelope's migration, Southern Pacific railroad tracks also doomed the animals; the antelope could easily cross the tracks, but instinct prevented them from doing this, and they soon perished from exposure to harsh winters and the shrinkage of their habitat.

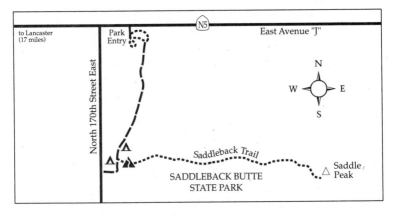

Today's park visitor may glimpse several other animals native to Antelope Valley, including coyote, jackrabbits, lizards, and the Antelope ground squirrel. Some fortunate hikers may even witness the unhurried progress of a desert tortoise.

Before you hike to the top of the butte, you may wish to hike the short nature trail located near the park entrance. It's a good introduction to the Joshua tree and other plant life found.

Guided walks are sometimes conducted along Joshua Trail during autumn and spring months on Sunday mornings. Check at the visitor center for more information.

The trail to the boulder-strewn summit of Saddleback Peak takes a straight-line course, with most of the elevation gain occurring in the last half-mile. Atop the peak, the hiker is rewarded with far-reaching desert views.

Directions to trailhead: From Highway 14 (Antelope Valley Freeway) in Lancaster, take the 20th Street exit. Head north on 20th and turn east (right) on Avenue J. Drive about 18 miles, past barren land and farmland, to Saddleback Butte State Park. Follow the dirt park road to the campground, where the trail begins. Park near the trail sign. There is a state park day-use fee.

The walk: The signed trail heads straight for the saddle. The soft, sandy track, marked with yellow posts (this may be the best-marked trail in the state park system), leads through an impressive Joshua tree woodland.

After 1½ miles, the trail begins to switch back steeply up the rocky slope of the butte. An invigorating climb brings you to the saddle of Saddleback Butte. To reach Saddleback Peak, follow the steep leftward trail to the summit.

From the top, you can look south to the San Gabriel Mountains. You may be able to spot Mount Baldy dominating the eastern end of the range. At the base of the mountains, keen eyes will discern the California Aqueduct, which carries water to the southland from the Sacramento Delta. To the east is the vast Mojave Desert, to the north is Edwards Air Force Base. To the west are the cities of Lancaster and Palmdale, and farther west the rugged Tehachapi Mountains.

Antelope Valley California Poppy Reserve

Antelope Loop Trail

> **Terrain:** Gentle hills of Antelope Valley
> **Highlights:** California's state flower in magnificent, seasonal bloom
> **Distance:** From Visitor Center to Antelope Butte Vista Point is 2H miles round trip with 300-foot elevation gain.
> **Degree of difficulty:** Easy to moderate

The California poppy blooms on many a grassy slope in the Southland, but only in the Antelope Valley does the showy flower blanket whole hillsides in such brilliant orange sheets. Surely the finest concentration of California's state flower (during a good wildflower year) is preserved at the Antelope Valley California Poppy Reserve in the Mojave Desert west of Lancaster.

The poppy is the star of the flower show, which includes a supporting cast of fiddlenecks, cream cups, tidy tips and gold fields. March through Memorial Day is the time to saunter through this wondrous display of desert wildflowers.

The poppy has always been recognized as something special. Early Spanish settlers called it *Dormidera,* "the drowsy one," because the petals curl up at night. They fashioned a hair tonic/ restorer by frying the blossoms in olive oil and adding perfume.

At the reserve, you

Map labels: Antelope Butte Vista Point; Kitanemuk Vista Point; Antelope Loop North; Antelope Loop South; Visitor Center; Lancaster Road; N W E S

can pick up a map at the Jane S. Pineiro Interpretive Center, named for the painter who was instrumental in setting aside the reserve to protect California's state flower for the enjoyment of future generations. Some of Pineiro's watercolors are on display in the center, which also has wildflower interpretive displays and a slide show.

Built into the side of a hill, the center boasts an award-winning solar design, windmill power, and "natural" air conditioning.

Antelope Loop Trail—and all trails in the reserve—are easy walking and suitable for the whole family. Seven miles of gentle trails criss-cross the 1,760-acre reserve; many hikers take every trail in the park without getting too tired.

Spring wildflower displays are always unpredictable. To check on what's blooming where, call the park at (805) 724-1180 before making the trip.

Directions to trailhead: From the Antelope Valley Freeway (California 14) in Lancaster, exit on Avenue I and drive west 15 miles. Avenue I becomes Lancaster Road a few miles before the Poppy Reserve.

The walk: Begin on the signed Antelope Loop Trail to the left of the visitors center. The trail passes through an orange sea of poppies and fiddlenecks, then climbs briefly to Kitanemuk Vista Point, ¾ mile from the visitor center. Atop Vista Point are those flowery symbols of faithfulness and friendship, forget-me-nots, and an unforgettable view of the Mojave Desert and the snow-covered Tehachapis.

After enjoying the view, continue on to Antelope Butte Vista Point, where another lookout offers fine desert panoramas. From here, join the south loop of the Antelope Loop Trail and return to the visitors center.

After you've circled the "upper west side" of the Poppy Reserve, you may wish to extend your hike by joining the Poppy Loop Trail and exploring the "lower east side."

Red Rock Canyon State Park
Hagen, Red Cliffs Trails

Terrain: Steep-walled gorges, badlands of El Paso Mountains
Highlights: Colorful cliffs, natural preserves
Distance: 1 to 2 miles round trip
Degree of difficulty: Easy to moderate
Precautions: Carry plenty of water, inquire about dirt road
conditions.

The view of Red Rock Canyon may very well seem like déjà vu. Cliffs and canyons in these parts have appeared in the background of many a western movie.

A black-and-white movie of Red Rock Canyon *would* be dramatic: shadow and light playing over the canyon walls. Technicolor, however, might more vividly capture the aptly named red rock, along with the chocolate brown, black, white, and pink hues of the pleated cliffs.

The park is situated at a biologic crossroads between the Mojave Desert to the south and the High Sierra to the northwest. Red Rock is also at a geologic crossroads between the Mojave and Great Basin deserts, having formations common to each.

The dramatic, eroded sedimentary cliffs we see today accumulated in a lake bed during Miocene times, some 10 million years ago. The soft sandstone rock is capped by a hard lava-cap rock, which protects the colorful formations and keeps them from eroding quite so fast.

Preserved in the cliffs is a fossel record fascinating to paleontologists. Millions of years ago, Red Rock Canyon was a freshwater lake, ringed by oak and even palm trees, where saber-toothed cats, elephants, and rhinoceroses roamed.

The first people, the Kawai'isu, lived in the Red Rock Canyon area more than 10,000 years ago. They occupied the land several hundred years before Europeans arrived.

Gold fever in the 1890s prompted exploration of almost all the canyons in the El Paso Mountains. During this era, Rudolph Hagen acquired much land in the Red Rock area. He named the little mining community/stage stop Ricardo after his son Richard. The Ricardo Ranger Station is located at the site of the once-thriving hamlet.

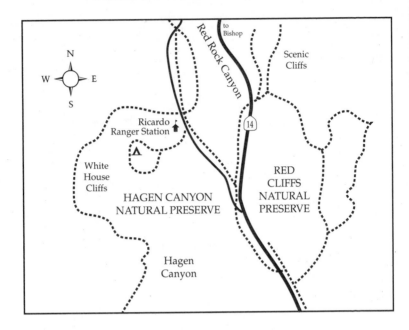

Red Rock Canyon became a state recreation area in 1969; when it became obvious off-road vehicles were damaging the hills and canyons, Red Rock was upgraded to a park in 1982.

Best places to hike are in the park's two preserves, which are closed to vehicles. You'll find some trails to hike, but this park lends itself to improvisation.

Hagen Canyon Natural Preserve is a striking badlands, the dramatic cliffs capped by a layer of dark basalt. A primitive one-mile loop trail explores the canyon.

Red Cliffs Natural Preserve protects the 300-foot sandstone cliffs east of Highway 14. No developed trail exists; however hikers can enjoy a mile or so of cross-country travel through the preserve.

The park nature trail, a ¾-mile path tells the geologic story of the area, and points out typical desert flora. It's keyed to an interpretive pamphlet available at the trailhead. Join the nature trail at the south end of the park campground.

Directions to trailhead: Red Rock Canyon State Park is located 25 miles north of the town of Mojave off Highway 14. Turn northwest off 14 onto the signed road for the park campground. Follow this road a short mile to Ricardo Ranger Station. The station has a small visitor

center with nature exhibits. Check with rangers about the condition of the many dirt roads that explore the park and surrounding desert. Guided nature walks are sometimes available during weekends during the spring and fall months.

Southern California Mountains

Southern California boasts a remarkably diverse collection of mountainous state parks from the Mediterranean-flavored flora of the Santa Monica Mountains to the alpine splendor of the San Jacinto Mountains.

A most memorable walk is the trek through lodgepole pine country to the top of 10,804-foot Mt. San Jacinto, high point of the state park system. The great naturalist John Muir found the view from the summit "the most sublime spectacle to be found anywhere on this earth!"

Semi-circling the Los Angeles-Orange County metropolis are several lesser-known ranges with state parks that provide much-needed open space and recreation for big basin residents: Bernasconi Hills surrounding Lake Perris State Recreation Area; Chino Hills (California's most expensive state park); Santa Susana Mountains, where walkers follow a stagecoach route known as the Devil's Slide.

Another highlight for the walker is the Santa Monica Mountains, the only relatively undeveloped mountain range in America that bisects a major metropolitan area. The mountains stretch from the heart of Los Angeles to Point Mugu, fifty miles away. State park lands—Will Rogers, Topanga, Malibu Creek, Leo Carrillo, and Point Mugu—have an extensive network of fire roads and footpaths that lead through native tall grass prairies and fern-lined canyons, and up to rugged, rocky ridgetops that seem far removed from the city below.

Cuyamaca Rancho State Park
Stonewall Peak Trail

Terrain: Forested shoulders of "Old Stoney"
Highlights: Vistas of Cuyamaca country, the park, desert
Distance: Paso Picacho Campground to summit is 4 miles
round trip with 900-foot elevation gain; return via California
Riding and Hiking Trail, Cold Stream Trail is 5½ miles round
trip.
Degree of difficulty: Moderate
Precautions: Stay off peak during thunderstorms

Plentiful rain and the Cuyamacas' geographical location between coast and desert make these mountains a unique ecosystem. The 4,000- to 6,500-foot peaks host rich forests of ponderosa and Jeffrey pine, fir, and incense cedar, as well as some wonderful specimens of live and black oak. In lower elevations, broad grasslands stretch toward the horizon. The Cuyamacas are a delight for birdwatchers because desert, coastal, and mountain species are all found in the range.

A good portion of the Cuyamaca Mountains are protected by the state park and William Heise Park. More than 110 miles of hiking trails pass through the old rancho. The Cuyamacas offer four-season hiking at its colorful best: fall with its brown, yellow, and crimson leaves; winter with snows on the higher peaks; spring with its wildflowers; summer with its sudden thunderstorms.

In 1870, trouble began when a Cuyamaca Mountains gold mine was named to honor Confederate General "Stonewall" Jackson. Although the Civil War had been over for five years, miners were ready to resume hostilities over the mere mention of the general's name. In the interest of harmony and high productivity, the mine's name was shortened to Stonewall, thereby identifying it with the prominent stony peak on the skyline above.

Rounded Mount Cuyamaca (6,512 feet) is the highest peak in the range, but Stonewall Peak is more prominent. "Old Stony" is about 1,000 feet lower, but its huge walls of granite and crown of stone make it stand out among neighboring peaks. The popular Stonewall

Peak Trail will take you to the top of the peak (5,730 feet) and give you grand views of the old Stonewall Mine Site, Cuyamaca Valley, and desert slopes to the east. An optional route lets you descend to Paso Picacho Campground via the California Riding and Hiking Trail and the Cold Stream Trail.

Directions to trailhead: From San Diego, drive east on Interstate Highway 8. Exit on Highway 79 north. The highway enters Cuyamaca Rancho State Park and climbs to a saddle between Cuyamaca and Stonewall peaks. Park near the entrance of Paso Picacho Campground. There's a state park day-use fee. The trail to Stonewall Peak begins just across the highway from the campground.

The walk: From Paso Picacho Campground, the trail ascends moderately, then steeply through oak and boulder country. The black oaks wear vivid colors in fall.

The trail switchbacks up the west side of the mountain. Hike through a thick cluster of incense cedar and when you emerge from the spicy-smelling trees, views from the north unfold. Cuyamaca Reservoir is the most obvious geographical feature. Before a dam was built to create the reservoir, Cuyamaca Lake, as it was called, was a sometime affair. Native Americans never trusted it as a dependable water source and the Spanish referred to it as *la laguna que de seco,* or "the lake that dries up." During dry years, the cows enjoy more meadow than reservoir.

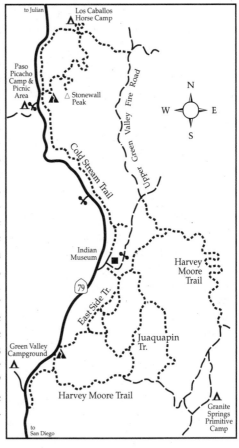

Vegetation grows more sparse and granite outcroppings dominate the high slopes as the trail nears the top of Old Stony. A hundred feet from the summit, a guardrail with steps hacked into the granite helps you reach the top. Far-reaching views to the east and west are not possible because a number of close-in mountains block your view. You can, however, orient yourself to Cuyamaca geography from atop Stonewall Peak. Major Cuyamaca peaks, from north to south, are North Peak, Middle Peak, and Cuyamaca Peak.

It's exciting (but risky) to be atop Stonewall Peak when a storm is brewing over the Cuyamacas. The peak has been known to catch a lightning strike or two. Black clouds hurtle at high speed toward the peak. Just as they are about to collide with the summit, an updraft catches them and they zoom up and over your head.

You can return the way you came or via the California Riding and Hiking Trail by backtracking 100 yards on the Stonewall Peak Trail to an unsigned junction. From here, bear right (north). The trail descends steeply at first, then levels off near Little Stonewall Peak (5,250 feet). It then descends moderately to the California Riding and Hiking Trail, which traverses the west side of the park. You travel for one mile on the California Riding and Hiking Trail, which is actually part of the Stonewall Peak Trail. It forks to the right and crosses Highway 79. Don't take the fork, but continue a half-mile down the Cold Stream Trail, paralleling the highway, back to Paso Picacho Campground.

Foot notes: Cuyamaca country, with more than a hundred miles of trail, has a number of great walks. Cuyamaca Peak Trail (6 miles round trip) climbs through a forest of oak, pine, and fir to a 6,512-foot summit offering views from the Pacific to the Salton Sea. Harvey Moore Trail (up to 12 miles round trip) meanders through grassy rolling hills. Middle Peak Trail (5¾ miles round trip) is the one to take for tall trees—big specimens of silver fir and cedar, plus Coulter, sugar, ponderosa, and Jeffrey pine. Kelly Ditch Trail (11 miles round trip) connects the state park with nearby William Heise Park; the black oaks en route provide one of the Southland's showiest displays of fall color.

San Pasqual Battlefield
State Historic Park
Battlefield Monument Trail

> **Terrain:** Cactus-dotted slopes above San Pasqual Valley
> **Highlights:** Mexican-American War history; wild land on the edge of San Diego
> **Distance:** 1 mile round trip
> **Degree of difficulty:** Easy

The Battle of San Pasqual had little military significance, historians surmise, but was nevertheless was an pivotal event during the Mexican-American War—a conflict that brought California under American control and eventually into the Union.

At dawn on December 6, 1846, American troops, led by General Stephen Kearny, peered through the fog at the Californios who were encamped in the San Pasqual Valley. Then they attacked. The Americans and their horses were in terrible condition (the result of an exhausting journey from New Mexico). To make matters worse, their gunpowder was wet.

The Californios, a superb group of horsemen under the command of General Andrés Pico, met the Americans' charge with gunfire and their deadly long lances.

Some 21 Americans were killed and many more wounded, including General Kearny, in the short but intense battle. About a dozen Californios were wounded as well before both sides withdrew.

A four-day standoff followed. Kearny sent Kit Carson to bring back U.S. Army reinforcements from San Diego. The reinforced Americans, with overwhelming numerical superiority, soon captured San Diego and, after a brief skirmish along the San Gabriel River, captured Los Angeles as well.

The state historic park interprets the battle—the most severe one of the Mexican-American War fought in California. A modern visitor center and museum tell the story of the conflict with maps, displays, and a video. Other exhibits feature the history and natural history of the San Pasqual Valley. The park's short nature trail and Battlefield

Monument Trail are also good introductions to the life and lore of San Pasqual Valley.

Most visitors rush through the valley on their way to the San Diego Wild Animal Park, located 1½ miles east of the park. But San Pasqual Valley and the state park are well worth a stop. The valley has for the most part resisted San Diego's eastward suburban sprawl by virtue of its agricultural zoning.

Directions to trailhead: From Highway 78, eight miles east of Escondido, take the turnoff to San Pasqual Battlefield State Historic Park. Leave your car in the lot by the visitor center.

The walk: Join the nature trail, which begins on the hillside behind the visitor center. After a quarter-mile, you'll join Battlefield Monument Trail and ascend a slope bristly with prickly pear cactus.

At a picnic ramada, you get an inspiring view of the wide San Pasqual Valley as well as fine place to eat lunch. Sometimes you can view some of the larger animals roaming through the nearby San Diego Animal Park. You can return the way you came back to the visitor center or continue west on Battlefield Monument Trail to a historic monument next to Highway 78.

GEN. ANDRES PICO

GEN. STEPHEN W. KEARNY

Palomar Mountain State Park
Scott's Cabin Trail

Terrain: Mixed forest, mountain meadows
Highlights: Pond-side picnicking, gentle, Sierra Nevada-like
  atmosphere.
Distance: Loop from Silver Crest Picnic Area to Scott's Cabin,
  Cedar Grove Campground, Boucher Lookout, is 3½ miles
  with 800-foot elevation gain.
Degree of difficulty: Easy to moderate

Palomar Mountain is a state park for all seasons. Fall offers dramatic color changes, and blustery winter winds ensure far-reaching views from the peaks. In spring, the dogwood blooms, and during summer, when temperatures soar, the park offers a cool, green retreat.

This day hike, a 3½-mile loop, is a *grande randonnée* of the park, a four-trail sampler that leads to a lookout atop 5,438-foot Boucher Hill.

Directions to trailhead: From Interstate 5 in Oceanside, drive northeast on State Highway 76 about 30 miles. Take County Road S6 north; at S7, head northwest to the park entrance. There is a day-use fee. Park in the lot at Silver Crest Picnic Area just inside the park. Scott's Cabin Trail takes off from the right side of the road about 20 yards beyond the lot entrance.

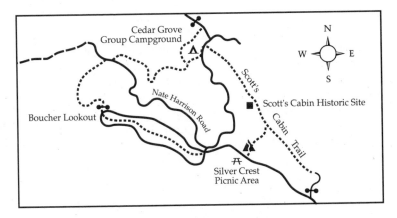

The walk: A trail sign points the way to Scott's Cabin, a half-mile away. Scott's Cabin, built by a homesteader in the 1880s, is found on your left. The crumpled remains aren't much to look at.

You'll descend steeply through a white-fir forest and reach the signed junction with the Cedar-Doane Trail, which heads right (east). If you go right, this steep trail, formerly known as the Slide Trail because of its abruptness, takes the hiker down oak-covered slopes to Doane Pond. The pond is stocked with trout, and fishing is permitted. A pond-side picnic area welcomes the hiker.

If you go left at the trail junction, it's a short walk to Cedar Grove Campground. Follow the trail signs and turn left on the campground road, and then right into the group campground. Look leftward for the signed Adams Trail, which cuts through a bracken fern meadow.

Once across the meadow, you'll encounter a small ravine where dogwood blooms during April and May. The trail winds uphill past some big cone spruce and reaches Nate Harrison Road.

The road is named in honor of Nathan Harrison, a Southern slave who followed his master to the California gold rush—and freedom—in 1849. Harrison laid claim to a homestead on the wild eastern edge of what is now state park land, and had a successful hay-making and hog-raising operation.

Across the road, your path becomes Boucher Trail, which ascends a north-facing slope through white fir, then through bracken ferns and black oaks, to the summit of Boucher Hill.

Atop the hill is a fire lookout and microwave facility. From the summit, you get a view of the surrounding lowlands, including Pauma Valley to the west.

Return to the parking area via Boucher Trail, which descends 0.6 mile between the two sides of the loop road that encircles Boucher Hill. The trail heads down an open ridgeline to a junction of five roads, where it's a mere hop, skip and a jump back to the Silver Crest Picnic Area.

Follow the paved road past the park cabin to the picnic area.

Foot notes: Most visitors to Mount Palomar drive their cars all the way to the top, visit the observatory and drive back down. Too bad! They miss a nice hike. Observatory Trail (4 miles round trip) climbs through the Cleveland National Forest to the summit and the observatory.

Mt. San Jacinto State Park
Mount San Jacinto Trail

Terrain: Fern-filled meadows, subalpine forest
Highlights: High point of state park system, second-highest peak in Southern California; outstanding views.
Distance: Mountain Station to Round Valley is 4 miles round trip with 600-foot elevation gain; to San Jacinto Peak is 11 miles round trip with 2,300-foot elevation gain.
Degree of difficulty: Moderate to strenuous
Precautions: High altitude hiking, wilderness permits required.

The San Jacinto mountain range is one of those magical places that lures hikers back year after year. Hikers enjoy the contrasts this range offers—the feeling of hiking in Switzerland while gazing down at the Sahara.

Palm Springs Aerial Tramway makes it easy for hikers to enter Mount San Jacinto State Wilderness. Starting in Chino Canyon near Palm Springs, a tram takes passengers from 2,643-foot Lower Tram-

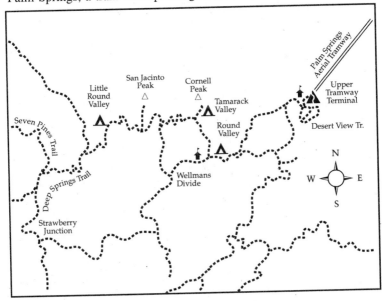

way Terminal (Valley Station) to 8,516-foot Upper Tramway Terminal (Mountain Station) at the edge of the wilderness.

The hiker accustomed to remote trailheads may find Valley Station, where excited tourists sip drinks and shop for souvenirs, a bit peculiar. The gondola rapidly leaves terra firma behind. Too rapidly, you think. It carries you over one of the most abrupt mountain faces in the world, over cliffs only a bighorn sheep can scale, over several life zones from palms to pines. When you disembark at Mountain Station, your ears will pop and you'll have quite a head start up Mount San Jacinto.

The wild areas in the San Jacinto Mountains are administered by both state park and national forest rangers. The middle of the region, including San Jacinto Peak, is part of the state park; most of it is managed as a wilderness area. On both sides of the peak, north and south, the wilderness is part of the San Bernardino National Forest.

The meadows and High Sierra-like scenery can be glimpsed on a moderate hike to Round Valley; the ascent through the lodgepole pine forest to the top of Mt. San Jacinto is absolutely splendid, as are the views from the peak.

Directions to trailhead: From Interstate 10, exit on California 111 (the road to Palm Springs). Proceed 9 miles to Tramway Road, turn right, and follow the road 2½ miles to Mountain Station. Contact the Tramway office for information about prices and schedules.

The walk: From Mountain Station, walk down the cement walkway through the Long Valley Picnic Area. Soon you will arrive at the state park ranger station. Obtain a wilderness permit here.

Continue west on the trail, following the signs to Round Valley. The trail parallels Long Valley Creek through a mixed forest of pine and white fir, then climbs into lodgepole-pine country. Lupine, monkeyflower, scarlet bugler and Indian paintbrush are some of the wildflowers that add seasonal splashes of color.

After passing a junction with a trail leading toward Willow Creek, another 0.3 mile of hiking brings you to Round Valley. There's a trail camp and a backcountry ranger station in the valley, and splendid places to picnic in the meadow or among the lodgepole pines.

An alternative to returning the same way is to retrace your steps 0.3 mile back to the junction with the Willow Creek Trail, take this trail a mile through the pines to another signed trail north back to Long Valley Ranger Station. This alternative route adds only about a quarter-mile to your day hike, and allows you to make a loop.

To Mount San Jacinto Peak: From Round Valley, peak-bound hikers follow the sign for Wellman Divide Junction. From the divide, a trail leads down to Humber Park. At the divide, you'll be treated to spectacular views of Tahquitz Peak and Red Tahquitz, as well as the more-distant Toro Peak and Santa Rosa Mountain. You continue toward the peak on some vigorous switchbacks. The lodgepole pines grow sparse among the crumbly granite. At another junction, a half-mile from the top, the trail continues to Little Round Valley but you take the summit trail to the peak. Soon you arrive at a stone shelter—an example of Civilian Conservation Corps handiwork during the 1930s—built for mountaineers who have the misfortune to be caught in winter storms. From the hut, you boulder-hop to the top of the peak.

Foot notes: Those walkers who have taken the tram to Mountain Station and find themselves short of time will enjoy Desert View Trail (2 miles round trip) which offers an introduction to the alpine environment of Mt. San Jacinto as well as a superb panorama of Palm Springs.

Lake Perris State Recreation Area
Terri Peak Trail

Terrain: Brushy, Bernasconi Hills
Highlights: Good clear-day views from Terri Peak
Distance: From Campfire Center to Terri Peak is 3½ miles
round trip with 800-foot elevation gain; to Indian Museum,
return via lakeshore, is 6 miles round trip.
Degree of difficulty: Moderate

Few nature lovers—or lovers of any kind—have discovered the romance of Perris. True, a million and a half visitors come to the lake each year, but the only nature most are interested in is that found wriggling on the end of a hook.

While the *parc* is oriented to *les autos et les bateaux,* there is a network of trails for those visitors who wish to explore Perris *à pied.* Perris pacesetters will enjoy the trek to Terri Peak, easily the most romantic spot in all of the Bernasconi Hills.

Springtime colors the hills with a host of wild fleurs, including goldfields, California poppy, fiddleneck, baby blue eyes and blue dicks. The view from Terri Peak on smog-free days is tres fantastique.

Directions to trailhead: From the Pomona Freeway (60), a few

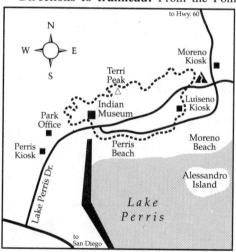

miles east of its intersection with I-215, exit on Moreno Beach Drive and proceed 4 miles to the park. Immediately after paying your state park day-use fee at the entry kiosk, turn right on Lake Perris Drive. Look sharply right for the strange-looking international symbol indicating a campfire and an amphitheater. Park in the campfire/interpretive center lot. The unsigned trail begins to the left of the campfire area.

The walk: The trail ascends gradually west and occasionally intersects a horse trail. The unsigned path is tentative at first but an occasional wooden post helps keep you on the trail, which climbs boulder-strewn slopes.

The coastal scrub community—sage, buckwheat, chamise and toyon predominates. Also much in evidence are weedy-looking non-native species, as well as mustard, prickly pear cactus, morning glory and Russian thistle.

The trail climbs to a small flat meadow, then turns southwest and climbs more earnestly to the peak. From atop Terri Peak, enjoy clear-day views of the San Bernardino Mountains to the northeast and the Santa Ana Mountains to the southwest. Below is fast-growing Moreno Valley, checkerboarded alternately with green fields and subdivisions. You can see all of Lake Perris, Alessandro Island, and hundreds of boaters, anglers and swimmers.

The trail from Terri Peak down to the Indian Museum is in poor condition. Beginning hikers may want to retrace their steps to the trailhead. The more experienced will begin their descent. Expect to lose the trail a couple of times; however you won't get lost because it's easy to stay oriented with the lakeshore on your left and the Indian Museum ahead.

After a steep descent, the trail bends sharply east and deposits you at the Indian Museum's parking lot. The museum includes exhibits interpreting the Cahuilla, Chemehuevi, Serrano and other desert tribes and how they adapted to life in the Mojave Desert region.

From the museum, you follow the asphalt road down to Lake Perris Drive, cross this main park road and continue down to Perris Beach. Here, and at Moreno Beach one mile to the west, you may cool off with a swim.

Improvise a route along the lakeshore using the sidewalk and bicycle trail until you spot the main campground entrance on your left. Enter the campground, pass the kiosk, then pick up the intermittent footpath that winds through the campground. This path and some improvisation will bring you to Lake Perris Drive and back to the trailhead.

Chino Hills State Park
Hills-for-Everyone Trail

Terrain: Rolling grassland, oak-lined canyon
Highlights: Wild side of SoCal, delightful in spring
Distance: Along Ranch Road to McDermont Spring is 4 miles
    round trip with 400-foot gain; to Carbon Canyon Regional
    Park is 7½ miles one way with 800-foot loss from
    McDermont Spring.
Degree of difficulty: Moderate

Chino Hills State Park, located in Orange, San Bernardino, and Riverside counties, preserves some much-needed "breathing room" in this fast-growing area. Nearly 3 million people live within sight of the Chino Hills and more than 9 million people live within a 40-mile radius of the park!

The park is the state's most expensive ever, with in excess of $50 million spent by the time it opened for full-time use in 1986. Some, but not too much, development is in store for Chino Hills; signs or facilities are being installed, but mostly the park will continue to be the province of horseback riders, mountain bikers and hikers.

The 12,000-acre park is located near the northern end of what geologists call the Peninsular Ranges Geomorphic Province. The Chino Hills are part of the group of hills that include the Puente Hills to the northwest. These hills form a roughly triangular area of approximately 35 square miles of valleys, canyons, hills and steep slopes.

High temperatures, often combined with heavy smog, suggest that a summer visit can be something of an ordeal. The park is much more pleasurable in the cooler months, and especially delightful in spring.

Hills-for-Everyone Trail was named for the conservation group that was instrumental in establishing Chino Hills State Park. The trail follows a creek to the head of Telegraph Canyon. The creek is lined with oak, sycamore and the somewhat rare California walnut.

Directions to trailhead: Despite its location so close to the metropolis, Chino Hills State Park can be a bit tricky to find. The park is located west of Highway 71 between the Riverside Freeway (91) and the Pomona Freeway (60). From Highway 71, Traveling south on

71 from 60, visitors should turn right on Los Serranos Road and then make a quick left onto Pomona-Rincon Road. (Visitors heading north on 71 from 91 will spot, before reaching Los Serranos Road, a left-turn lane leading directly to Pomona-Rincon Road.) A half-mile of travel brings you to Soquel Canyon Road. Take this road to Elvinar Road and turn left.

Just after Elvinar turns east and becomes Sapphire Road, you'll see the signed dirt park road on your right. Enter the park on this road (which returns to pavement in two miles) and follow signs to the park office and ranger station. The road forks just before the ranger station. To the right is the ranger station and visitor center. Bear left one-half mile on the dirt road to a vehicle barrier and trailhead parking. The signed trailhead is located a short distance past the vehicle barrier on the right of the road.

The walk: Hills-for-Everyone Trail descends to a small creek and follows the creek up-canyon. Shading the trail—and shielding the hiker from a view of the many electrical transmission lines that cross the park—are oaks, sycamores and walnuts. Of particular interest is the walnut; often the 15- to 30-foot-tall tree has several dark brown trunks, which gives it a brushy appearance.

The trail, which can be quite slippery and muddy after a rain,

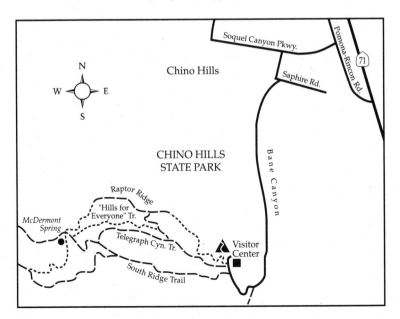

passes a small (seasonal) waterfall. The slopes above the creekbed are carpeted with lush grasses and miners lettuce.

Along the trail is found evidence of the park's ranching heritage, including lengths of barbed-wire fence and old cattle troughs. For more than a century this land was used exclusively for cattle ranching.

Near its end, the trail ascends out of the creekbed to the head of Telegraph Canyon and intersects a dirt road. McDermont Spring is just down the road. Some of the livestock ponds, constructed during the area's ranching days, still exist, and hold water year-round. McDermont Spring—along with Windmill and Panorama ponds—provides water for wildlife.

To Carbon Canyon Regional Park: Telegraph Canyon Trail (a dirt road closed to public vehicular traffic) stays close to the canyon bottom and its creek. It's a gentle descent under the shade of oak and walnut trees. The walnuts are particularly numerous along the first mile of travel and the hiker not inclined to hike the length of Telegraph Canyon might consider exploring this stretch before returning to the trailhead.

The route passes an old windmill. Farther down the canyon, the walnuts thin out. A lemon grove, owned by the state park but leased to a farmer, is at a point where the dirt road intersects Carbon Canyon Road. Walk along the broad shoulder of the latter road half a mile to Carbon Canyon Regional Park.

Foot notes: Raptor Canyon Trail (4 miles round trip) traverses one of the more natural areas of the park. Water Canyon Trail (4½ miles round trip), shaded by huge oaks and sycamores, and dotted with the Chinese tree-of-heaven, is about the coolest spot in the Chino Hills to walk. Brush Canyon Trail (5 miles round trip) tours oak woodland and grassland environments.

Silverwood Lake State Recreation Area
Miller Canyon Trail

Distance: To Serrano Beach is 3½ miles round trip; to Marina
is 6 miles round trip
Terrain: Brush-covered and pine-dotted lakeshore
Highlights: Birds to watch, fish to catch, trails to trek
Degree of difficulty: Easy to moderate family hike
Precautions: Lake is crowded on summer weekends. Don't use
park map to plan your hike; it's not to scale!

Silverwood Lake has a noisy side and a quiet side, a developed side
and a wild side. "No doubt about it—the lake has a split personality,"
declares Ranger Mike Wisehart, who patrols Silverwood Lake State
Recreation Area. "On summer weekends, it's a place to water ski and
party down. During other seasons, people come for quieter pursuits—
bird-watching, fishing, hiking."

The lake was formed twenty years ago when Cedar Springs Dam
was constructed and waters from the State Water Project filled a little
valley that was formed long ago by the meandering West Fork of the
Mojave River. Water for the lake comes more than 400 miles from
northern California through a truly astonishing maze of plumbing.

Early in this century, at the bottom of what is now Silverwood
Lake, about a hundred families worked the land and founded the town

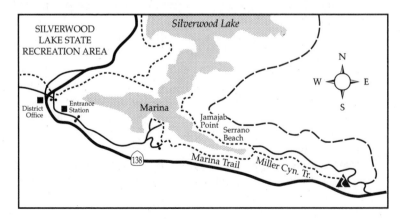

of Cedar Springs. Strawberries put the town on the map; tourists traveled for miles to buy jars of strawberry jam. Some of the more entrepreneurial farmers froze their strawberries and shipped them to Los Angeles ice-cream makers.

By the mid-1920s, Seventh-Day Adventists, who developed a small tuberculosis sanitarium in the area, were the pillars of the community. Cedar Springs remained a popular weekend outing through the Depression years. The rustic community was razed, then covered, when Silverwood Lake was filled in 1972.

Around the lake is a diversity of habitats. Thick chaparral—manzanita, ceanothus, chamise, mountain mahogany, plus oak and scrub oak—crowds the lakeshore. Alder, willow and sycamore line nearby creeks. On higher slopes is a thriving forest of ponderosa pine, fir and incense cedar.

A diversity of habitats means many different bird species: bluebirds, rufous-sided towhee, Western tanager, and many more songbirds. The red-tailed hawk and great horned owl are dramatic sights. A small, but growing number of bald eagles have become winter residents at the lake.

Of course, the lake hosts many varieties of native and migratory waterfowl: great blue heron, western grebe, snowy egret, Canadian geese, and a zillion ducks. The serious birder will pick up a bird checklist at the park's entrance station.

At first glance at the park map, it looks like a hike around Silverwood Lake's 13-mile shoreline might be good fun. However, the park map is not drawn to proper scale; it's a difficult 25-mile trek on dirt roads to circle the lake—not much fun.

Silverwood Lake's trail system surprises. Experienced hikers might figure the park's premier path is the Pacific Crest Trail, which crosses a portion of the recreation area; actually, this stretch of PCT offers a less-than-thrilling day hike. PCT fans will much prefer day hiking along the nearby Deep Creek section of the trail.

The walker might also figure that the lakeside bikepath is not for pedestrians; actually, walkers are welcome to use the paved path, which is officially known as "Bike and Hike Trail." The aesthetically pleasing trail gives access to portions of lakeshore that cannot be reached by auto. Silverwood's best hike is the part footpath/part bikepath route through Miller Canyon. Miller Canyon Trail leads to some woodsy retreats, grand views, and Serrano Beach, an inviting sand strand and picnic area.

Directions to trailhead: From Interstate 15 at Cajón Junction, take the Highway 138/Silverwood Lake exit. Drive ten miles east to the main entrance of Silverwood Lake State Recreation Area. Continue four more miles past the entrance on Highway 138 to the signed Miller Canyon turnoff. Turn left. The actual signed trail head is at the edge of the Miller Canyon Group Camp; however, parking is awkward hereabouts and rangers suggest you leave your car a short way up Miller Canyon Road at the Devil's Pit parking area.

The walk: From the signed trailhead at the Miller Canyon Group Camp, join the footpath dropping into the canyon. You soon begin sauntering along Miller Creek, one of the far-flung tributaries of the Mojave River.

First stop along the trail is Devil's Pit, a not-very-appropriate name for what can be a heavenly swimming hole in spring and summer. Above this "pit" is an observation platform, offering views down Miller Canyon and up at nearby peaks of the San Bernardino Mountains.

At Lynx Point (another inappropriate name; there aren't any lynx in the area) is another vista point. The panorama includes a view of Mt. Baldy, highest summit in the nearby San Gabriel Mountains.

Below Lynx Point, Miller Canyon Trail intersects the paved bike and hike trail. A short walk on the left fork of the trail brings you to a little-used Hike/Bike camp—perfect for a picnic. From the camp, you can continue on the Bike and Hike Trail along the south lakeshore to park's marina.

Taking the right fork of the trail leads to Miller Canyon Road. Follow the road a few hundred feet to its end, then resume walking on the paved Bike and Hike Trail. Serrano Beach is a short quarter-mile up the trail.

After another quarter-mile, the paved Bike and Hike Trail ends at Jamajab Point, which offers good views across the lake to the park's marina. A narrow trail, used mostly by fishermen, winds another half-mile along the lakeshore.

Santa Susana Mountains State Park
Stagecoach Trail

> **Terrain:** Sandstone peak, grassy slopes
>
> **Highlights:** Hiking part of the old stagecoach route from San Francisco to Los Angeles, an infamous stretch through Santa Susana Pass known as the Devil's Slide.
>
> **Distance:** From Chatsworth Park South to Devil's Slide is 2½ miles round trip with 500-foot elevation gain
>
> **Degree of difficulty:** Easy to moderate

One of the major obstacles to stagecoach travel between Los Angeles and San Francisco was a route out of the west end of the San Fernando Valley over the Simi Hills. About 1860, a steep road was carved out of the rock face of the hills. The steepest stretch, a peril to man and beast, was known as Devil's Slide.

The slide, the old stage road, and a portion of the Simi Hills are preserved in a park-in-the-making located just west of Chatsworth. In 1989, the state purchased 400 acres in the Santa Susana Pass area and added it to another 400 acres of state-owned parkland. Eventually Santa Susana Mountains State Park will be staffed with rangers, and have recreation facilities. The park represents two decades of organizing and lobbying efforts by local environmentalists, spearheaded by the Santa Susana Mountain Park Association.

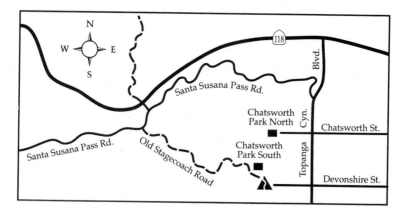

A network of trails loop through the park, but the trails are unsigned and more than a little confusing. During your first visit to the park, expect to improvise a bit. Once you get the lay of the land, subsequent visits will be easier.

As you drive up Devonshire you'll notice signed Stagecoach Trail, an equestrian trail. Leave your car and pick up this trail if you wish, but it's more convenient continuing to the ample parking area in the main part of Chatsworth Park South.

Directions to trailhead: From the Ventura Freeway (101) in Woodland Hills, exit on Topanga Canyon Boulevard and drive 6¼ miles north to Devonshire St. Turn left and proceed ¾ mile to Chatsworth Park South, a city-owned park with wide lawns and picnic areas, located next to the new state park. If you're coming from the Simi Valley-San Fernando Valley Freeway (118), take the Topanga Canyon Boulevard exit in Chatsworth, drive 1½ miles to Devonshire and turn right to the park.

The walk: From the parking lot, walk across the wide lawn (or take one of the dirt paths that border the lawn). With the park recreation center directly behind you, navigate toward a couple of oaks and join a gravel path that begins just below a water tower on your right.

Begin a moderate ascent. When presented with confusing choices and unsigned junctions, try to keep ascending straight up the hill. Don't drift too far to the south where there's a line of electrical transmission towers, or too far to the north where the Southern Pacific railroad tracks penetrate the mountains.

A half-mile from the trailhead you'll intersect a paved road, which winds up to a small hydroelectric pumping plant. You, however, will almost immediately abandon this road at a break in a chain link fence by two telephone poles. Here you'll find the old stage road and begin to climb more earnestly toward Devil's Slide.

Near the top of the slide is a historical marker commemorating "Old Santa Susana Stagecoach Road, 1859-90." This is a great place to pull up a rock, sit a spell and survey the San Fernando Valley. Just below is Chatsworth, a mixture of old ranchland and new townhouses. If you're lucky, you'll sight a freight or passenger train snaking through the Simi Hills and disappearing into the Santa Susana tunnel.

Continue another quarter-mile up the Stagecoach Trail and inspect the rest of Devil's Slide. Or you can retrace your steps and take one the side trails leading southeast over to the park's intriguing rock formations.

Will Rogers State Historic Park
Will Rogers Trail

Terrain: Brushy Santa Monica Mountains
Highlights: Tour Cowboy Philosopher's home, then enjoy the
  coast, mountain and metropolis views from Inspiration Point.
Distance: To Inspiration Point is 2 miles round trip with a 300-
  foot elevation gain
Degree of difficulty: Easy

Will Rogers, often called the "Cowboy Philosopher," bought a
spread in the Santa Monica Mountains in 1922. He and his family
enlarged their weekend cottage to 31 rooms.

The Oklahoma-born Rogers toured the country as a trick roper,
punctuating his act with humorous comments on the news of the day.
His roping act led the humorist to later fame as a newspaper columnist, radio commentator and movie star.

Today, the ranch is maintained as Will Rogers State Historic Park,
set aside in 1944. You can see a short film on Rogers's life at the visitor center and tour the ranch house, still filled with his prized possessions.

Directions to trailhead: From Sunset Boulevard in Pacific
Palisades, 4½ miles inland from Sunset's junction with Pacific Coast
Highway, turn inland on the access road leading to Will Rogers State
Historic Park. Park your car near the polo field or near Rogers' house.

The walk: Join the path near the tennis courts west of park headquarters and begin ascending north into the mountains. (You'll see a
couple of different trails; you want to join the main, wide bridle path.)

Rogers Trail ascends a ridge overlooking nearby Rivas Canyon and
leads to a junction, where you take the turnoff for Inspiration Point.
Not really a point at all, it's actually more of a flat-topped knoll; nevertheless, clear-day views are inspiring: the Santa Monica Bay, the
metropolis, the San Gabriel Mountains, and even Catalina Island.

Foot notes: Rustic Canyon Trail (6 miles round trip) loops through
Will Rogers SHP and a canyon every bit as woodsy and secluded as
its name suggests.

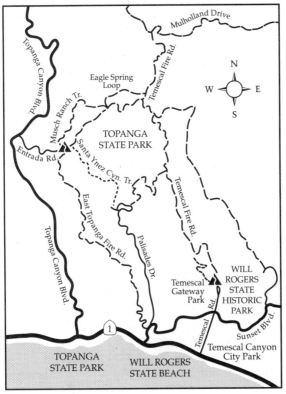

Topanga State Park
Eagle Rock Loop Trail (Backbone Trail)

> **Terrain:** Heart of state park, surrounded by suburban sprawl but retaining its rural character.
> **Highlights:** Pleasant sampling of Santa Monica Mountains
> **Distance:** To Eagle Rock via Eagle Rock/Eagle Springs Loop is 6½ miles round trip with 800-foot gain; to Will Rogers SHP via Eagle Rock, Fire Road 30, Rogers Road is 10½ miles one way with a 1,800-foot loss
> **Degree of difficulty:** Moderate to strenuous

Topanga Canyon is a quiet retreat, surrounded by L.A. sprawl but retaining its rural character. The state park is sometimes billed as "the largest state park within a city limit in the U.S."

The name Topanga is from the Shoshonean Indian dialect. Until the 1880s, there was little permanent habitation in the canyon. Early settlers tended vineyards, orchards, and cattle ranches. In the 1920s, the canyon became a popular weekend destination for Los Angeles residents. Summer cabins were built along Topanga Creek and in subdivisions in the surrounding hills. For a $1 round-trip fare, tourists could board a Packard auto stage in Santa Monica and be driven up Pacific Coast Highway and Topanga Canyon Road to the Topanga Post Office and other more scenic spots.

In the heart of the state park, the walker will discover Eagle Rock, Eagle Spring and get topographically oriented to Topanga. The energetic will enjoy the one-way journey from Topanga to Will Rogers State Historic Park.

The Topanga State Park to Will Rogers Park section of the Backbone Trail has been finished for quite some time and has proved very popular. The lower reaches of the trail offer a fine tour of the wild side of Topanga Canyon while the ridgetop sections offer far-reaching inland and ocean views.

Directions to trailhead: From Topanga Canyon Boulevard, turn east on Entrada Road; that's to the right if you're coming from Pacific Coast Highway. Follow Entrada Road by turning left at every opportunity until you arrive at Topanga State Park. The trailhead is at the end of the parking lot.

(For map and information about the end of this walk, consult the Will Rogers State Historic Park write-up and directions to the trailhead on the preceding pages.)

The walk: From the Topanga State Park parking lot, follow the distinct trail eastward to a signed junction, where you'll begin hiking on Eagle Springs Road. You'll pass through an oak woodland and through chaparral country. The trail slowly and steadily gains about 800 feet in elevation on the way to Eagle Rock. When you reach a junction, bear left on the north loop of Eagle Springs Road to Eagle Rock. A short detour will bring you to the top of the rock.

To complete the loop, bear sharply right (southwest) at the next junction, following the fire road as it winds down to Eagle Spring. Past the spring, you return to Eagle Spring Road and retrace your steps back to the trailhead.

Three-mile long Musch Ranch Trail, which passes from hot chaparral to shady oak woodland, crosses a bridge and passes the park pond, is another fine way to return to the trailhead.

To Will Rogers State Historic Park: Follow the loop trip directions to the northeast end of Eagle Rock/Eagle Spring Loop, where you bear right on Fire Road 30. In one-half mile you reach the intersection with Rogers Road. Turn left and follow the dirt road (really a trail) for 3½ miles, where the road ends and meets Rogers Trail. Here a level area and solitary oak suggest a lunch stop. On clear days enjoy the spectacular views in every direction: To the left is Rustic Canyon and the crest of the mountains near Mulholland Drive. To the right, Rivas Canyon descends toward the sea.

Stay on Rogers Trail, which marches up and down several steep hills, for about two more miles, until it enters Will Rogers Park near Inspiration Point.

Foot notes: Santa Ynez Trail offers ferns, waterfalls and dramatic sandstone cliffs on a 2½ mile round trip route to Santa Ynez Canyon Falls. Los Liones Canyon Trail (6 miles round trip) climbs to The Overlook, which offers grand views of West Los Angeles and Santa Monica Bay. Garapito and Bay Tree Trails offer a 7½ mile loop that explores the back side (Mulholland Drive approach) of the state park and roams the wild tributaries of Rustic and Garapito Canyons.

Malibu Creek State Park

Malibu Creek Trail

Terrain: Gorge and riverbed of Malibu Creek in middle of
  Santa Monica Mountains
Highlights: "The Gorge" of Malibu Creek; site of "M*A*S*H"
  television series
Distance: To Rock Pool is 3½ miles round trip with 150-foot
  elevation gain; to Century Lake is 4½ miles round trip with
  200-foot elevation gain
Degree of difficulty: Easy to moderate

Before land for Malibu Creek State Park was acquired in 1974, it was divided into three parcels belonging to Bob Hope, Ronald Reagan, and 20th Century-Fox. Although the park is still used for moviemaking, it's primarily a haven for day hikers and picnickers.

Today Malibu Creek State Park preserves more than 7,000 acres of rugged country in the middle of the Santa Monica Mountains. Malibu

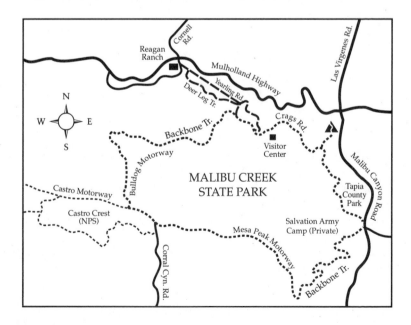

Creek winds through the park. The creek was dammed at the turn of the century to form little Century Lake.

The trail along Malibu Creek explores the heart of the state park. It's an easy, nearly level walk that visits a dramatic rock gorge, Century Lake and several locales popular with moviemakers.

Directions to trailhead: From Pacific Coast Highway, turn inland on Malibu Canyon Road and proceed 6½ miles to the park entrance, one-quarter mile south of Mulholland Highway. If you're coming from the San Fernando Valley, exit the Ventura Freeway (101) on Las Virgenes Road and continue four miles to the park entrance.

The walk: From the parking area, follow the wide fire road. You'll cross the all-but-dry creek. The road soon forks into a high road and a low road. Go right and walk along the oak-shaded high road, which makes a long, lazy left arc as it follows the north bank of Malibu Creek. You'll reach an intersection and turn left on a short road that crosses a bridge over Malibu Creek.

You'll spot the Gorge Trail and follow it upstream a short distance to the gorge, one of the most dramatic sights in the Santa Monica Mountains. Malibu Creek makes a hairpin turn through 400-foot volcanic rock cliffs and cascades into aptly named Rock Pool. The "Swiss Family Robinson" television series and some Tarzan movies were filmed here.

Return to the trailhead or retrace your steps back to the high road and bear left toward Century Lake. As the road ascends you'll be treated to a fine view of Las Virgenes Valley. When you gain the crest of the hill, you'll look down on Century Lake. Near the lake are hills of porous lava and topsy-turvy sedimentary rock layers that tell of the violent geologic upheaval that formed Malibu Canyon. The lake was scooped out by members of Crag's Country Club, a group of wealthy, turn-of-the-century businessmen who had a nearby lodge.

You can call it a day here, or continue on the fire road past Century Lake. You'll pass the location of the now-removed set for the "M*A*S*H" television series. The Goat Buttes that tower above Malibu Creek were featured in the opening shot of each episode.

Foot notes: A grand 14-mile loop of the park can be made by connecting both the high and low routes of the Backbone Trail. The high road—Mesa Peak Motorway—climbs Castro Crest; the low road descends with Malibu Creek. Ronald Reagan's Ranch, now part of the state park, is a delight for hikers, who can tour the ranch's rolling meadowland and grand old oaks on a four-mile round trip trail.

Leo Carrillo State Beach
Nicholas Flat Trail

Terrain: Coastal scrub-covered upland area back of state beach
Highlights: Coastal views, grassy Nicholas Flat
Distance: To Nicholas Flat is 7 miles round trip with 1,600-foot
  elevation gain
Degree of difficulty: Moderate to strenuous.

Leo Carrillo State Beach has always been a popular surfing spot. Surfers tackle the well-shaped south swell, while avoiding the submerged rocks and kelp beds. In recent years, the state added a large chunk of Santa Monica Mountains parkland to the state beach, and now Leo Carrillo is a pleasing place to take a hike.

Nicholas Flat Trail departs from Pacific Coast Highway and climbs inland up steep, scrub-covered slopes to a wide meadow and a small pond. From its high points, the trail offers good views of the coast.

Nicholas Flat Trail can also be savored for one more reason: In Southern California, very few trails connect the mountains with the sea. About eighty-five percent of all Californians live within thirty miles of the coast; in the Southland, most of the extensive coastal trail

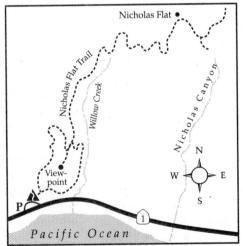

system that existed a hundred years ago has been covered with pavement or suburbs. Nowadays, to find a lot of trails that lead from Coast Highway into the mountains, you'd have to travel to the Big Sur region or the parklands north of San Francisco.

Get an early start on the Nicholas Flat Trail. Until you arrive at oak-dotted Nicholas Flat itself, there's not much shade en route. In good wildflower-watching years, you might spot such spring blooms as monkeyflowers, coyote brush, golden yarrow, bush sunflowers, hummingbird sage, and a lot of lupine along the trail.

Directions to trailhead: From the west end of the Santa Monica Freeway in Santa Monica, head up-coast on Pacific Coast Highway about 25 miles to Leo Carrillo State Beach. There's free parking along Coast Highway, and fee parking in the park's day use area. Signed Nicholas Flat trailhead is located a short distance past the park entry kiosk, opposite the day use parking area.

The walk: If the state park hasn't mowed its "lawn" lately, the first fifty yards of Nicholas Flat Trail will be a bit indistinct. Immediately after its tentative beginning, the trail junctions. The right branch circles the hill, climbs above Willow Creek, and after a mile, rejoins the main Nicholas Flat Trail. Enjoy this option on your return.

Take the left branch, which immediately begins a moderate to steep ascent of the grassy slopes above the park campground. The trail switchbacks through a coastal scrub community up to a saddle on the ridgeline. Here you'll meet the alternate branch of Nicholas Flat Trail. From the saddle, a short side trail leads south to a hilltop, where there's a fine coastal view. From the viewpoint, you can see Point Dume and the Malibu coastline.

Following the ridgeline, Nicholas Flat Trail climbs inland over chaparral-covered slope. Keep glancing over your right shoulder at the increasingly grand coastal views, and over your left at the open slopes browsed by the park's nimble deer. In the spring, the fast-fading wildflower population is dominated by morning glory vines with white trumpet-shaped flowers.

After a good deal of climbing, the trail levels atop the ridgeline and you get your first glimpse of grassy, inviting Nicholas Flat. The trail descends past a line of fire- blackened, but unbowed, old oaks and joins an old ranch road that skirts the Nicholas Flat meadows. Picnickers may unpack lunch beneath the shady oaks or out in the sunny meadow. The trail angles southeast across the meadow to a small pond. The man-made pond, used by cattle during the region's ranching days, is backed by some handsome boulders.

Return the way you came until you reach the junction located ¾ mile from the trailhead. Bear left at the fork and enjoy this alternate trail as it descends into the canyon cut by Willow Creek, contours around an ocean-facing slope, and returns you to the trailhead.

Point Mugu State Park
Sycamore Canyon Trail

Terrain: One of California's finest sycamore savannas
Highlights: Wondrous sycamores, autumn leaves, monarch
  butterfly migration.
Distance: Big Sycamore Canyon to Deer Camp Junction is 6½
  miles round trip with 200-foot gain; return via Overlook Trail
  is 10 miles round trip with 700-foot gain
Degree of difficulty: Easy to moderate
Precautions: Trail gets heavy mountain bike use

Every fall, millions of monarch butterflies migrate south to the forests of Mexico's Transvolcanic Range and to the damp coastal woodlands of Central and Southern California. The monarch's awe-inspiring migration and formation of what entomologists call over-wintering colonies are two of nature's most colorful autumn events.

All monarch butterflies west of the Rockies head for California in the fall; one of the best places in Southern California to observe the arriving monarchs is the campground in Big Sycamore Canyon at Point Mugu State Park.

The monarch's evolutionary success lies not only in its unique abil-

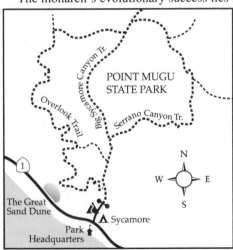

ity to migrate to warmer climes, but in its mastery of chemical warfare. The butterfly feeds on milkweed—the favored poison of assassins during the Roman Empire. This milkweed diet makes the monarch toxic to birds; after munching a monarch or two and becoming sick, they learn to leave the butterflies alone.

The butterflies advertise their poisonous nature with their conspicuous coloring. They have brownish-red wings with black veins. The outer edge of the wings are dark brown with white and yellow spots. While one might assume the monarch's coloration would make them easy prey for predators, just the opposite is true; bright colors in nature are often a warning that a creature is toxic or distasteful.

Sycamore Canyon Trail takes you through a peaceful wooded canyon, where a multitude of monarchs dwell, and past some magnificent sycamores. The sycamores that shade the canyon bearing their name are incomparable. The lower branches, stout and crooked, are a delight for tree-climbers. Hawks and owls roost in the upper branches.

The trail follows the canyon on a gentle norther traverse across Point Mugu State Park, the largest preserved area in the Santa Monica Mountains. This trail, combined with Overlook Trail, gives the hiker quite a tour of the park.

During October and November, Sycamore Canyon offers the twin delights of falling autumn leaves and fluttering butterflies. (Ask park rangers where the monarchs cluster in large numbers.)

Directions to trailhead: Drive up-coast on Highway 1, 32 miles from Santa Monica, to Big Sycamore Canyon Campground in Point Mugu State Park. Outside the campground entrance is an area where you may park. Walk past the campground entrance through the campground to a locked gate. The trail begins on the other side of the gate.

The walk: Take the trail up-canyon, following the creek. Winter rains cause the creek to rise, and sometimes keeping your feet dry while crossing is difficult. Underground water keeps the creekside vegetation green year-round—so this is a fine hike in any season.

One half-mile from the campground you'll spot Overlook Trail, which switchbacks to the west up a ridge and then heads north toward the native tall grass prairie in La Jolla Valley. Make note of this trail, an optional return route.

A second half-mile of nearly level canyon walking brings you to another major hiking trail that branches right—Serrano Canyon Trail, an absolute gem.

Another easy mile of walking beneath the sycamores brings you to a picnic table shaded by a grove of large oak trees. The oaks might be a good turnaround spot for a family with small children. The total round trip distance would be a little over 4 miles.

Continuing up the canyon you'll pass beneath more of the giant sycamores and soon arrive at Wood Canyon Junction, the hub of six trails which lead to all corners of the park. Bear left on signed Wood Canyon Trail and in a short while you'll reach Deer Camp Junction. Drinking water and picnic tables suggest a lunch stop. Oak trees predominate over the sycamores along Wood Canyon Creek; however, the romantic prefer the sycamores, some of which have large clumps of mistletoe in the upper branches.

You can call it a day here and return the way you came. As you hike down the canyon back to the campground, the large and cranky blue jay population will scold you, but don't let the squawking birds stop you from enjoying one of California's finest sycamore savannas.

To return via Overlook Trail: Continue past the junction with Wood Canyon Trail and Deer Camp Junction on the Wood Canyon Trail, which becomes Pumphouse Road. You'll climb over the divide between Sycamore Canyon and La Jolla Valley. Upon reaching a junction, you'll head south on the Overlook Trail, staying on the La Jolla Canyon side of the ridge. True to its name, Overlook Trail offers good views of grassy mountainsides, Boney Peak and Big Sycamore Canyon.

You'll pass an intersection with Scenic Trail, a rough path that hugs the ridge separating La Jolla and Big Sycamore Canyon, where you'll bear right and follow the fire road one-half mile back to the trailhead.

Foot notes: Ringed by ridges, the native grassland of La Jolla Valley welcomes the walker with its drifts of oak and a peaceful pond; a 7 mile round trip on La Jolla Valley Loop Trail and Ray Miller Trail tours the valley.

Serrano Canyon Trail (8½ mile loop) journeys to the sweeping grasslands of Serrano Valley, as beautiful and as quiet a place as you'll find in the Santa Monica Mountains.

Southern California Coast

San Diego, Orange, Los Angeles, Ventura and Santa Barbara county shores have long served as resort areas for Californians, as well as for visitors from around the nation and around the world. Though some state beaches are crowded blanket-to-blanket with sun worshipers, many offer a much more relaxing, even remote environment for a day at the beach.

The state beaches begin at the Mexican border with Borderfield State Park and continue past "America's Riviera" (Santa Barbara) to Refugio and El Capitan state beaches.

Each Southern California beach has its own character—best surfing clearest water, panoramic view, most bird-life. The air and water temperatures are Mediterranean, the place-names Spanish.

The coast includes not only such sand strands as the "Sans"—Elijo, Onofre, Clemente and Buenaventura—but some nature preserves as well. Monarch butterflies migrate to a woodland on the bluffs above El Capitan State Beach. Birds and bird-watchers flock to the mouth of the Santa Clara River at McGrath State Beach. On the bluffs south of Del Mar grows the rare Torrey Pine, set aside in a state reserve that shelters a rich native plant community.

Border Field State Park
Border Field Trail

> **Terrain:** Estuary, sand beach
> **Highlights:** Good birding and beach-walking at the southwest corner of the United States.
> **Distance:** To Tijuana River is 3 miles round trip; to Imperial Beach is 6 miles round trip.
> **Degree of difficulty:** Easy
> **Precautions:** Tijuana River can flood and is dangerous to cross at high water; occasional sewage spills have polluted river/estuary and closed the park.

At the very southwest corner of America is a monument marking the border between Mexico and California. When California became a territory at the end of the Mexican-American War, an international border became a necessity. American and Mexican survey crews determined the boundary, and the monument of Italian marble was placed in 1851 to mark the original survey site. Today the monument stands in the shadow of the Tijuana Bull Ring and still delineates the border between the United States and Estados Unidos Mexicanos.

Much of the Tijuana River Estuary, one of the few salt marshes left in Southern California and one of the region's most important bird habitats, is within Border Field State Park's boundaries.

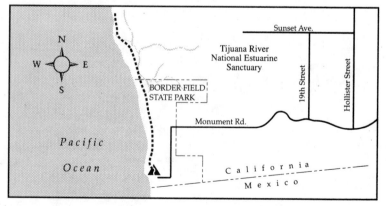

Stop in at the visitor center and check out the natural history exhibits that interpret this unique environment.

This walk explores the dune and estuary ecosystems of the state park and takes you to wide sandy Imperial Beach. Wear an old pair of shoes and be prepared for the soft mud of the marsh.

Directions to trailhead: Border Field State Park is located in the extreme southwestern corner of California, with Mexico and the Pacific Ocean as its southern and western boundaries. From Interstate 5 (San Diego Freeway) south, exit on Hollister Street, proceed to a T-intersection, bear west (right) 2 miles on Monument Road to the state park. The park closes at sunset.

The walk: Follow the short bluff trail down to the beach, which is under strict 24-hour surveillance by the U.S. Border Patrol. The beach is usually deserted, quite a contrast to crowded Tijuana Beach a few hundred yards to the south. As you walk north on Border Field State Park's 1½-mile-long beach, you'll pass sand dunes anchored by salt grass, pickleweed and sand verbena.

On the other side of the dunes is the Tijuana River Estuary, an essential breeding ground, feeding and nesting spot for more than 170 species of native and migratory birds. At Border Field, the salt marsh is relatively unspoiled, unlike so many wetlands encountered farther north, which have been drained, filled or used as dumps.

A mile and a half from the border you'll reach the mouth of the Tijuana River. Only after heavy storms is the Tijuana River the wide swath pictured on some maps. Most of the time it's fordable at low tide, but use your best judgement.

Continue north along wide, sandy Imperial Beach, past some houses and low bluffs. Imperial beach was named by the South San Diego Investment Company to lure Imperial Valley residents to build summer cottages on the beach. Waterfront lots could be purchased for $25 down and $25 monthly, and developers promised the balmy climate would cure an assortment of ailments.

In more recent times, what was once a narrow beach protected by a seawall has been widened considerably by sand dredged from San Diego Bay. There's good swimming and surfing along Imperial Beach and the waves can get huge. The beach route reaches Imperial Pier, built in 1912 and the oldest in the county.

Torrey Pines State Reserve
Parry Grove, Guy Fleming Trails

Terrain: Sandstone bluffs
Highlights: Rare Torrey pines, native plants
Distance: 0.4 to 1 mile trails; a couple miles to criss-cross the Reserve
Degree of difficulty: Easy
Precautions: Protect the fragile ecology by staying on the trail

Atop the bluffs of Torrey Pines State Reserve lies a microcosm of old California, a garden of shrubs and succulents, an enclave of life that the Indians lived.

Most visitors come to view the 3,000 or so *Pinus torreyana,* which grow only here and on Santa Rosa Island, but the reserve also offers the walker a striking variety of native plants.

Be sure to check out the interpretive displays at the park museum and the native plant garden near the head of the Parry Grove Trail. Plant and bird lists, as well as wildflower maps are available for a small fee.

Parry Grove Trail, named in honor of Dr. C.C. Parry, takes you through a handsome grove of Torrey pines. Parry was a botanist assigned to the boundary commission that surveyed the Mexican-American border in 1850. While waiting for the expedition to start, Parry explored the San Diego area. He investigated a tree that had been called the Soledad pine for the nearby Soledad Valley. Parry sent samples to his teacher and friend, Dr. John Torrey of Princeton, and asked that if it proved to be a new species, it be named for Torrey. The Soledad pine became *Pinus torreyana,* or Torrey pine, in honor of the famous botanist and taxonomist.

The 0.4-mile loop trail also leads past toyon, yucca, and many other coastal shrubs.

Broken Hill Trail visits a drier, chaparral-dominated landscape, full of sage and buckwheat, ceanothus and manzanita. From Broken Hill Overlook, there's a view of a few Torrey pines clinging to life in an environment that resembles a desert badlands.

Beach Trail leads to Yucca Point and Razor Point and offers precip-

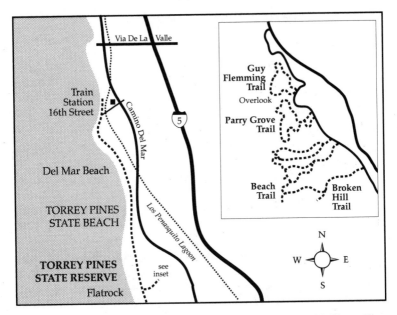

itous views of the beach below. The trail descends the bluffs to Flat Rock, a fine tidepool area.

Guy Fleming Trail is a 0.6-mile loop that travels through stands of Torrey pine and takes you to South Overlook, where you might glimpse a migrating California gray whale.

Directions to trailhead: From Interstate 5, exit on Carmel Valley Road and head west to North Torrey Pines Road (also known as old Highway 101). The main entrance to the reserve is at the base of the bluffs, where the park road climbs to a parking area near the reserve visitor center. You can also leave your car along the highway next to Torrey Pines State Beach and walk up the park road.

Foot notes: The 6-mile round trip beach walk south from Del Mar Train Station to Torrey Pines State Reserve is a winner. Board a southbound train from Los Angeles or another station along the line, and get off at Del Mar.

San Clemente State Beach
Trestles Trail

Terrain: Dramatic coastal bluffs, wide beach
Highlights: Mellow beach walking
Distance: To San Mateo Point is 3 miles round trip
Degree of difficulty: Easy

"Our beach shall always be free from hurdy-gurdies and defilement. We believe beauty to be an asset as well as gold and silver, or cabbage and potatoes."

This was the pledge of Norwegian immigrant Ole Hanson, who began the town of San Clemente in 1925. It was quite a promise from a real estate developer, quite a promise in those days of shameless boosterism a half-century before the California Coastal Commission was established.

Thanks in part to Hanson's vision, some of the peaceful ambiance of San Clemente, which he regarded as "a painting five miles long and a mile wide" has been preserved. And some of it's isolation, too. Most everyone in the real estate community thought Hanson crazy for building in a locale 66 miles from San Diego and 66 miles from Los

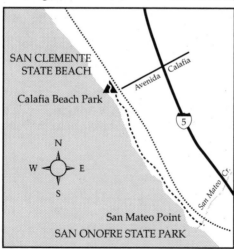

Angeles, but today this isolation attracts rather than repels. This isolation was one of the reasons President Richard Nixon (1969–74) established his Western White House on the bluffs above San Clemente Beach.

San Clemente State Beach is a great place for a walk. The beach is mercifully walled off from the din of the San

Diego Freeway and the confusion of the modern world by a handsome line of tan-colored bluffs. Only the occasional train passing over Santa Fe Railroad tracks, located near the shore, interrupt the cry of the gull, the roar of the breakers. The trestles located at the south end of the beach at San Mateo Point give Trestles Beach its name.

Trestles Beach is one of the finest surfing areas on the West Coast. When the surf is up, the waves peel rapidly across San Mateo Point, creating a great ride. Before the area became part of the state beach, it was restricted government property belonging to Camp Pendleton Marine Base. For well over twenty-five years, surfers carried on guerrilla warfare with U.S. Marines. Trespassing surfers were chased, arrested, and fined, and on many occasions had their boards confiscated and broken in two. Find a veteran surfer and he'll tell you about escapes from jeep patrols and guard dogs. Many times, however, the cool marines would charitably give surfers rides while out on maneuvers.

This walk's destination, San Mateo Point, is the northernmost boundary of San Diego County, the beginning of Orange County. When the original counties of Los Angeles and San Diego were set up in 1850, the line that separated them began on the coast at San Mateo Point. When Orange County was formed from southern Los Angeles County in 1889, San Mateo Point was established as the southern point of the new county.

The enthusiastic, with the time and inclination, can easily extend this beach-walk several miles south to San Onofre State Beach. Another option worth considering is to take the train to San Clemente and walk south from the Amtrak station.

Directions to trailhead: From the San Diego Freeway (I-5) in San Clemente, exit on Avenida Calafia and head west a half-mile to Calafia Beach Park, where there is metered parking. You can also park (for a fee) at San Clemente State Beach. A limited amount of free parking is available in the residential area near the state beach.

Northbound motorists on I-5 will exit at Cristianitos Road, turn left and go over the freeway onto Avenida del Presidente and drive a mile north to Calafia Beach Park.

The walk: From Calafia Beach Park, cross the railroad tracks, make your way down an embankment and head south. As you'll soon see, San Clemente State Beach is frequented by plenty of shorebirds, as well as plenty of surfers, body surfers, and swimmers.

At distinct San Mateo Point, which marks the border of Orange and

San Diego counties, you'll find San Mateo Creek. The headwaters of the creek rise way up in the Santa Ana Mountains above Camp Pendleton. A portion of the creek is protected by the Cleveland National Forest's San Mateo Canyon Wilderness. Rushes, salt grass and cattails line the creek mouth, where sand pipers, herons and egrets gather.

You can ford the creek mouth (rarely a problem except after winter storms) and continue south toward San Onofre State Beach and the giant domes of San Onofre Nuclear Power Plant. Or you can return the same way.

Or here's a third alternative, an inland return route: Walk under the train trestles and join the park service road, which is usually filled with surfers carrying their boards. The service road takes you up the bluffs, where you'll join the San Clemente Coastal Bike Trail, then wind through a residential area to an entrance to San Clemente State Beach Campground.

Improvise a route through the campground to the park's entry station and join the self-guiding nature trail (brochures available at the station). The path descends through a prickly pear- and lemonade berry-filled draw to Calafia Beach Park and the trailhead. The wind and water-sculpted marine terraces just south of the trailhead resemble Bryce Canyon in miniature and are fun to photograph.

If you want to walk the whole nature trail, you'll walk up to site #70 in the campground, then retrace your steps (100 yards or so) back to the Calafia Beach parking lot.

Crystal Cove State Park
Moro Canyon Trail

Terrain: Oak woodland, grassy slopes of San Joaquin Hills
Highlights: Undeveloped Orange County; coastal vistas
Distance: Park headquarters to top of Moro Canyon is 7 miles
round trip with 700-foot elevation gain
Degree of difficulty: Moderate

Extending three miles along the coast between Laguna Beach and Corona del Mar, and inland over the San Joaquin Hills, Crystal Cove State Park attracts birdwatchers, beachcombers, and hikers.

Former Irvine Ranch roads now form a network of hiking trails that loop through the state park. An especially nice trail travels the length of Moro Canyon, the main watershed of the park. An oak woodland, a seasonal stream and sandstone caves are some of the attractions of a walk through this canyon. Bird-watchers may spot the roadrunner, quail, Cooper's hawk, wrentit and many more species.

After exploring inland portions of the state park, allow some time to visit the park's coastline, highlighted by grassy bluffs, sandy beaches, tidepools and coves. The Pelican Point, Crystal Cove, Reef Point and Moro Beach areas of the park allow easy beach access. An offshore area adjacent to the park has been designated an underwater park for divers.

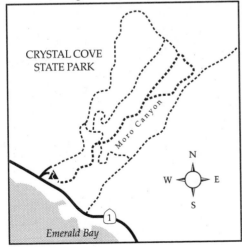

Directions to trailhead: Crystal Cove State Park is located off Pacific Coast Highway, about two miles south of the town of Corona Del Mar or one mile north of Laguna Beach.

Turn inland on the short park road, signed "El Moro Canyon." Drinking water, restrooms, interpretive displays and plenty of parking are available at the ranger station.

Pick up a trails map at the ranger station. At the station, you can consult the schedule of ranger-led interpretive walks, which explore both inland and coastal sections of the state park.

The walk: Below the ranger station, near the park entry kiosk pick up the unsigned Moro Canyon Trail, which crosses the grassy slopes behind a school and trailer park down into Moro Canyon. At the canyon bottom, you meet a fire road and head left, up-canyon.

The walker may observe such native plants as black sage, prickly pear cactus, monkeyflowers, golden bush, lemonade berry and deer weed. Long before Spanish missionaries and settlers arrived in Southern California, a Native American population flourished in the coastal canyons of Orange County. The abundance of edible plants in the area, combined with the mild climate and easy access to the bounty of the sea, contributed to the success of these people; anthropologists believe they lived here for more than four thousand years.

The canyon narrows, and you ignore fire roads joining Moro Canyon from the right and left. You stay in the canyon bottom and proceed through an oak woodland, which shades a trickling stream. You'll pass a shallow sandstone cave just off the trail to the right.

About 2½ miles from the trailhead, you'll reach the unsigned junction with a fire road. If you wish to make a loop trip out of this day hike, bear left on this road, which climbs steeply west, then northeast toward the ridgetop that forms a kind of inland wall for Muddy, Moro, Emerald and other coastal canyons.

When you reach the ridgetop, unpack your lunch and enjoy the far reaching views of the San Joaquin Hills and Orange County coast, Catalina and San Clemente Islands. You'll also have a raven's-eye-view of Moro Canyon and the route back to the trailhead. After catching your breath, you'll bear right (east) along the ridgetop and quickly descend back into Moro Canyon. A ¾-mile walk brings you back to the junction where you earlier ascended out of the canyon. This time you continue straight down-canyon, retracing your steps to the trailhead.

Malibu Lagoon State Beach
Malibu Beach Trail

Terrain: Sand and stone beach, lagoon at mouth of Malibu Creek
Highlights: Good surfing, great birding, quintessential Southland beach experience.
Distance: A mile or so to walk around Malibu Lagoon and down-coast a ways to Malibu Pier. Depending on the tide, you can walk 2 to 3 miles up-coast from Malibu Lagoon.
Degree of difficulty: Easy

When Southern California natives say "Malibu Beach" this popular surfing spot is what they mean: it's the site of beach-blanket movies and Beach Boys songs. The state beach—formerly known as Surfrider—is a mixture of sand and stone. More than 200 bird species have been observed at Malibu Lagoon.

For Los Angeles businessman Frederick Hastings Rindge, owner of 22 miles of southern California coast, life in the Malibu of a century ago was divine. "The ennobling stillness makes the mind ascend to heaven," he wrote in his memoir, *Happy Days in Southern California,* published in 1898.

Long before Malibu meant good surfing, a movie-star colony and some of the most expensive real estate on earth, "The Malibu" was a shorthand name for Topanga Malibu Sequit, an early-nineteenth-century rancho. This rancho extended from Topanga Canyon to the southeast to Ventura County on the northwest, from the tideline to the crest of the Santa Monica Mountains.

Malibu Lagoon hosts many different kinds of waterfowl, both resident and migratory. The beach is rock cobble on the ocean side of the lagoon. To the landward side of the lagoon stretches the alluvial fill flatland deposited by Malibu Creek. The city of Malibu is situated here. Malibu—the city and the creekbed—suffered some fire damage as a result of the serious 1993 brushfire that burned from the crest of the Santa Monica Mountains down to the coast highway.

Across from the lagoon is a stunning California landmark, the Adamson House, a beautiful Spanish-style home built by Rhoda

Adamson, daughter of Frederick Rindge. The house, built in 1929, makes lavish use of ceramic "Malibu Tile." The grounds have been restored to their former beauty, with many ornamental trees and shrubs. Fountains and flagstone pathways wind through the landscaped grounds. Guided tours (fee) are available 11 a.m. to 3 p.m., Wednesday through Saturday.

Adjoining the Adamson House is the Malibu Lagoon Museum, which contains a collection of artifacts and rare photographs that depict the various eras of "The Malibu," as this section of coastal Southern California was known.

Directions to trailhead: Malibu Lagoon State Beach is located at Pacific Coast Highway and Cross Creek Road in Malibu.

The walk: First follow the nature trails around the lagoon.

Down-coast the walker will soon reach the historic 700-foot Malibu Pier, built in 1903. It's a favorite of fishermen and tourists. Sportfishing boats depart from the pier.

Farther down-coast is Zonker Harris Accessway, long the focus of debate between the California Coastal Commission, determined to provide access to the coast, and some Malibu residents who would prefer the public stay out. The original sign read "Zonker Harris Memorial Beach," honoring a character from the Doonesbury comic strip whose longtime primary goal was to acquire the perfect tan.

Up-coast, you'll pass Malibu Point; here the strong southwest swell refracts against a rock reef and creates the waves that makes Malibu so popular with surfers. Next you walk (stay below the high tide line and respect the privacy of the homeowners) the narrow and sandy beach lined by the exclusive Malibu Colony residences, home to many a movie star. Toward the west end of The Colony, the beach narrows considerably and houses are built on stilts, with the waves sometimes pounding beneath them.

As you walk along Malibu Beach, rejoice that you do not see State Highway 60, the Malibu Freeway. In the 1960s a plan was hatched to build a causeway along Malibu Beach, supported on pilings offshore. A breakwater would have converted the open shore into a bay shore. The wonderful pounding surf would have been reduced to that of a lake.

The beach is wider and more public at Corral State Beach, located between the mouths of Corral and Solstice Canyons.

McGrath State Beach
McGrath Beach Trail

> **Terrain:** Sandy beach, shore of estuary
> **Highlights:** Uncrowded beach; great birding at small lake and Santa Clara Estuary
> **Distance:** to McGrath Lake is 4 miles round trip; to Oxnard Shores is 8 miles round trip; to Channel Islands Harbor is 12 miles round trip
> **Degree of difficulty:** Easy to moderate

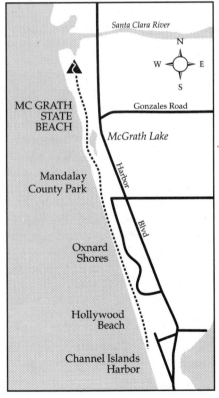

McGrath State Beach and McGrath Lake were named for the McGrath family which had extensive coastal land holdings in the Ventura coastal area dating from 1874. Located on the western city limits of Oxnard, the two-mile-long state beach extends south from the Santa Clara River.

Near the state beach entry kiosk, a small visitor center features exhibits about the area's plants and wildlife.

This walk takes you on a nature trail through the Santa Clara River Estuary, visits McGrath Lake and travels miles of sandy beach to Channel Islands Harbor.

Directions to trailhead: To reach McGrath State

Beach, visitors southbound on Highway 101 take the Seaward Avenue offramp to Harbor Boulevard, turn south on Harbor and travel 4 miles to the park. Northbound visitors exit Highway 101 on Victoria Avenue, turn left at the light to Olivas Park Drive, then right to Harbor Boulevard. Turn left on Harbor and proceed ¾ mile to the park. The signed nature trail leaves from the day use parking lot. Signposts along the nature trail are keyed to a pamphlet, available at the entry kiosk.

The walk: From the parking lot, follow the nature trail through the estuary. The riverbank is a mass of lush vegetation: willow, silverweed and yerba mansa. In 1980, the Santa Clara River area was declared a natural preserve, primarily to protect the habitat of two endangered birds—the California least tern and Belding's Savannah sparrow.

When you reach nature trail signpost 11, join a nearby trail that leads atop an old levee, first along the river, then down-coast along the periphery of the state beach campground. This trail joins a dirt road and continues down-coast, but the far more aesthetic route is along water's edge, so trudge over the low dunes and walk along the shoreline. Along the beach, visitors enjoy sunbathing or surf fishing for bass, corbina, or perch. In two miles, if you head inland a short ways, you'll spot McGrath Lake, tucked away behind some dunes.

As you continue south, more sandy beach and dunes follow. You pass a huge old Edison power plant, and arrive at Oxnard Shores, a development famous for getting clobbered by heavy surf at high tide. Past Oxnard Shores, a mile of beach walking brings you to historic Hollywood Beach. *The Sheik,* starring that great silent movie idol Rudolph Valentino, was filmed on the desert-like sands here. Real estate promoters of the time attempted to capitalize on Oxnard Beach's instant fame and renamed it Hollywood Beach. They laid out subdivisions called Hollywood-by-the-Sea and Silver Strand, suggesting to their customers that the area was really a movie colony and might become a future Hollywood, but it never became a mecca for the stars or their fans.

This walk ends another mile down-coast at the entrance to Channel Islands Harbor.

El Capitan State Beach, Refugio State Beach
El Capitan Beach Trail

Terrain: Pleasant beaches and bluffs of two state beaches
Highlights: Monarch butterflies, mellow beaches
Distance: 6 mile round trip walk from El Capitan to Refugio State Beach
Degree of difficulty: Easy to moderate
Precautions: Best at low tide

El Capitan is a narrow beach at the mouth of El Capitan Creek. Shading the creek is a woodland of coast live oak and sycamore. During autumn, monarch butterflies congregate and breed in the trees here. (Ask park rangers where the monarchs cluster in large numbers.)

"El Capitan" refers to Captain José Francisco de Ortega, a rotund Spanish Army officer who served as trail scout for the Portolá expedition. When he retired from service to the Crown in 1795, he owed the

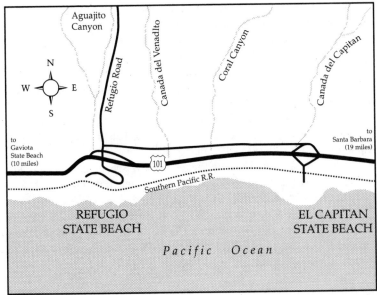

army money and offered to square things by raising cattle. The government granted him his chosen land: a coastal strip, two miles wide and twenty-five miles long extending from just east of Pt. Conception to Refugio Canyon. He called his land Nuestra Señora del Refugio, "Our Lady of Refuge." Alas, Captain Ortega's retirement was short-lived; he died three years later and was buried at the Santa Barbara Mission.

After the death of El Capitán, the Ortega family continued living in Refugio Canyon for many years. The mouth of the canyon at the Pacific was the major contraband-loading point for Southern California during the early years of the nineteenth century when Spanish settlers were forbidden to trade with Americans. From the Ortega Ranch, hides, tallow, leather goods and wine were loaded onto Boston-bound sailing ships.

Beach, bluff, and bike trails link El Capitan and Refugio State Beaches. Depending on the tide, you can usually travel up-coast along El Capitan Beach as far as Coral Canyon Beach. Then you can join the bluff trails or the bike path, which is also open to hikers, for the balance of the trip to Refugio Beach.

El Capitan and Refugio are popular beach campgrounds and nice places to spend a weekend.

Directions to trailhead: From Highway 101, 19 miles up-coast from Santa Barbara, take the El Capitan State Beach exit. Park in one of the day use areas; the park day use fee is also honored at Refugio and Gaviota State Beaches.

The walk: Descend one of the paths or staircases to the shore, then head up-coast along the mixed sandy and rocky beach. Sea cliffs are steep here because they are constantly being cut back by wave erosion. You'll pass wide Coral Canyon, its walls covered with beds of highly deformed light-colored shales.

At Coral Beach, the tides often discourage beach-walking, so head up to the bluffs and follow the bike path.

Approaching Refugio State Beach, you'll see abundant kelp just offshore. If a breeze is blowing over the water, note how areas with kelp are smooth and kelpless areas are rippled.

Refugio State Beach, at the mouth of Refugio Canyon, is a rocky beach with tidepools. Turn around here, or continue beach-walking up-coast (it's 10 more miles to Gaviota State Beach) for as long as time and tides permit.

La Purísima Mission State Historic Park
El Camino Real Trail

> **Distance:** 2 to 5 miles or more round trip
> **Terrain:** Gentle, oak-dotted Purísima Hills
> **Highlights:** Most enjoyable, best restored mission; best mission walking tour
> **Precautions:** Some poison oak along trails

Of California's twenty-one missions, the most fully restored is La Purísima, located four miles north of Lompoc in northwest Santa Barbara County. La Purísima is the only mission with a sizeable amount of land preserved around it—and the only one with hiking trails.

You could spend a fun day at La Purísima Mission State Historic Park in the Lompoc Valley—first heading for the Purísima Hills for a hike, then touring the mission. If you plan your visit for one of the park's "Mission Life Days" or "Purísima People Days," you'll find vol-

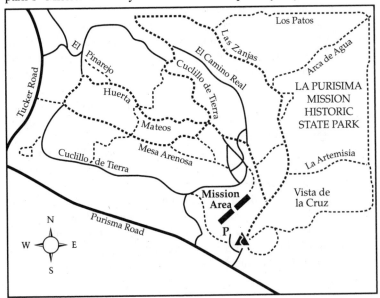

unteer docents costumed as padres, soldiers, and Indians and recreating mission life of the 1820s. Members of the volunteer group Prelado de los Tesoros (Keeper of the Treasures) act out their parts well.

Wandering the thousand acres of hill and dale preserved in the state park will help you grasp that, apart from the mission's religious purpose, it was a large commercial enterprise as well—early nineteenth century agribusiness. You'll walk where crops were grown and cattle grazed, view the mission's far-flung waterworks system, and even see the ruts that are reminders of where the old El Camino Real passed through the mission compound.

Following secularization of the mission system, La Purísima was abandoned in 1834 and soon fell into ruin. In 1934, exactly 100 years after the padres left, the Civilian Conservation Corps began reconstructing the church and a whole complex of buildings. Other restoration projects continued intermittently ever since, and today La Purísima is the most completely restored of California's missions.

Besides the church, you'll see the soldiers' barracks and the priests' quarters. On the mission grounds are reconstructions of the granary, bakery, olive press, and soap factory. Pens and corrals hold Mexican sheep and cattle, similar to the breeds of the mission period.

At the mission entrance is a small museum that displays historical information and artifacts recovered from the mission ruins. In a shady grove near the museum is a picnic ground.

Twelve miles of park trail explore three different ecosystems. Los Berros Creek flows north-south through Purísima Canyon. West of Purísima Canyon is a large oak-dotted mesa that rises a hundred feet above the canyon floor. East of Purísima Canyon are the stream-cut Purísima Hills.

Local joggers and exercise walkers stick to the park's flatlands by joining El Camino Real, then rounding the barley fields and returning via Las Zanjas Trail. That's a circuit of about 3 miles.

Hikers often use the narrower footpaths—Huerta Mateo and Mesa Arenosa Trails—and make a 2-mile loop. Add the 2-mile loop and the 3-mile together for a fine 5-mile walk in the park.

Directions to trailhead: From Highway 101 in Buellton, exit on Highway 246 and head west 13½ miles to Purísima Road. Turn right and proceed a mile to La Purísima Mission State Historical Park on your right. Limited free parking is available near the trailhead alongside Purísima Road or inside the park closer to the mission buildings (fee).

The walk: From Purísima Road, join La Ranchería Trail to the park museum, walk toward the picnic area, then join paved El Camino Real to signed Huerta Mateo Trail. This footpath leads over sandy terrain. Thriving in the sandy soil is coastal scrub vegetation that normally grows only on dune systems much closer to the coast. Occupying the slopes and ridge crests nearby is a flourishing oak woodland.

Stick with Huerta Mateo Trail past several signed junctions until you reach Cucillo de Tierra, a fire road. Turn left and walk a short quarter-mile to signed Mesa Arenosa Trail. Down you go along this sandy trail until you reach a signed junction with Las Canerias Trail; join this path heading west a quarter-mile to wide Cucillo de Tierra Trail. You can turn right here and head back to the mission buildings; however, those hikers wishing to see more the backcountry will turn left (north) and walk 0.4 mile to El Chaparral Trail, which provides a short connecting route to El Camino Real. Turn left and walk along the flat bottomland of Purísima Canyon, which has been cultivated since the construction of the mission and today supports an annual crop of wheat and barley.

El Camino Real runs out at the park boundary and you turn right (east) on Last Zanjas Trail. This path offers a lovely walk near Los Berros Creek. You'll pass a pond and portions of the old mission aqueduct as you enjoy the 1¼-mile walk back to the mission compound and the trailhead.

Point Sal State Beach
Point Sal Trail

Terrain: Beaches and bluffs
Highlights: Wild and remote beach, dramatic point for observing seals and sea lions
Distance: From the state beach to the point, it's 5 miles round trip; can continue several miles up-coast to Nipomo Dunes
Degree of difficulty: Moderate
Precautions: Trails leading along bluffs usually in rough shape

When your eye travels down a map of the Central California coast, you pause on old and familiar friends—the state beaches at San Simeon, Morro Bay, and Pismo Beach. Usually overlooked is another state beach—remote Point Sal, a nub of land north of Vandenberg Air Force Base and south of the Guadalupe Dunes. Windy Point Sal is a wall of bluffs rising 50 to 100 feet above the rocky shore. The water is crystal-clear, and the blufftops provide a fine spot to watch the boisterous seals and sea lions.

The trail system in the Point Sal area is in rough condition. The narrow bluff trails should not be undertaken by novice hikers, the weak-kneed or those afraid of heights. Families with small children and less experienced trekkers will enjoy beachcombing and tidepool-watching.

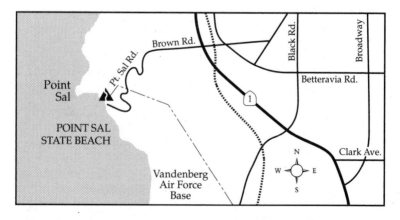

Directions to trailhead: From Highway 101 in Santa Maria, exit on Betteravia Road. Proceed west past a commercial strip and then out into the sugar beet fields. Betteravia Road twists north. About eight miles from Highway 101, turn left on Brown Road. Five miles of driving on Brown Road (watch for cows wandering along the road) brings you to a signed junction; leftward is a ranch road, but you bear right on Point Sal Road, partly paved, partly dirt washboard (impassable in wet weather). Follow this road 5 miles to its end at the parking area above Point Sal State Beach.

Be advised that Point Sal Road is sometimes closed during the rainy season. The Air Force sometimes closes the road for short periods during its missile launches.

The walk: From the parking area, follow one of the short steep trails down to the beautiful crescent-shaped beach. Hike up-coast along the windswept beach. In ⅓ mile, you'll reach the end of the beach at a rocky reef, difficult to negotiate at high tide. A second reef, encountered shortly after the first, is equally difficult. Atop this reef, there's a rope secured to an iron stake to aid your descent to the beach below. The rope is also helpful in ascending the reef on your return.

Unless it's very low tide, you'll want to begin following the narrow bluff trail above the reefs. The trail arcs westward with the coast, occasionally dipping down to rocky and romantic pocket beaches sequestered between reefs.

About 1½ miles from the trailhead, you'll descend close to shore and begin boulder-hopping. After a few hundred yards of boulder-hopping, you'll begin to hear the bark of sea lions and get an aviator's view of Lion Rock, where the gregarious animals bask in the sun.

Your trek continues on a pretty decent bluff trail, which dips down near a sea lion haul-out. (Please don't approach or disturb these creatures.) You'll then ascend rocky Point Sal. From the point, you'll view the Guadalupe Dunes complex to the north and the sandy beaches of Vandenberg Air Force Base to the south. Before returning the same way, look for red-tailed hawks riding the updrafts and admire the ocean boiling up over the reefs.

Energetic hikers can follow a trail which passes behind Point Sal, joins a sandy road, and descends to a splendid beach north of the point. Here you'll find a two-mile-long sandy beach to explore. This unnamed beach is almost always deserted except for a few fishermen and lots of pelicans.

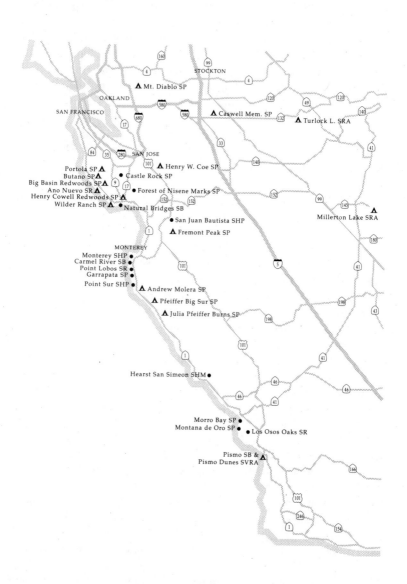

160
99
4
STOCKTON
▲ Mt. Diablo SP
4
OAKLAND
120
49
120
SAN FRANCISCO
580
132
140
17
680
580
▲ Caswell Mem. SP
▲ Turlock L. SRA
33
41
84 35
280 SAN JOSE
140
101
▲ Henry W. Coe SP
Portola SP ▲
● Castle Rock SP
152
152
99
143
Butano SP ▲
Big Basin Redwoods SP ▲
9
Ano Nuevo SR ▲
17
● Forest of Nisene Marks SP
▲
Henry Cowell Redwoods SP ▲
152
Millerton Lake SRA
Wilder Ranch SP ▲
● Natural Bridges SB
● San Juan Bautista SHP
180
1
▲ Fremont Peak SP
MONTEREY
5
Monterey SHP ●
Carmel River SB ●
101
Point Lobos SR ●
41
Garrapata SP ●
Point Sur SHP ●
▲ Andrew Molera SP
198
▲ Pfeiffer Big Sur SP
43
▲ Julia Pfeiffer Burns SP
198
101
1
41
Hearst San Simeon SHM ●
46
46
46
46
41
Morro Bay SP ●
Montana de Oro SP ● ● Los Osos Oaks SR
Pismo SB & ▲
166
Pismo Dunes SVRA
101
246
154
1

Central California

92

Central Valley

Five hundred miles long, the Central Valley, or the Great Central Valley as it is often known, is one of the richest agricultural regions in the world, some 25,000 square miles of farms and fields, levees and reservoirs, towns and cities. The Central Valley is commonly divided into the Sacramento Valley in the north and the San Joaquin Valley in the south.

The waters of the Sacramento River and its tributaries, which drain the Sacramento Valley are collected in such mega-reservoirs as Lake Oroville and Folsom Lake; these lakes offer abundant water-oriented recreation, as well as some shoreline hiking.

The Sacramento River itself hosts a couple of parks with riverside trails, including Woodson Bridge State Recreation Area and Colusa-Sacramento State Recreation Area.

High Sierra snowmelt flows west in a network of rivers to the San Joaquin Valley. Supplying water for agriculture—and for a little fun, too—are Turlock and Millerton lakes.

Before the San Joaquin Valley was cleared for cultivation, it was dotted with woodland. Most of this woodland has disappeared, but at Caswell Memorial State Park, hikers can explore an oak woodland on the banks of the Stanislaus River.

Millerton Lake State Recreation Area
South Shore Trail

> **Terrain:** Foothills around Millerton Lake
> **Highlights:** Views of lake, historic Millerton courthouse
> **Distance:** South Bay Picnic Area to the marina is 4 miles round trip.
> **Degree of difficulty:** Moderate

The state recreation area has Gold Tours, with a chance to pan for gold, on Saturdays during November and March. On Saturdays in December, January, and February, the park offers Eagle Tours; visitors board boats and glimpse wintering bald eagles, as well as dozens of other bird species.

Just as the San Joaquin River flows down from the High Sierra foothills into the Central Valley, it's dammed by Friant Dam. Built across the river canyon in 1944, the dam created Millerton Lake.

The lake inundated the historic town of Millerton. The town evolved from an Army camp, Fort Miller, established to battle the

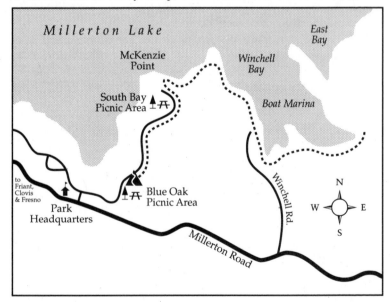

local Yokut people, angered by the intrusion of settlers and Forty-niners on their territory. The small town of Millerton grew and served for awhile as the Fresno County seat, complete with an impressive courthouse built in 1867.

As Millerton Lake began to fill, preservationists rescued the courthouse by dismantling and rebuilding it on higher ground. The courthouse, built of massive granite blocks, includes the reconstructed offices of the tax collector, sheriff, and assessor. It's open to visitors.

Millerton Lake measures about a mile wide near the dam site, three miles wide at its widest point. The lake backs up 16 miles into its river canyon.

Best hike is South Shore Trail, sometimes called Winchell Ridge Trail, which follows the contours of Winchell Bay on its way to the Marina at Winchell Bay. The trail extends some four miles from Blue Oak Camp Picnic Area to its end a bit past the marina. Because the first half of the trail closely parallels the road (on the inland side of the road) most hikers will find the second half of South Shore Trail more satisfying and thus begin the walk at South Bay Picnic Area.

The park has ambitious plans to extend South Shore Trail another ten miles to Temperance Flat and a BLM camp near Kerckhoff Powerhouse.

Directions to trailhead: From Highway 99 in Fresno, take Highway 41 north and proceed twenty miles to the Highway 145 turnoff. Follow the signs five miles east to the main park entrance on the south shore of Millerton Lake State Recreation Area. The park road follows the lakeshore to Blue Oak Picnic Area, where there's trailhead parking. Start your hike here or, better yet, continue another two miles to South Bay Picnic Area.

The walk: From the picnic area, the trail turns east to round McKenzie Point. It's mellow walking with little elevation gain, as the path contours over oak-dotted grassy slopes.

You'll get fine vistas of the lake, as well as over-the-shoulder views of the Millerton Courthouse. After skirting Winchell Bay, you'll reach the marina, a no-nonsense facility that holds little interest for the hiker. Signs help walkers stay on the trail, which crosses Winchell Road, just below another park entrance station and continue a bit farther along the lakeshore before passage is forbidden due to private property problems.

Turlock Lake State Recreation Area
Tuolomne Trail

Terrain: Oak-dotted Sierra foothills, banks of Tuolomne River.
Highlights: Native plants, quiet stretch of river.
Distance: Half a mile or so round trip
Degree of difficulty: Easy
Precautions: Trails very overgrown.

Bordered on the north by the Tuolomne River and on the south by Turlock Lake, the State Recreation Area offers many opportunities for outdoor recreation: boating, fishing, swimming, waterskiing on the lake; plus walking, camping, and blackberry-picking along the river.

This tributary of the San Joaquin River still has places that display the kind of native plant life that was once common along the banks of the great rivers of the valley. Along the Tuolomne, a tangle of blackberries and wild grape grow at the river's edge, accompanied by wildflowers and Woodwardia ferns.

Trails have been cut (and made by use) to the river's edge by blackberry fanciers, who enjoy picking the native fruit from July through October. The paths, which receive little or no maintenance and are overgrown, explore a woodsy environment around the campground, between the river and the lake. Not only are the paths poor, but access is difficult; there's no day use area on the river side of the park. Best bet is to ask rangers if you can leave your car near the park entrance station and walk into the campground where the trail begins.

Join the unmarked trail at campsite six. The hiking is improvisational; wander at will as far as your energy and the condition of the trail allows. Eventually your passage will be halted by blackberry thickets.

Directions to trailhead: From Highway 99 in Modesto, drive east on Highway 132 (Yosemite Boulevard) some 21 miles to Camp Road. Turn right, cross the Tuolomne River on an old iron bridge, and fork left onto Lake Road, which soon leads to Turlock Lake State Recreation Area. The lake is on the south side of the road; the campground, Tuolomne River, and the brief hiking trail are on the north side of the road.

Caswell Memorial State Park

Oak Forest Trail

> **Terrain:** Wooded banks of Stanislaus River
> **Highlights:** Rare oak woodland
> **Distance:** 1 mile or so round trip, plus optional longer walks
> **Degree of difficulty:** Easy

Before the San Joaquin Valley was cleared for cultivation, it was dotted with forests. Most of these woodlands have vanished, but at Caswell Memorial State Park, a remnant oak forest is preserved, a reminder of how the great valley appeared in days gone by.

Along the Stanislaus River banks is a thriving grove of valley oaks. Some specimens stand 60 feet high and 17 feet in circumference.

Most visitors come to Caswell for the bass (striped, largemouth and smallmouth) fishing. The park's beach and swimming areas are popular on summer days.

The park also offers an opportunity to exit busy highways 99 and I-5 and stretch your legs.

Spring and fall are the most comfortable times to meander Oak Forest Nature Trail through stands of valley oak, then along the Stanislaus River. Heed all warning signs and stay well away from the nesting birds.

The nature trail once was an interpreted path, but isn't any longer. Instead, the walker will find a path that loop the loops through tangles of wild grape and blackberry bushes on the banks of the Stanislaus. Rangers conduct nature walks on Saturday mornings in the summer.

The hiking is strictly improvisational; loop as long as you wish (you could actually get a few miles of hiking along the river and through the woods) before returning to the parking area or the park's swimming beach.

Directions to trailhead: From Highway 99, some 10 miles north of Modesto, take the Ripon exit. Follow West Main Street through the little town, then past kiwi groves and produce stands to Austin Road. Turn left and travel 2½ miles to the park. The trail departs from the park's day use area.

Folsom Lake State Recreation Area
Western States Trail

> **Terrain:** Wooded, brushy lakeshore
> **Highlights:** Bird-watching, wooded section of lake
> **Distance:** Rattlesnake Bar to Horseshoe Bar is 3 miles round
>   trip
> **Degree of difficulty:** Easy to moderate

Closest to a metropolitan area of all the big reservoir parks, Folsom Lake attracts 4 million visitors a year. Situated in the Sierra Nevada foothills, just 25 miles from Sacramento, the lake is popular with those who like to camp, water-ski, boat, swim and fish.

Folsom Lake, formed by Folsom Dam, has 75 miles of shoreline. The dam is located near the confluence of the north and south forks of the American River; this has created two long arms extending deep into the foothills with a peninsula in between.

In a popular state recreation area like Folsom Lake, rangers have lots of law enforcement duties; they've even been known to hold "VFW" reunions—that's Veterans of Folsom Wars.

Still, even the most law-and-order-style rangers like to point out the natural beauty of the 6,000 or so acres of land around the lake. Oak woodland and grassland sprinkled with spring wildflowers are part of the intriguing terrestrial habitat.

Hikers and horseback riders enjoy the park's 80 miles of trail. One stretch is part of the Western States Pioneer Express Trail between Carson City, Nevada, and Sacramento. This path also connects Folsom Lake with Auburn State Recreation Area.

Folsom has a number of environmental camps that are only accessible by foot, boat or bicycle.

The more isolated hiking is along the North Fork and the South Fork of the America River, those two long arms of Folsom Lake. Trails north and south from Folsom Dam also offer good walking.

One fine stretch of Western States Trail is between Rattlesnake Bar and Horseshoe Bar. The "bars" refer to wide turns in the river where miners often found gold. There's enough lake traffic to remind you're hiking in a giant recreation area, but not so much that you can't enjoy a natural experience.

Directions to trailhead: From Auburn-Folsom Road (which runs between its two namesake communities on the west side of the lake), turn east on Horseshoe Bar Road and follow it to its end at a gravel road, a parking area for horse trailers.

The walk: Before entering the woods, the path meanders a meadowland and offers a curious sight: palm trees. On a humid day, you can imagine you're on a tropical isle.

The trail ascends into a woodland and crosses a wooden bridge over a creek flowing into the lake. Notice the tangles of wild grape hanging from the trees.

For the first mile and a half, the main trail (wider than a couple of confusing side paths along the way) rises and falls a few times, passing close to some private property and fence lines.

The trail reaches a somewhat level area by the water. Turn around here or continue with the lakeside trail for a few more miles

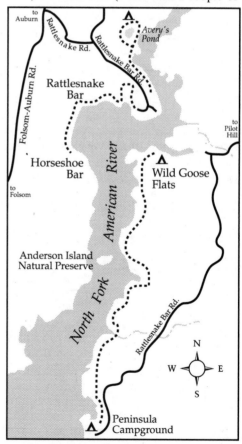

Auburn State Recreation Area
Western Pioneer Trail

> **Terrain:** Banks of American River
> **Highlights:** Dramatic stretch of river
> **Distance:** From Ruck-a-Chucky Campground to rapids is 4 miles round trip
> **Degree of difficulty:** Easy to moderate

The dam builders didn't get their way on the American River.

In 1967, construction began on Auburn Dam, which would have turned the gorges and canyons along this stretch of the river into Auburn Lake. But a Montana dam, similar in design to the one under construction at Auburn, collapsed. This incident, along with conservation efforts by such groups as Friends of the River, put a halt to the project. The federal Bureau of Reclamation then allowed the state of California to use a portion of the river as a recreation area.

Since it's possible, though unlikely, the project could be revived (the dam was conceived in the 1940s and a few die-hard locals have been pushing for its construction ever since), no expensive roads or facilities have been constructed in the 30,000-acre recreation area; any such improvements would be covered by water if Auburn Lake came into existence.

Fishing, river-rafting, hiking and camping are popular activities at

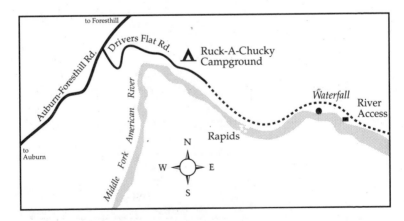

the park, which is located along more than 30 miles of the north and middle forks of the American River. Rafting excursions are available by commercial tour operators.

In this guide, I've placed Auburn State Recreation Area in a chapter with other parks in California's Great Central Valley, primarily because of its proximity to metro-Sacramento and to Folsom Lake. Folsom, one of the state's big reservoir parks and part of California's vast waterworks system, seems very much part of the Central Valley; however, adjacent Auburn, sans dam, has a wilder vibe and seems temperamentally, if not geographically, to be linked with the nearby Gold Country parks. Scenic Highway 49 winds through the recreation area and offers a glimpse of the sharp canyons and rugged countryside characteristic of the Mother Lode foothills.

A major part of the recreation area's 58-mile trail system is the Western Pioneer Trail, which travels from Sacramento to Lake Tahoe. Weekend backpackers can pitch a tent at a number of trail camps along the river.

Trail information and permits are available at a field office, located just off Highway 49, one-half mile south of the Auburn city limits.

One of Ranger Jordan Fisher-Smith's favorite walks is a stretch of trail along the American River from Ruck-a-Chucky Campground to the Ruck-a-Chucky rapids. Early spring wildflowers—fairy lanterns, Indian paintbrush, lupine and many more—brighten the pathway.

Ruck-A-Chucky got its name from late 1800s' gold miners, who found the "rotten chuck" served at most mining camps hard to digest. Over the years, this slang became the even more colorful ruck-a-chucky.

Directions to trailhead: From Interstate 80 on the outskirts of Auburn, exit on Auburn-Foresthill Road and head east eight miles. Turn right on dirt Drivers Flat Road (bumpy, but suitable for passenger cars with good ground clearance) and proceed to 2½ miles to Ruck-a-Chucky Campground and road's end at the trailhead.

Note: Drivers Flat Road may be closed during inclement weather.

The walk: From the signed trailhead, follow the closed road along the "warm side" of the river. The American River, which has its headwaters in the deep snows of the Sierra Nevada, has deposited quite a collection of sand, rounded cobblestones and great boulders en route, and carved an impressive canyon here as well.

The mighty American River broke off and carried away bits of gold from up stream quartz veins. It was this placer gold that brought 10,000 miners to the area, shortly after its discovery on the south fork of the American in 1848.

As you look down at the river, you might spot a merganser, one of those large diving ducks common on American River. If you look up high above the river banks, you might see some little platforms marked by rock walls; Gold Rush-era miners lived way up there.

Ruck-a-Chucky rapids is not a stretch of river that sane river-rafters run, so there is a portage trail that leads along the banks to get around the rapids. A lookout point over the rapids is a good turnaround point. For a longer hike, you can continue another two miles to Fords Bar.

Lake Oroville State Recreation Area
Loafer Creek, Roy Rogers Trails

> **Terrain:** Chaparral-oak-pine dotted hillsides
> **Highlights:** Intimate view of lake and shoreline, monument to state water system
> **Length:** 2-mile loop or 4¾-mile loop
> **Degree of difficulty:** Easy to moderate

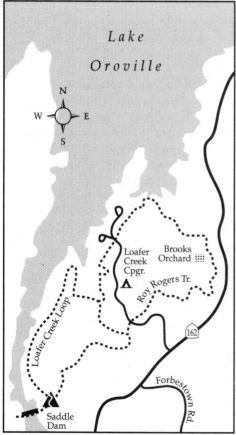

Feather River-fed Lake Oroville offers lots to do, both on and off the water. Boating and water-skiing, fishing and swimming are popular forms of recreation on the big lake, while camping, picnicking, hiking and horseback riding are among the enjoyable pursuits along Oroville's lengthy (167 mile) shoreline.

To learn about the lake and surrounding environs, check out the displays and observation tower at the visitor center. Here you'll find positively worshipful exhibits about western water-seekers, California's gigantic water system, and the role of water in our present-day civilization. My favorite exhibit is the one comparing the relative height of Oroville Dam in relation to the Statue of Liberty and the Eiffel Tower.

The state recreation area has a couple of short hiking trails that can be linked to provide a 2-mile jaunt, a more ambitious 4¾-mile loop, or something in between.

Directions to trailhead: From Highway 70 (Business), otherwise known as Oroville Dam Boulevard, in Oroville, head east to Highway 162 (Olive Highway) and continue five miles to Kelly Ridge Road. Turn left and drive a half-mile. Just after the turnoff to the water treatment plant, turn right on the dirt road leading to a parking area.

The walk: Head back toward the water treatment plant and small dam. Ignore the signed trail beckoning you to hike to the visitor information center and walk across the dam to the signed trailhead on the other side.

Take the "Brooks Orchard" leg of the loop trail and begin a modest climb through a woodland of oak and digger pine.

After a mile, the trail forks. A left means you loop back another mile to the trailhead.

The right fork crosses the Loafer Creek Campground Road, then gently travels a mile to Brooks Orchard, a popular resting and watering place for the many horses and riders on Oroville's trails.

A quarter-mile past this rest stop, you'll cross a creek, then meander down toward the lakeshore. You'll skirt Loafer Creek Campground, then ascend oak- and ponderosa pine-covered slopes.

When you meet up with Loafer Creek Loop Trail, you'll swing right, over grass slopes on a mellow descent back to the trailhead.

Foot notes: From Lake Oroville's visitor information center, you can join Chaparral Trail (an interpretive nature trail), then follow Kelly Ridge Trail to a lookout point above the lake; this lots-to-see loop is 2¾ miles.

Outside the park, in Plumas National Forest, is Feather Falls Trail (7½ miles round trip) that leads to a most impressive waterfall. The 640-foot high waterfall is the sixth highest in the United States; it's particularly impressive in the spring after a good rainy winter.

Colusa-Sacramento River State Recreation Area

Nature, Levee Trails

Terrain: Banks of California's largest river, wide expanses of agricultural land
Highlights: Scenic Sacramento River, quaint Colusa
Distance: 1 mile loop nature trail, plus 1½ to 3 miles along levee
Degree of difficulty: Easy

The campers, boaters, fishermen and hikers who enjoy this delightful park on the west side of the Sacramento River rarely can the previous use of the land now included in a state recreation area. It was—literally—a dump.

Beginning in 1955, the dump was filled, graded, and improved. In 1964 the area was opened as a park.

The banks of the river were once occupied by the River Patwin, who were noted for their fine feather work and basketry. In warfare, they went into battle wearing elk hide and reed body armor to protect against spears and arrows. The Patwin followed the Ghost Dance Movement, which held that white men would disappear and the land would return to its original pristine state.

But the Patwin were wrong. The area's climate, generous winter

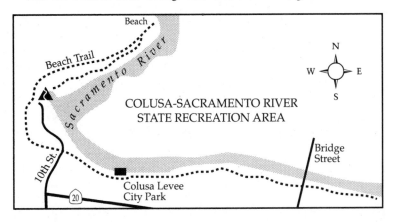

rains and fertile climate attracted scores of farmers, particularly after the Gold Rush when thousands of settlers homesteaded along the banks of the Sacramento River.

The Sacramento, lined by cottonwoods and willows, wild grapes and figs, may look placid as a lake, but in winter the river often becomes a raging torrent. Great quantities of silt, which helps create some of the richest farmland in the nation, are left behind after flood season. Sometimes the park's boat ramp and picnic ground end up covered with mud.

The park is a nice place for fishing off the riverbank or as a base for fishing expeditions up and downriver.

For hikers, Colusa is a walk in the park, an easy saunter down to the river and a sandy beach. During the summer, you can swim, if you don't mind cold water.

The trail is the old campground road; in 1980, the campground was moved to its present location to avoid the Sacramento River's annual flooding—and the rebuilding costs associated with the floods.

From the park's southern boundary, a levee extends up-river and down. Head downriver (south, then east) on the levee and you'll pass through a city park and get great views of Colusa, with its Victorian homes and historic buildings, as well as the ag-country beyond.

Directions to trailhead: From Interstate 5 in Williams, some 60 miles north of Sacramento, exit on Highway 20 and drive east 9 miles to the quaint town of Colusa. As Highway 20 bends sharply south, you'll continue straight onto 10th Street and soon arrive at the state recreation area. The trail begins near a gate at the far side of the park.

The walk: Take the right or left fork: the two paths link one-half mile later, just before the river. Make your way among the tall cottonwoods to the sandy beach on the river's edge.

Loop back and join the levee, which passes through Colusa Levee City Park and offers views of Colusa's old buildings. Towering above the river to the east are the 2,000-foot Sutter Buttes; to the west are the more than a mile-high peaks of the Coast Range.

A good turnaround point (¾ mile from the park) is a bridge over the Sacramento and aptly named Bridge Street; however, you can continue walking the levee for several more miles past farms and fields.

Woodson Bridge State Recreation Area
Sacramento River Trail

> **Terrain:** Banks of Sacramento River
> **Highlights:** Interstate 5 escape, tubing
> **Distance:** 1½ miles round trip
> **Degree of difficulty:** Easy
> **Precautions:** Some poison oak

Canoers, rafters and inner-tubers float down to Woodson Bridge State Recreation Area, located in an oak woodland on the Sacramento River between Chico and Red Bluff.

The park is often the day's-end destination for the above-mentioned flotilla, which puts in up river at Los Molino or Red Bluff. For fishermen, out for shad, striped bass, catfish and salmon, Woodson Bridge is not so much a destination as a departure point for launching a boat on the Sacramento.

Walkers stroll beneath the grand old oaks growing along the river. Joining the oaks are walnut, sycamore, and cottonwood. The park's trees muster quite a display of fall color. Beneath the trees grow a tangle of elderberry and wild grape.

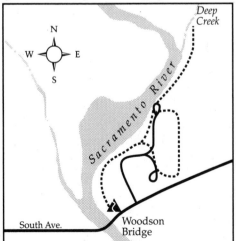

The 428-acre park straddles both sides of the river; the west bank is undeveloped while the east bank offers 46 campsites amidst the oaks.

Immediately south of Woodson Bridge is Tehama County Park which offers a boat-launching ramp and picnic ground. The county park's beach adjoins the state beach.

Woodson Bridge is open year-round, but the best times to visit are in spring and autumn when the days are warm, but not scorching, as they are in summer.

The trail system is not extensive, but does offer a leg-stretcher of a walk along the Sacramento River. On a clear day in the North Sacramento Valley, you can look up and see the Trinity Alps, Mount Shasta and Mount Lassen towering in the distances.

Directions to trailhead: From Interstate 5 in Corning, exit on South Avenue and head east 6 miles to Woodson Bridge.

From Highway 99 in Vina (about 15 miles north of Chico), exit on South Avenue and proceed 3 miles west to the park.

Best place to park and begin the walk is actually next door to the state park at Tehama County Park.

The walk: Below the bridge, you'll notice a gravel bar where local tubers put in and take out. Above the bar, on the river bank, two trails head into the thick undergrowth.

Take either trail and you'll curve east with the river, soon joining the state park's nature trail. The nature here is willow, alder and cottonwood trees, along with wild grape and thickets of blackberry bushes.

Eventually you'll reach a small picnic area, a good turnaround point. You can extend your hike by walking a half-mile along the riverbank to the mouth of Deer Creek.

Central California Mountains

Paralleling much of California's magnificent Central Coast is the equally magnificent Coast Range. The range rises to an extrordinary viewpoint—Mt. Diablo—near San Francisco Bay.

The Coast Range is better known by the names of its component parts, including the Santa Cruz Mountains and the Santa Lucia Mountains of Big Sur. In the young, geologically active Santa Cruz Mountains, generous rains support impressive redwood groves, some of which are preserved in state parks: Portolá, Henry Cowell Redwoods, and a forest undergoing restoration—The Forest Of Nisene Marks. The magnificent grove at Big Basin became California's first state park in 1902.

Linked to Big Basin by the superb Skyline-to-the-Sea Trail is striking Castle Rock State Park. This trail—and many local volunteers—made history when the first "Trails Day" event was held in 1969 to help restore the trail.

Ever since Highway 1 was constructed in 1937, dramatic Big Sur has been a magnet for visitors from around the world. Some of the southernmost stands of redwood, along with oak-studded portreros and wildflower-strewn meadows are preserved in the Big Sur state parks—Garrapata, Pfeiffer Big Sur, and Julia Pfeiffer Burns. Andrew Molera State Park in particular, has an international flavor with many languages heard in its walk-in campground and along its trails.

Julia Pfeiffer Burns State Park
Waterfall, Overlook, Partington Cove Trails

> **Terrain:** Steep coastal bluffs
> **Highlights:** Whale-watching; waterfall
> **Length:** ½ to ¾ miles each
> **Degree of difficulty:** Easy

For most visitors, "Big Sur" is synonymous with popular Pfeiffer Big Sur State Park. Often overlooked is a smaller slice of Big Sur located ten miles south—Julia Pfeiffer Burns State Park.

It's a shame to overlook it. A redwood grove, dramatic coastal vistas, and the only major California waterfall to tumble into the Pacific are some of the park's attractions.

The park is a tribute to hardy pioneer Julia Pfeiffer Burns, remembered for her deep love of the Big Sur backcountry. Her father, Michael Pfeiffer, started a ranch in the Santa Lucia Mountains in 1869.

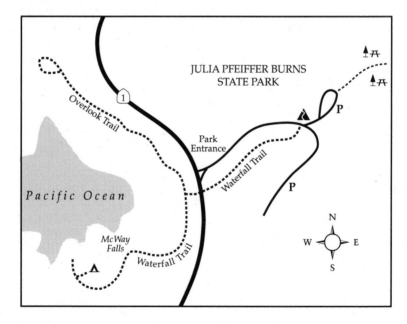

In 1915, Julia Pfeiffer married John Burns, and the two ran a cattle ranch while living at their home located south of the present park.

During the 1920s, New York congressman and confidante to Franklin Roosevelt, Lathrop Brown, and his wife Helen, built "Waterfall House" on the bluffs above McWay Falls. Built before the completion of Coast Highway, the isolated residence was surrounded by a lush garden of plants and flowers imported from around the world.

Easterner Helen Brown was an admirer of westerner Julia Pfeiffer Burns, and in 1962, more than three decades after her friend's death, she donated the Brown's property to the state. Helen Brown requested that Waterfall House become a park museum; however, the parks department insisted that it lacked sufficient funds to operate a museum and bulldozed the house into the sea.

You can easily sample the coastal charms of four-square-mile Julia Pfeiffer Burns State Park by following the short Waterfall and Partington Cove Trail.

The park's coastal trails are great "leg-stretcher" jaunts to break up the coastal drive. They're particularly fine paths to hike in winter because they provide fine observation points from which to sight migrating California gray whales.

Directions to trailhead: Julia Pfeiffer Burns State Park straddles Highway 1, about 36 miles south of Carmel and some 10 miles south of Pfeiffer Big Sur State Park. Turn inland into the park and proceed to the day use lot.

To join Partington Cove Trail, the second walk described below, head north on Coast Highway 1.8 miles past the state park entrance to a turnout near where the highway bridge crosses Partington Creek. The trail starts from the west end of Partington Creek bridge.

The walk: From the Julia Pfeiffer Burns State Park lot, take the signed trail toward Scenic Overlook. Along McWay Creek you'll spot some eucalyptus, quite a botanical contrast to the redwoods growing up-creek. (During spring, ceanothus and dogwood splash color along the trail.) The path leads through a tunnel under Coast Highway and emerges to offer the walker grand panoramas of the Big Sur coast.

You'll soon reach the overlook, where you can observe slender, but dramatic McWay Falls tumbling a hundred feet from the granite cliffs into McWay Cove.

On your return, you can take a side trail and meander over to the park's cypress-shaded environmental campsites, which are perched on the former site of Waterfall House. When you arrive back at the trailhead, consider following Ewoldsen Trail a short distance to a picnic area located in a lovely redwood grove. (Unfortunately, Ewoldsen Trail, beyond the picnic area, was seriously burned in the 1985 Rat Creek Fire and has not been reopened.)

Next, it's time to visit another part of the state park—Partington Cove. (See trailhead directions above.) The cove was once the site of a dock where tanbark was loaded onto waiting ships. Woodsmen stripped the bark from the tanbark oak, a kind of cross between an oak and a chestnut. Before synthetic chemicals were invented to tan leather, gathering and shipping of the bark was a considerable industry along the Big Sur coast. During the 1880s, homesteader John Partington operated a landing here.

From the iron gate on the coast side of Highway 1, follow the dirt road that drops down into the canyon cut by Partington Creek. (A steep side trail continues down to the tiniest of beaches at the creek mouth.) The main trail crosses the creek on a wooden footbridge and passes through a hundred-foot-long tunnel that was blasted through the rocky cliffs.

At Partington Cove are the remains of a dock. The not-so-placid waters of the cove stir the seaweed about as if in a soup, and you wonder how boats moored here actually managed to load their cargo of bark and lumber.

Offshore, between Partington Cove and McWay Creek to the south, is Julia Pfeiffer Burns Underwater Park, placed under state protection in 1970. Kelp forests provide habitat for abalone, lingcod and many more sea creatures, as well as for otters, which you may glimpse if you follow the crumbling cliffside trail from the dock site to the end of Partington Point.

Foot notes: If you want more of a workout and a tour of the red-woods, the park also has some inland trails. Tan Bark Trail, which leads through a redwood grove and a forest of tanbark oaks is one of my favorite Big Sur trails. This 6½-mile round trip trail leads to the aptly named "Tin House" and offers superb coastal views. Tan Bark Trail begins at the east end of Partington Creek bridge.

Pfeiffer Big Sur State Park
Valley View Trail

Terrain: Redwood slopes of Santa Lucia Mountains
Highlights: Classic Big Sur
Distance: Big Sur Lodge to Pfeiffer Falls, Valley View, is 2
    miles round trip with 200-foot elevation gain
Degree of difficulty: Easy

For most visitors, "Big Sur" means Pfeiffer Big Sur State Park. The state park—and its brief but popular trail system—is dominated by the Big Sur River, which meanders through redwood groves on its way to the Pacific Ocean, five miles away.

John Pfeiffer, for whom the park was named, homesteaded 160 acres of mountainous terrain between Sycamore Canyon and the Big Sur River. In 1884, he moved into a cabin perched above the Big Sur River Gorge. (You can see the reconstructed "Homestead Cabin," which is located on the park's Gorge Trail.) John Pfeiffer sold and

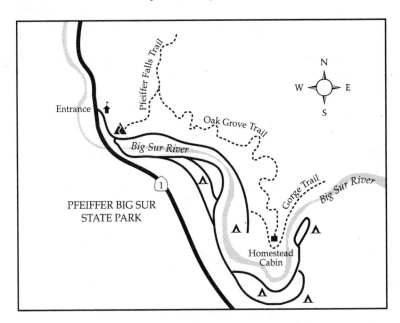

donated some of his ranchland to the state in the 1930s, and it became the nucleus of the state park.

This walk, which follows the Pfeiffer Falls Trail and Valley View Trail, is an easy "leg stretcher" suitable for the whole family. It visits Pfeiffer Falls and offers a good introduction to the delights of the state park.

Directions to trailhead: Pfeiffer Big Sur State Park is located off Highway 1, some 26 miles south of Carmel and two miles south of the hamlet of Big Sur. Beyond the entry booth, turn left at the stop sign, then veer right (uphill). Very soon, you'll find some day use parking. A much larger parking area is located near the store and restaurant at the bottom of the hill.

The walk: From the signed trailhead, follow the trail to Pfeiffer Falls. Very shortly, on your left, you'll spot a trail heading left to Valley View; this will be your return path. The walk continues under stately redwoods and meanders along with Pfeiffer-Redwood Creek.

You'll soon ascend a redwood stairway to a junction with Oak Grove Trail, which leads rightward 1½ miles through oak and madrone woodland over to the Mt. Manuel Trail. Stay left at this junction and follow Pfeiffer Falls Trail through the forest and past a second branch of the Valley View Trail.

A stairway leads to an observation platform at the base of the falls. Pfeiffer-Redwood Creek cascades over a 40-foot precipice to a small grotto.

After enjoying the falls, descend the stairway and bear right on the Valley View Trail, which leaves behind the redwoods and ascends into a tanbark oak and coast live oak woodland.

At a signed junction, turn right and follow the pathway along a minor ridge to a lookout. The Pacific Ocean pounding the Point Sur headlands and the Big Sur River Valley are part of the fine view.

Backtrack along Valley View Trail and at the first junction stay right and descend on Pfeiffer Falls Trail back to Pfeiffer-Redwood Canyon. Another right at the canyon bottom brings you back to the trailhead.

Pt. Sur State Historic Park
Pt. Sur Lightstation Trail

Terrain: Dramatic Big Sur bluffs
Highlights: Century-old lighthouse, guided tour
Distance: ½ mile guided walk
Degree of difficulty: Easy

During the nineteenth century, when coastal roads were few and poor, most cargo was transported by ship. Ships traveled close to shore so that they could take advantage of the protection offered by bay and point. This heavy coastal trade—and its dangers—prompted the U.S. Lighthouse Service Board to establish a series of lighthouses along California's coast located about 60 miles apart.

Point Sur had been the death of many ships, and mariners had been petitioning for a beacon for many years when the government in 1885 appropriated $50,000 to construct a lightstation. The Point Sur light joined the one at Piedras Blancas situated 60 miles south and the one located 60 miles north at Pigeon Point.

The first light, which became operational in 1889, used one of the famed Fresnel lenses designed by French physicist Augustin Jean Fresnel. A whale oil lantern was the first light source. In later years, kerosene fueled the operation. Soot problems from the not-very-clean burning kerosene kept the keepers busy polishing the glass and worrying about surprise visits from supervisors who conducted "white glove" inspections.

The lighthouse became fully automated in 1975. The original light, visible for 23 miles out to sea, is now on display in the Maritime Museum of Monterey.

The century-old stone buildings, when viewed from Highway 1, are intriguing; they're even more so when viewed up close on one of the tours conducted by volunteer docents. While the station undergoes restoration, the only way to see the facility—the only intact lightstation with accompanying support buildings on the California coast—is by guided tour.

The tour includes the lighthouse itself, the keepers' houses, the blacksmith shop and the barn, where livestock was kept. You'll learn the fascinating story of the isolated life lived by the four keepers and their families.

Docent-led tours are currently offered on weekends. There's a fee for the tours, which have a limited number of slots—available on a first-come, first-served basis. Suggestion: Arrive early.

The walk to the lighthouse is interesting for more than historical reasons. Geology buffs will call the path to the light the "Tombolo Trail"; a tombolo, rare on the California coast, is a sand bar connecting an island to the mainland.

The view from atop the 360-foot-high basaltic rock is superb. You're eyeball-to-eyeball with the gulls and cormorants. To the south is False Sur, named for its confusing resemblance to Point Sur, when viewed from sea.

In 1980, Point Sur Lightstation was designated a state historic landmark, and in 1984 the U.S. Department of the Interior turned it over to the California Department of Parks and Recreation. The old Lighthouse Service Board was long-ago absorbed by the U.S. Coast Guard, and the kerosene lamp and steam-driven warning whistle have been replaced by a computer-directed electric beam and radio beacon, but Point Sur Lightstation, as it has for a century, continues to warn ships of the treacherous Big Sur Coast.

Andrew Molera State Park

Beach, Bluff, Panorama, Ridge Trails

> **Terrain:** Meadows, rugged coastal bluffs
> **Highlights:** Big Sur River mouth, redwoods, dramatic coast
> **Distance:** 2½ to 9½ miles round trip; 900-foot elevation gain
> **Degree of difficulty:** Easy to moderate

Mountains, meadows and the mouth of Big Sur River are some of the highlights of a walk through Andrew Molera State Park, largest state park along the Big Sur coast.

More than 20 miles of trail weave through the park, which has a diversity of ecosystems. You can hike along the bluffs overlooking three miles of beach, and climb through meadows and oak woodland. At the river mouth are a shallow lagoon and beautiful sandy beach.

In 1855, Yankee fur trader Juan Bautista Roger Cooper acquired this land, formerly part of the Mexican land grant Rancho El Sur. Acquaintances of his day—and historians of today—speculate that Cooper used his "Ranch of the South" as a landing spot, bringing cargo ashore at the Big Sur River mouth to avoid the high custom fees of Monterey Harbor.

Grandson Andrew Molera, who inherited the ranch, had a successful dairy operation. His Monterey Jack cheese was particularly prized. He was a hospitable fellow, popular with neighbors who camped along the river while awaiting shipments of supplies from San Francisco.

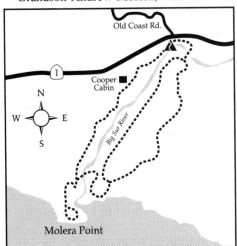

A good leg-stretcher walk is to take Beach Trail to the beach at the mouth of the Big Sur River, then return via Creamer Meadow Trail.

Beach Trail and a number of other park roads are old dirt roads, which allow side-by-side walking, thus appealing to sociable hikers.

During summer, you'll see surfers heading for the beach. You may also hear a number of foreign languages en route. The state park's walk-in campground is very popular with European visitors.

A longer tour of the park can be made via the Bluff, Panorama and Ridge trails. The coastal views from these trails are magnificent.

Note that the roundtrip loop described below relies on seasonal (late spring to early fall) footbridges. At other times, you'll have to make this trip an out-and-back or get your feet (and possibly much more) wet by crossing the river.

Directions to trailhead: Andrew Molera State Park is just off California 1, some 21 miles south of Carmel.

The walk: From the parking lot, cross the Big Sur River on the seasonal footbridge. Walk 100 yards of so along a broad path that soon splits. Bear right onto Beach Trail. (The left fork joins Creamery Meadow Trail, an ideal return route for those who like loop trails.) The trail stays near the river, whose banks are crowded with thimbleberry and blackberry, honeysuckle vines, willow and bay laurel.

At the river mouth is a small beach and shallow lagoon, frequented by sanderlings, willets and many more shorebirds. A short path (Headlands Trail) leads above the beach to Molera Point, where you can watch for whales (January through April) or passing ships.

Bluff Trail heads east from Beach Trail and immediately climbs steeply up the coastal bluff. Soon the path turns south as it wanders over the bluff, a marine terrace cloaked in coyote bush and grasses. About 1¾ miles from the mouth of the Big Sur River, Bluff Trail gives way to Panorama Trail, a more rigorous path that soon drops into a deep gully, then climbs steeply up a ridge where some wind-stunted redwoods cling to life.

Your reward for gaining about 900 feet in elevation are great views of the state park, the coast to the south and triangular-shaped Cone Peak, one of the high points of the Santa Lucia Mountains.

Panorama Trail gives way to Ridge Trail, which descends northwest along the park's main ridge nearly four miles, almost back to the beach, to Creamery Meadow Trail. Swing right on this path and walk a mile back to the trailhead and parking lot.

Garrapata State Park
Rocky Ridge, Soberanes Canyon Trails

> **Terrain:** Steep Santa Lucia Mountains
> **Highlights:** Grand Big Sur coastal views, redwoods.
> **Distance:** 7 miles round trip with 1,200-foot elevation gain
> **Degree of difficulty:** Moderate to difficult
> **Precautions:** Steep trail, poison oak; *garrapata* means tick in
> Spanish—watch out for them.

Undeveloped and usually overlooked, Garrapata State Park offers a lot of Big Sur in a compact area. The park features two miles (probably closer to four miles counting the twists and turns) of spectacular coastline and a steep sampling of the Santa Lucia Mountains.

Rocky Ridge Trail quickly leaves Highway 1 behind and offers far-reaching views of the Santa Lucia Mountains and the sea. A grand loop of the state park can be made by returning to the trailhead via redwood-lined Soberanes Canyon.

The name Soberanes is linked with the early Spanish exploration of California. Soldier Jose Maria Soberanes marched up the coast to Monterey with the Gaspar de Portolá expedition of 1769. Seven years later, Soberanes served as a guide for Juan Bautista De Anza, whose party pushed north to San Francisco Bay. Grandson José Antonio Ezequiel Soberanes acquired the coastal bluff and magnificent backcountry that became known as the Soberanes Ranch.

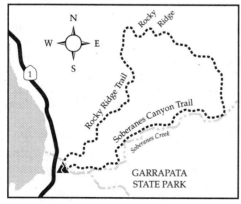

Garrapata State Park offers a variety of hiking options. The coast lover can loop around aptly named Whale Peak, which is not only cetacean-shaped, but offers good views of migrating gray whales from about March through April. The whales can be seen swimming—usually fairly close to shore—as they head back to Arctic waters. The most popular whale-watching spot in the park, however, is Soberanes Point. Bring your binoculars.

Rocky Ridge Trail will be more enjoyable for the gung-ho hiker than the novice. The trail ascends very steeply as it climbs Rocky Ridge. Then, after gaining the ridge, hikers must descend an extremely steep mile (we're talking about a 20 to 30 percent grade here) to connect to Soberanes Canyon Trail.

The leg-weary, or those simply looking for an easier walk, will simply stroll through the redwoods of Soberanes Canyon and not attempt Rocky Ridge Trail.

Directions to trailhead: Garrapata State Park is seven miles south of Carmel Valley Road, off Highway 1 in Carmel. There's a highway turnout at mileage marker 65.8.

The walk: From the gate on the east side of Highway 1, walk inland over a dirt road to a nearby barn, then a wee bit farther to cross Soberanes Creek and reach a trail junction. Soberanes Canyon heads east along the creek, but Rocky Ridge-bound hikers will keep with the closed road, heading north and dipping in and out of a gully.

Hikers rapidly leave the highway behind as the path climbs the rugged slopes, which are dotted with black sage, golden yarrow and bush lupine. The route uses few switchbacks as it ascends 1,435-foot Rocky Ridge. From atop the ridge are good views to the east of Soberanes Creek watershed, to the west of Soberanes Point, and to the north of Carmel and the Monterey Peninsula.

The route contours eastward around the ridge. To the north is the steep canyon cut by Malpaso Creek. After leveling out for a time, the grassy path reaches a small cow pond, then begins to descend over steep but pastoral terrain.

The trail is cut by cattle paths, a reminder of a century of grazing. The route plunges very steeply down the bald north wall of Soberanes Canyon. The mile-long killer descent finally ends when you intersect Soberanes Canyon Trail and begin descending gently to the west.

Soberanes Canyon Trail stays close to the creek and enters the redwoods. Western sword fern, redwood sorrel, blackberry bushes and Douglas iris decorate the path.

Near the mouth of the canyon, the trail becomes gentler. Willow, watercress and horsetail line the lower reaches of Soberanes Creek. Soon after passing some out-of-place mission cactus, brought north from Mexico by Spanish missionaries, hikers return to the trailhead.

The Forest of Nisene Marks State Park
Loma Prieta Grade Trail

Terrain: Maze of ridges and canyons filled with second-growth redwood forest and oak woodlands

Highlights: A rugged, little-developed park with 30 miles of hiking trails.

Distance: From Porter Picnic Area to Hoffman's Historic Site is 6 miles round trip with a 400-foot elevation gain. Several longer hikers are possible.

Degree of difficulty: Moderate

Precautions: Lots of poison oak

One of the largest state parks in Central California, the Forest of Nisene Marks has few facilities, but this very lack of development makes it attractive to anyone looking for a quiet walk in the woods. The woods, in this case, are second-growth redwoods. The park is on land near Santa Cruz that was clear-cut during a lumber boom lasting from 1883 to 1923.

Loma Prieta Lumber Co. had quite an operation. Using steam engines, oxen, skid roads and even a railway, loggers ventured into nearly every narrow canyon of the Aptos Creek watershed. After the loggers left Aptos Canyon, the forest regenerated. Today a handsome second generation of redwoods is rising to cover the scarred slopes.

The Marks, a prominent Salinas Valley farm family, purchased the land in the 1950s. In 1963, the three Marks children donated the property to the state in the name of their mother, Nisene Marks. As specified in the deed, the forest must not be developed and the natural process of regeneration allowed to continue.

Ferocious winter storms in 1982 and 1983 battered the canyons and ruined part of the park's trail system, in particular the paths in the upper reaches of Aptos Canyon. Railroad grades and trestles that had withstood a century of storms were washed away. Volunteers and the California Conservation Corps repaired the damage.

Loma Prieta Grade Trail follows parts of an old railway bed. A narrow-gauge steam railway ran from a mill to China Camp. A few ramshackle wooden buildings are all that's left of this turn-of-the-century

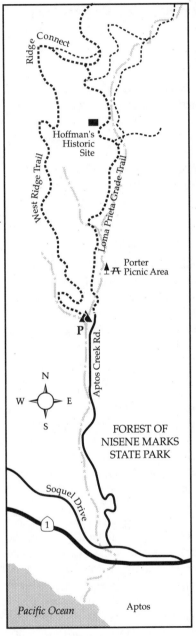

lumber camp that once housed 300 workers.

Directions to trailhead: From Highway 1 in Aptos, take the Aptos/ Seacliff exit to Soquel Drive. Turn right (east) and proceed a half-mile into Aptos. Turn left on Aptos Creek Road and drive four miles to a locked gate at the Forest of Nisene Marks' Porter Picnic Area.

The walk: From the picnic area, follow Aptos Creek 0.4 mile to the Loma Prieta Grade trailhead. (An old mill site is a short walk up the road.)

For a short stretch, the trail stays near Aptos Creek. This creek, which rises high on Santa Rosalia Ridge, is joined by the waters of Bridge Creek, then spills into Monterey Bay at Rio Del Mar Beach. Silver salmon and steelhead spawn in the creek.

The old railway bed makes a gentle trail except for a few places where the old bridges have collapsed into ravines. Your destination of China Camp, now called Hoffman's Historic Site, has a few wooden structures.

You can return the same way or take the Ridge Connector Trail over to West Ridge Trail. This latter trail runs south and connects with Aptos Creek near the trailhead. Be warned that Ridge Trail is sometimes crowded by large amounts of poison oak.

Henry Cowell Redwoods State Park

River, Eagle, Pine, Ridge Trails

> **Terrain:** Redwood groves, oak woodland
> **Highlights:** Grand redwoods, coastal views
> **Distance:** 4 miles round trip with 500-foot elevation gain
> **Degree of difficulty:** Moderate

Henry Cowell Redwoods State Park preserves first- and second-growth redwoods in a tranquil Santa Cruz Mountains setting.

Henry Cowell and Joseph Welch, who in the 1860s acquired the former Mexican land grant Rancho Cañada de Rincón, shared a similar commitment to protect the Big Trees Grove (now Redwood Grove). Welch's holdings were purchased by Santa Cruz County in 1930 and became parkland; in the 1950s this land was combined with 1,500 acres donated by Cowell's heirs to become a state park.

Thanks to the preservation efforts by these men, the "Big Trees" are as stirring a sight now as they were a century ago when railroad pas-

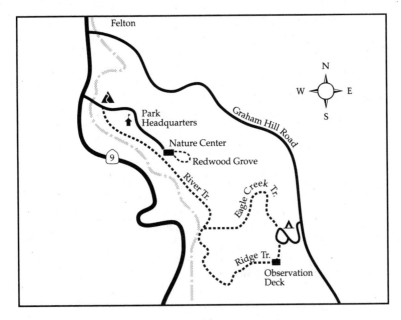

sengers bound for Santa Cruz from San Jose made a lunch stop amongst the tall trees.

The short Redwood Grove Nature Trail, which visits one of the finest first-growth groves south of San Francisco, is a good place to start your exploration of the Santa Cruz Mountains. This popular trail, complete with interpretive leaflet, loops along the San Lorenzo Riverbank among the redwoods, some of which have been given names. One of the larger commemorative redwoods honors President Theodore Roosevelt, who enjoyed his 1903 visit to the grove.

The state park is hilly and with changes in elevation come changes in vegetation. Moisture-loving redwoods predominate on the lowlands while the park's upper ridges are cloaked with oak woodland and chaparral.

By connecting four of the park's trails, you can walk through all of the park's diverse ecosystems. You'll begin in the redwoods and ascend chaparral-covered slopes to an observation deck located in the middle of the park. Great mountain and coastal views are your reward for the ascent. Be sure to stop in at the park interpretive center, which has exhibits and sells maps and books. Redwood Grove Nature Trail begins near the center.

Directions to trailhead: Henry Cowell Redwoods State Park is located just south of Felton on Highway 9. You can pick up River Trail near the park entrance at Highway 9, or from the picnic area.

The walk: River Trail meanders down river along the east bank of the San Lorenzo. You may hear the whistle of the Roaring Camp & Big Trees Railroad, a popular tourist attraction located adjacent to the park. The steam-powered train takes passengers through the Santa Cruz Mountains on a narrow gauge track.

About a quarter-mile after River Trail passes beneath a Southern Pacific railroad trestle, you'll intersect Eagle Creek Trail and begin ascending out of the redwood forest along Eagle Creek. Madrone and manzanita predominate on the exposed sunny slopes.

Bear right on Pine Trail (the pines you'll see en route are ponderosa pine) and climb steeply up to the observation deck. Enjoy the view of the Monterey and Santa Cruz coastline, the redwood forests, and that tumbled-up range of mountains called Santa Cruz.

On the return trip, take Ridge Trail on a steep descent to River Trail. Both River Trail and its nearly parallel path—Pipeline Road—lead back to Redwood Grove and the picnic area.

Big Basin Redwoods State Park
Skyline to the Sea Trail

Terrain: Deep woods, wet world of Waddell and Berry creeks
Highlights: Redwoods, evergreen forest, even a beach in
  California's oldest state park
Distance: 12 miles one way with 1,200-foot elevation loss
Degree of difficulty: Moderate to strenuous
Precautions: Slippery trail bring drinking water

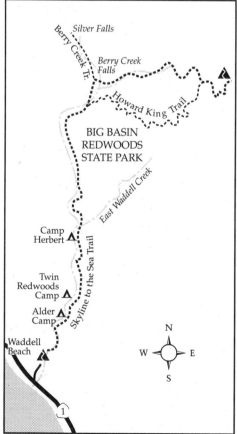

In 1902, the California state park system was born with the establishment of the California Redwood Park at Big Basin Redwoods State Park in Santa Cruz County.

California preserved many more "redwood parks" during the twentieth century, but the redwoods at Big Basin remain one of the gems of the park system.

And one of the gems of the state's trail system — Skyline to the Sea Trail—explores Big Basin Redwoods State Park. As its name suggests, the path drops from the crest of the Santa Cruz Mountains to the Pacific Ocean.

For the most part, it runs downhill on its

scenic 35-mile journey from Castle Rock State Park to Big Basin Redwoods State Park to Waddell Beach. Views from the Skyline—redwood-forested slopes, fern-smothered canyons and the great blue Pacific—are superb.

This gem of a trail has many friends. During one weekend in 1969, dedicated members of the Sempervirens Fund and the Santa Cruz Trails Association turned out more than 2,000 volunteers to dig, clear, prune and otherwise improve the trail. Area volunteers put together an annual Trails Day that is now a model for trails organizations throughout the state.

A fine backpacking trip for a three-day weekend would be to trek the 35 miles of Skyline from Castle Rock State Park to Big Basin, then onward to the sea.

The wildest and most beautiful part of the Skyline stretches from park headquarters at Big Basin to Waddell Creek Beach and Marsh. It winds through deep woods and explores the moist environments of Waddell and Berry Creeks.

Springtime, when the creeks are frothy torrents and Berry Creek Falls cascades at full vigor, is a particularly dramatic time to walk the Skyline to the Sea Trail. During summer, the cool redwood canyons are great places to beat the heat.

Directions to trailhead: From Santa Cruz, drive 12 miles north on Highway 9. Turn west on Highway 236 and proceed nine miles to Big Basin Redwoods State Park.

If you're hiking from Big Basin to the sea, you'll need to arrange a car shuttle. Waddell Beach, at trail's end, is 18 miles up-coast from Santa Cruz on Highway 1.

Better yet, take the bus, which stops at both the state park and Waddell Beach.

One suggestion: Leave your car at the Santa Cruz bus station (920 Pacific Avenue) and take the 7:45 a.m. (weekends) bus bound for the state park. You'll arrive about 9 a.m. Hit the trail and take the 5:15 p.m. bus from Waddell Beach back to Santa Cruz. Schedules are different on weekends and weekdays and change frequently. Call the Santa Cruz Metropolitan Transit District at (408) 425-8600 for the latest bus schedule.

The walk: The trail begins in the nucleus of the park on Opal Creek flatlands at the bottom of the basin. From park headquarters, join Redwood Trail, which crosses a bridge and travels a few hundred yards to a signed junction with Skyline to the Sea Trail. You'll turn toward the sea and begin a stiff climb out of the basin, passing junctions with other park trails.

After climbing, the trail descends through deep and dark woods, first with Kelly Creek, then along the west fork of Waddell Creek. Ferns and mushrooms, salamanders and banana slugs occupy the wet world of the trail.

Some four miles from the trailhead, just short of the confluence of Waddell Creek and Berry Creek, you'll intersect Berry Creek Falls Trail. The falls cascade over fern-covered cliffs into a frothy pool.

An ideal lunch stop, or turnaround spot is Sunset Trail Camp, located a mile up Berry Creek Falls Trail and near another falls—Golden Falls.

Skyline to the Sea Trail descends with Waddell Creek and passes through the heart of the beautiful Waddell Valley. Rancho del Oso, "Ranch of the Bears," as this region is known, has second-generation redwoods, Douglas fir and Monterey pine, as well as lush meadows.

A mile and a half from the ocean, you'll reach Twin Redwoods Camp. As you near the sea, the redwoods give way to laurel groves and meadow land. Near trail's end is a freshwater marsh, a favorite stopping place for migratory birds on the Pacific flyway.

A wildlife sanctuary, Theodore J. Hoover Natural Preserve, has been established in the heart of the marsh area for more than 200 kinds of native and migratory birds.

The trail ends at Highway 1. West of the highway is a bus stop and windswept Waddell Beach.

Castle Rock State Park

Saratoga Gap, Ridge Trails

Terrain: Steep slopes with sandstone outcroppings, mixed
evergreen forests, redwood groves
Highlights: Dramatic rock formations, vistas, waterfall
Distance: 5½ miles round trip
Degree of difficulty: Moderate
Precautions: Some poison oak; narrow trail on steep slopes no
place for acrophobes

Perched high on the western slope of the Santa Cruz Mountains,
among frequent fogs (and just above occasional smogs) Castle Rock
State Park offers dramatic rock formations and quiet forest paths.

Castle Rock, the park's 3,214-foot high point, is a sandstone formation that appeals to rock-climbers, geologists and photographers. A
thick evergreen forest obstructs the view from Castle Rock.

Much better panoramas are to be had atop Goat Rock, a sandstone
outcropping that offers hikers clear-day views of the San Lorenzo
Valley and Pacific Ocean.

For a pleasant loop through the park, join Saratoga Gap Trail,
which visits Castle Rock Falls and leads to Castle Rock Trail Camp.
Your return is via Ridge Trail, which parallels Saratoga Gap Trail at
higher elevation and offers grand clear-day views.

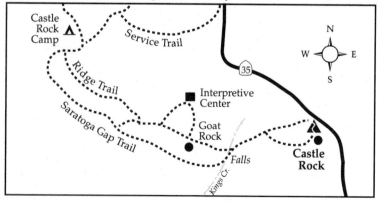

Directions to trailhead: From Highway 17 just north of Los Gatos, exit on Highway 9, winding through the town of Saratoga and ascending the Santa Cruz Mountains to meet Highway 35. From the junction of Highway 9 and Highway 35 (Skyline Blvd.) drive south on 35 for 2½ miles to the signed state park lot on the right. The signed trail begins at the west end of the lot.

The walk: Begin descending on Saratoga Gap Trail under the shade of oaks and ferns. Soon a side trail offers the opportunity to visit Castle Rock.

The main path follows a creek and crosses on a footbridge. You'll pass a signed trail (your return route) leading to Goat Rock, and continue to Castle Rock Falls, ¾ mile from the trailhead.

Take a look down-canyon to the San Lorenzo River watershed and the wide blue Pacific; this view may have been the main reason for the construction of an observation platform.

The path ascends wooded hillsides and, a half-mile beyond the waterfall, leaves behind the trees and climbs into the chaparral. From this elfin forest, hikers get clear-day views of Monterey Bay.

The trail alternates between brushy hillsides and madrone- and oak-filled canyons on the slope of Varian Peak, named for physicist-conservationist Russell Varian, instrumental in the creation of the state park.

Russell Point Overlook offers a good view, but a nicer rest/lunch stop is a quarter-mile farther at Castle Rock Trail Camp. The camp, located in a knobcone pine forest, has water and picnic tables.

From the camp, you'll retrace your steps as far as the junction with Ridge Trail, which you'll join on an ascent of oak-, madrone-, and boulder-dotted slopes. This path leads a mile to another observation point and to a terrific interpretive center, a collection of outdoor exhibits that really show the lay of the land. (The geography lesson is particularly valuable when fog blankets the Santa Cruz Mountains, as if often does.)

On the final segment of this day hike, you'll loop past Goat Rock, a favorite of local climbers, then descend to rejoin Saratoga Gap Trail. Turn left and return to the trailhead.

Portola State Park
Iverson, Summit, Slate Creek Trails

> **Terrain:** A little basin full of redwoods, mixed evergreen forest
> **Highlights:** Family outing in overlooked park
> **Distance:** 6 miles round trip; longer and shorter options possible
> **Degree of difficulty:** Moderate

You could call this tranquil park, perched on the opposite side of the Santa Cruz Mountains from nationally renowned Big Basin Redwoods State Park, "Little Basin Redwoods State Park"; like its well-known cousin, this park is a natural basin forested with coast redwoods.

Portola State Park it is, however, its name honoring explorer Don Gaspar de Portolá, who led an expedition in search of Monterey Bay (he discovered San Francisco Bay instead) in 1769.

The California landscape has changed immeasurably since Portolá's time, but places like Portola State Park still evoke the feeling of wild California. This wild feeling begins outside the park boundaries as you travel Alpine Road. The view is of wide open spaces, of uncluttered valleys and ridges topped with nothing more than grass and cows.

The state park centers around two creeks—Peters and Pescadero—which meander through a basin. Douglas fir and oaks cloak the ridges while redwoods, accompanied by huckleberry and ferns, cluster in cooler bottomlands.

Most of the redwoods in the area are second-growth trees; this land, like most in the Santa Cruz Mountains, was logged during the last century. Some large trees, considered unsuitable for timber at that time, escaped the lumbermen's axes and saws and may be seen today inside the park.

The Islam Temple Shrine of San Francisco used the property as a summer retreat for its members from 1924 until 1945 when the state acquired the land. During the 1960s, Portola had an almost amusement-park feeling. Pescadero Creek was dammed, providing a large fishing and swimming area. One year, 150,000 people poured into the small park.

In 1974, the dam was removed and Portola reverted to quieter pursuits—camping, hiking, nature study. Rangers sometime refer to Portola as a "neighborhood park" meaning thus far only locals have discovered this ideal-for-a-family outing small redwood forest.

Fourteen miles of trail loop through the park. My favorite day hike is a six-mile "walkabout" that utilizes five different trails.

Drop in at the park visitor center to view the nature and history exhibits. The park has an active interpretive program with some guided nature walks.

Alas, two park highlights are no more. Magnificent 17-foot-high Shell Tree, almost completely gutted by fire, was a 2,000-year-old redwood that lived on and on . . . until a careless camper's fire finished it off in 1989. Iverson Cabin, built in 1868 by homesteader Christian Iverson, was a casualty of the 1989 earthquake, and today is little more than a pile of boards.

Directions to trailhead: From Interstate 280 (Junípero Serra Freeway), about six miles north of San Jose, exit on Saratoga Avenue and head south, joining Highway 9 in the town of Saratoga. Highway 9 ascends west into the mountains to a junction with Skyline Drive (Highway 35). Turn right (northwest) on Skyline and follow it to a

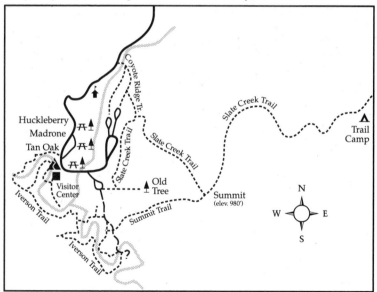

junction with Alpine Road and the signed turnoff to Portola State Park. Turn onto Alpine Road. After four miles, turn left on the state park road and continue 3½ more miles to the park.

Leave your car at Tan Oak or Madrone picnic areas just across the road from the visitor center.

The walk: Join Sequoia Nature Trail, which begins behind the park visitor center. Tramp through the redwood forest, cross Pescadero Creek, and loop around Louise Austin Wilson Grove, site of the Shell Tree.

Next join Iverson Trail, which meanders along Pescadero Creek. A short side trail leads to diminutive, fern-framed Tip-Toe Falls.

Iverson Trail visits the ruins of Iverson Cabin as it meets a park service road. A right leads to Old Haul Road which in turn leads five miles to San Mateo Memorial County Park. You turn left, cross Pescadero Creek on a bridge, and soon arrive at a signed junction with Summit Trail.

True to its name, Summit Trail ascends some 500 feet in elevation to a rather undistinguished summit. It then dips briefly to a saddle and a signed junction with Slate Creek Trail. It's another mile to the park's trail camp, a pleasant, though waterless, rest stop.

From the saddle, Slate Creek Trail descends a pleasant mile west, then contours south to Old Tree Trail and the park's campground. Walk through the campground, then join the park road for a brief walk back to the park visitor center.

Foot notes: If hiking Portola's paths agree with you, you'll want to return to hike adjacent Pescadero Creek County Park and nearby San Mateo Memorial County Park.

Butano State Park
Mill Ox, Goat Hill, Año Nuevo Trails

> **Terrain:** Redwoods, fern canyon
> **Highlights:** Mellow hiking, views of coast, Año Nuevo Island
> **Distance:** 4 miles round trip with 700-foot elevation gain
> **Degree of difficulty:** Easy to moderate

According to Native American lore, *butano* means "a gathering place for friendly visits." Visitors who find out-of-the-way Butano State Park will no doubt agree with this assessment.

On the map, Butano State Park seems rather close to the bustling Santa Clara Valley, and to the Bay area. But this 2,800-acre park, tucked between sharp Santa Cruz Mountains ridges, has a remote feeling. This feeling of remoteness is heightened by a twenty-mile trail network that leads through redwoods and a fern canyon, and climbs to some great vista points.

While most of the redwoods in the park are second-growth, some grand old first-growth specimens remain. The land was logged during the 1880s, but did not endure the devastating clear-cuts common to other coastal ridges of the Santa Cruz Mountains. The steep terrain nixed conventional transportation, so the woodsmen had to settle for

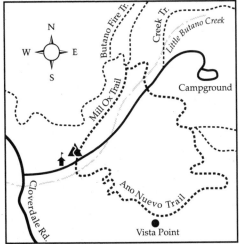

cutting shakes, posts, and fence rails—products that could be more easily hauled to market.

On lower slopes, just above Butano Creek, the walker encounters the forest primeval: redwoods, trillium, sword ferns. Moss-draped Douglas fir, tangles of blackberry bushes, and meadowland, are some of the environments visited by the park's diverse trail system. Año Nuevo Lookout offers fine views of the elephant seal reserve, and of the San Mateo coastline.

Directions to trailhead: From Highway 1, turn inland on Pescadero Road, and drive 2½ miles to Cloverdale Road. Drive south 3 miles to Butano State Park Road and turn left into the park. Leave your car near the entry kiosk.

The walk: Signed Jackson Flats Trail begins just across from the park entry kiosk. The path starts out in meadowland, but soon enters redwoods.

The trail follows the north slope of the canyon cut by Little Butano Creek, and junctions with Mill Ox Trail. Take Mill Ox Trail to the right, down to the canyon bottom. Cross Butano State Park Road, and join an unmarked (except for an "authorized vehicles only" sign) paved road. Ascend through redwoods on this access road. The route soon junctions with Goat Hill Trail, which you follow into a mixed forest of oak and madrone. Follow this trail to the next intersection: Goat Hill Trail heads left and melts into the woods, but you take the short connector path to Olmo Fire Trail. Turn right. Olmo Fire Trail leads to a junction with Ano Nuevo Trail on your left. Take this path over fir- and blackberry bush-covered slopes to Año Nuevo Viewpoint, located in a clearing. On clear days, you can look south to Año Nuevo Island, the elephant seal rookery.

From the viewpoint, the trail descends with enough switchbacks to make a snake dizzy, back to the park entrance.

Fremont Peak State Park
Fremont Peak Trail

Terrain: Steep mountaintop, pine and oak woodlands
Highlights: Grand views of surrounding countryside and
  Monterey Bay; favorite spot for amateur astronomers
Distance: 1 mile round trip
Degree of difficulty: Easy
Precautions: Poison oak along trail

The view. That's the reason—really, just about the only reason—travelers go so far out of their way to visit Fremont Peak State Park.

From atop 3,169-foot Fremont Peak, hikers are treated to a tremendous panorama of San Benito Valley, Monterey Bay and the rugged Santa Lucia Mountains back of Big Sur.

The park also offers two more views: One is a glimpse into history and the part Captain John Charles Frémont played in the drama of California's struggle for statehood.

Another view from the park is into the heavens. Fremont Peak Observatory houses a 30-inch reflecting telescope, one of the largest telescopes available for public use. Call the park for information about astronomy programs held during the spring, summer, and early fall viewing seasons.

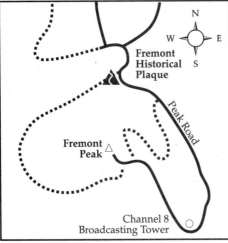

In March of 1846, Captain Frémont and his men were camped near Monterey, then the capital of the Mexican province of Alta California. Mexican military leaders demanded that the Americans leave the territory. Frémont not only refused, but planted the American flag atop the tallest peak in the area and built a small fort nearby. A war of nerves ensued before Frémont and his men finally broke camp. The incident reflects the kind of tension and jockeying for position between the rebellious Americans and the Mexican government in the years prior to the Bear Flag Revolt and California's entry into the Union.

Frémont ultimately returned to California as military governor for a short time. His colorful career included a short stint as a U.S. Senator from California, a run for the presidency in 1856 as the first presidential nominee of the infant Republican party, and service as a general in the Civil War.

Fremont Peak's northern slope is cloaked with manzanita, toyon and scrub oak, while the exposed southern slope is covered with knee-high grassland that is bright green and dotted with wildflowers in spring, golden brown in summer. Soaring above the tops of Coulter pine and madrone on the upper ridges are eagles, hawks and turkey vultures. More than a hundred birds have been sighted in the park.

In light of Frémont's talent as an explorer, trailblazer, naturalist and mapmaker (he was captain of the U.S. Topographic Engineers) the state park's trail system is disappointing—both by its extent (barely a mile of trail) and its condition (usually mediocre).

Nevertheless, the aforementioned grand view is reason enough for a walk in this off-the-beaten-path park.

For a nice day, combine this short hike with a walking tour of San Juan Bautista State Historic Park, which features adobes, the original town plaza, Mission San Juan Bautista and the old Plaza Hotel.

Directions to trailhead: From Highway 101 north of Salinas and south of Gilroy, exit on Highway 156 and travel miles to the town of San Juan Bautista. From the outskirts of town, take the signed turnoff for the state park (San Juan Canyon Road) and travel 11 miles to road's end at Fremont Peak State Park. Park in the uppermost lot.

The walk: You'll see both a road and a trail beginning from the parking lot. The half-mile trail, signed with a hiker's symbol, does not go to the peak but instead, dips into then climbs out of a ravine, before switchbacking up to the park's observatory.

Walk up the road for a short distance then join the signed Peak Trail, a footpath that contours around the mountain. Enjoy the view of Monterey Bay, as the path climbs to a saddle and meets a short summit trail that ascends to rocky Fremont Peak.

After taking in the view, return via the road, which passes by a communications facility before returning you back to the trailhead.

Henry W. Coe State Park
Monument, Middle Ridge, Fish Trails

Terrain: Steep canyons, oak savannahs, pine-topped ridges
Highlights: Diverse ecology in one of California's largest state parks
Distance: 6-mile loop, 9¼-mile loop
Degree of difficulty: Moderate
Precautions: Spring and fall most comfortable times for a visit

---

Henry W. Coe State Park welcomes visitors with a diverse ecology: grasslands, conifer forests, oak woodlands. The park features some unusual flora, including magnificent manzanita, growing more than fifteen-feet high on Middle Ridge and on well-named Manzanita Point.

Despite the area's long pre-park use as grazing land, assorted native grasses, including purple needle grass and Western rye, survive.

Henry Willard Coe, Jr., pioneered hereabouts in 1880, and over the years increased his holdings. His daughter Sada Coe Robinson gave

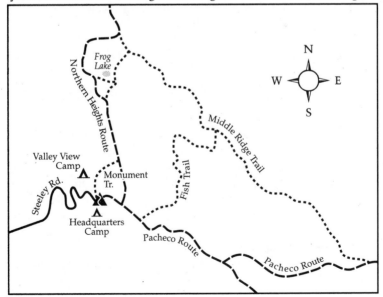

12,230 acres of the family ranch for a park in 1953. Subsequent additions have increased the park to more than 68,000 acres.

Henry W. Coe is one of California's largest state parks. About one-third of the park is classified as wilderness, where few man-made structures remain.

Best times to visit the park are in spring when wildflowers—Mariposa lilies, poppies, fiddlenecks, buttercups, shooting stars and more—pop out all over, and in autumn when the black oaks glow golden and the temperature is just right for hiking.

Stop at the park visitor center, located next to an old ranch house, and view the natural and cultural history exhibits. Pick up a map and inquire about trail conditions here.

Most of the park's trails are old ranch roads, open to hikers, cyclists and equestrians. The park has a somewhat astonishing 100-plus miles of trail. Day hikers departing from the visitor center can fashion a trip from the more than 40 miles of trail emanating from the headquarters' area through the original nucleus of the park.

The park visitor center, at about 2,600 feet in elevation is one of the highest parts of the park. In other words, most trails lead downhill, meaning return trips are an uphill climb.

I have two favorite loops through the main part of the park. One is a 6-mile jaunt to Middle Ridge, around Frog Lake, with a return on Fish Trail. A longer 9½-mile loop takes off from the junction with Fish Trail and continues 2½ miles to Poverty Flat; its oak- and sycamore-shaded trail camps are ideal for a midday picnic/rest stop.

Directions to trailhead: From Highway 101 in Morgan Hill (south of San Jose, north of Gilroy), exit on East Dunne Avenue. Drive 13 miles east on the narrow winding road to the park visitor center and hiker parking lot.

The walk: From the visitor center, walk a hundred yards back up the park entrance road and join the gated (but hikers may pass) dirt road (called Pacheco Route) on your right. At the first bend in the road, you'll join signed Monument Trail, a footpath.

Monument Trail ascends fairly steeply over oak-dotted grasslands and soon reaches a signed junction. At this point, one may take a short spur trail to the west for a great view of the Santa Clara Valley, before returning to the main trail which leads leads a few hundred yards east to a monument to park namesake Henry W. Coe.

Here you are on the crest of Pine Ridge. Ponderosa pine—unusual in the Diablo Range—give the ridge its name.

Your path joins a major dirt road, known as the Northern Heights Route, and begins a descent down the back side of Pine Ridge into a black oak forest. The road crosses the Little Fork of Coyote Creek and you pass a side trail on your right leading to Frog Lake. There's fine picnicking on the shores of this little green reservoir.

Continue up the road to Middle Ridge (longer, but with more scenic vistas) or join the steeper, but shorter footpath for the climb to the ridgetop and a meeting with Middle Ridge Trail.

Middle Ridge Trail descends, then ascends before entering a stand of truly gargantuan manzanita. A few pine trees grow up through the manzanita—a weird sight.

At the signed junction with Fish Trail, those ambitious hikers following the longer loop will continue descending on Middle Ridge Trail, cross the Middle Fork of Coyote Creek twice to Pacheco Route dirt road, following the road a short distance down to the Poverty Flat trail camps. Your return to the trailhead will be via the Pacheco Route, the new madrone- and laurel-shaded Forest Trail and the Corral Trail.

Those hikers on the shorter loop will descend through the woods to recross the Little Fork of Coyote Creek, then head across an inspiring valley oak-studded meadow. The trail meets, then crosses the Pacheco Route. You link up very briefly with Springs Trail, then join Corral Trail for a westward walk over a buckwheat-covered slope and through an oak woodland back to the trailhead.

Foot notes: The state park—and its trail system—keeps growing and growing. The park serves all trail users: a half-dozen mountain bike routes have been established, horse camps and hiker's trail camps have been set up in the backcountry.

Some of the dirt roads designated as mountain bike routes have nearby footpath alternatives for hikers. Backpackers will enjoy touring the northern boundary of the park on the Northern Heights Route, then setting off into the park's Orestimba wilderness area.

Two shorter, favorite hikes: the 5-mile loop from Manzanita Point to Poverty Flat, with a stop at the swimmin' hole at China Hole; also, from Manzanita Point, the 6-mile loop to Mahoney Meadows.

Mt. Diablo State Park
Juniper, North Peak Trails, "The Grand Loop"

Terrain: Brush-covered, pine-dotted slopes
Highlights: From Diablo's summit, the second-best view on earth
Distance: 7 miles round trip; 500-foot elevation gain
Degree of difficulty: Moderate
Precautions: Horribly hot in summer, snow in winter. Park is closed at sunset, except for campers

From the Golden Gate to the Farallon Islands, from the High Sierra to the Central Valley—this is the sweeping panorama you can savor from atop Mt. Diablo. Geographers claim that hikers can see more of the earth's surface from the top of Mt. Diablo than from any other peak in the world with only one exception: Africa's legendary 19,340-foot Mt. Kilimanjaro.

The far-reaching panorama from Mt. Diablo is all the more impres-

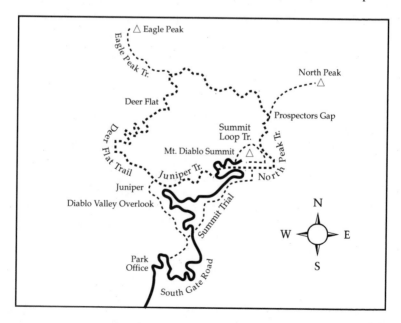

sive considering the mountain's relatively short (elevation 3,849 feet) height. Two reasons for the grand views: (1) the mountain rises solo very abruptly from its surroundings and (2) the land surrounding the mountain—the San Franciso Bay and Central Valley—is nearly flat.

Several colorful yarns describe how the mountain got its name. The most popular account supposedly arose from an 1806 expedition of Spanish soldiers from San Francisco Presidio who marched into the area to do battle with the local Indians. In the midst of the fighting, a shaman clad in striking plumage appeared on the mountain. The Spaniards were convinced they saw Diablo—the Devil—and quickly retreated.

In 1851, Mt. Diablo's summit, long a landmark for California explorers, was established as the official base point for California land surveys. Even today, Mt. Diablo's base line and meridian lines are used in legal descriptions of much California real estate.

Toll roads up the mountain were opened in the 1870s and a fancy hotel was built. In order to make their California holiday complete, tourists of the time just had to climb Mt. Diablo and take in the majestic view.

In 1931, the upper slopes of Mt. Diablo were preserved as a state park. In more recent years, the lower slopes were added to the park, thanks in a large measure to the efforts of Save Mt. Diablo, a local conservation organization.

Today the park consists of some 19,000 acres of oak woodland, grassland and chaparral. Stands of knobcone and Coulter pine, as well as scattered digger pine, are found all over the mountain.

Mt. Diablo boasts some fine trails but the state park is primarily oriented to the automobile. Something of the majesty of conquering Diablo is lost for hikers when they're joined at the top by dozens of visitors stepping from their cars.

Still, there are plenty of places on Diablo's flanks where cars can't go. And the road to the summit, while intrusive, does allow hikers to easily customize the length of their day hike.

Want an easy hike? Start walking just below the summit. Want a vigorous aerobic workout? Start hiking at the base of the mountain and trek all the way to the top.

A relatively easy way to the top is via two-mile round trip Juniper Trail. Ambitious hikers will tackle the 6-mile round trip Summit Trail.

A great way to tour the park is to follow what park rangers call "The Grand Loop," a seven-mile circuit that connects several trails and fire roads and offers views of—and from—Diablo in every direction.

Directions to trailhead: From Highway 680 in Danville, exit on Diablo Road and go east. After three miles, go north on Mt. Diablo Scenic Boulevard, which becomes South Gate Road, then Summit Road, and winds 8½ miles to Laurel Nook Picnic Area. Park in the wide turnout (Diablo Valley Overlook), then join signed Juniper Trail, which departs from the picnic area.

The walk: From the picnic area, the path ascends northeast over brushy slopes. After crossing paved Summit Road, the path climbs some more up to the lower summit parking lot.

Plan to spend some time on the summit enjoying of the view. A couple of handy locator maps help identify cities and natural features near and far.

After you've enjoyed the view, join the trail heading east from the south side of the parking lot. The path parallels the road for a short distance, then reaches a junction. Summit Trail heads southwest down the mountain, but you join the eastward-trending trail to North Peak.

Enjoy the awesome view of the Central Valley as you march over a rocky, juniper-dotted slope. The red-brown rock formation above looks more than a little diabolical; the most prominent rock formation is known as Devil's Pulpit. A half-mile from the above-mentioned intersection, the trail, sometimes called Devil's Elbow Trail, sometimes called North Peak Trail, angles north and descends to a distinct saddle, Prospectors Gap. At the gap is a junction with the rugged ¾-mile-long dirt road leading to North Peak.

Our path contours along the bald north slope of Diablo, passing junctions with Meridian Ridge Fire Road and Eagle Peak Trail, and arriving at Deer Flat, a pleasant rest stop shaded by blue oak.

Intersecting Deer Flat Trail, you'll switchback up to Juniper Campground, then continue a short distance farther to Laurel Nook Picnic Area, where you began your hike.

Central California Coast

Highway 1, from Carmel south to the Monterey/San Luis Obispo County line, was designated California's first official Scenic Highway in 1965. "Scenic" would be the least of the superlatives used by those who get to know the Central Coast.

Of course, as superlatives go, it's hard to top landscape artist Francis McComas's description of Point Lobos: "The greatest meeting of land and sea in the world."

Dominating the seascape of San Luis Obispo County is the "Gibraltar of the Pacific," Morro Rock. The 50-million-year-old volcanic peak is now a wildlife preserve and part of the state park system. Morro Bay is a tremendously rich coastal ecosystems; a good view of the bay is seen from the Morro Bay Sand Spit, part of Morro Bay State Park.

On the bluffs of Montaña de Oro State Park grow fields of mustard and poppies that give the park its "Mountain of Gold" name. Brightening the Pismo Dunes in springtime are yellow and magenta sand verbena, coreopsis and white-fringed aster. Part of the Pismo Dunes, California's most extensive dune system, is protected in a state preserve.

The Central Coast hosts two wildlife dramas that attract visitors from around the world. At Año Nuevo State Reserve, walkers on guided tours get close-up looks at a large population of elephant seals. During autumn, the eucalyptus grove in Natural Bridges State Beach hosts the largest gathering of monarch butterflies in America.

Pismo State Dunes Natural Preserve, Pismo Dunes State Vehicular Recreation Area

Pismo Dunes Trail

> **Terrain:** Wind-sculpted sand dunes
> **Highlights:** Largest set of coastal dunes in California
> **Distance:** 2 or more miles round trip
> **Degree of difficulty:** Easy to moderate

Pismo Beach has a little something for everyone. Digging for the famed but now scarce Pismo clam has long been a popular pastime. Two campgrounds at the state beach are favorites of families looking for weekend getaways. Pismo Dunes State Vehicular Recreation Area is a sandy playground for street vehicles and off-highway vehicles.

For walkers, the attraction is Pismo State Dunes Natural Preserve, a region of tall sand hills where vehicles are prohibited, and you can wander for miles in a Sahara-by-the-sea.

The Pismo Dunes—or Nipomo Dunes these days—is one of the largest relatively undisturbed dune complexes in California. The dunes, which stretch 18 miles from the northern end of Pismo State

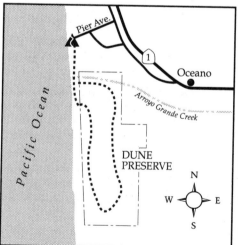

Beach to Point Sal State Beach, are a treasure.

The dunes, one to three miles wide, are a dynamic ecosystem: they have been building up and shifting in response to the prevailing northwest winds for 18,000 years. Some dunes are forming today. The active ones have little or no vegetation.

This walk explores the dune preserve inland

from Pismo Beach State Vehicular Recreation Area. The shoreline is often a traffic jam of cars, trucks and off-highway vehicles, filled with families, low-riders, and what seems to be half the population of Bakersfield. A few hundred yards inland, it's quiet, even lonely. Few bother to walk into the dune preserve to see Nature's handiwork.

Directions to trailhead: From Highway 101 in Arroyo Grande, exit on Grand Avenue and follow it westward to Highway 1. Head south a mile to the community of Oceano, just south of Grover Beach, and turn west on Pier Avenue. Pismo Dunes State Vehicular Recreation Area entrance station is a short distance ahead. Vehicles are allowed on the beach so, if you choose, pay the entrance fee and drive south a half-mile. The beach is signed with numbered markers. Park near the first marker you see—Marker 1.

If you're not keen on driving the beach, park along Pier Avenue short of the entrance kiosk. You may then (1) walk a half-mile south along water's edge (not as treacherous or as awful as it looks from a distance with all those vehicles on the beach) to the dune preserve entrance; or (2) walk a quarter-mile or so along Strand Way, a residential street paralleling the beach, then continue south along the banks of Arroyo Grande Creek, which near its mouth is flowing north-south, to the dune preserve entrance. (Walking to the trailhead from Pier Avenue adds about another mile to this walk.)

The walk: Head inland to the fence that marks the boundary of the Pismo State Dunes Natural Preserve. Take any of the meandering southbound trails that cross the dunes. A ridgeline of sand shields walkers from the sights and sounds of the busy beach below.

Continue southward through the dunes for a mile or so, the ascend out of the foredunes toward the crest of the great dunes to the east. You can then return north via the crest of the large dunes. When you reach Arroyo Grande Creek, the northern boundary of the preserve, return to the beach. At this point you're a couple hundred yards north of Marker #1, so head south back to the trailhead.

Foot notes: A one-mile dune trail extends from the Pismo State Beach entry kiosk at Grand Avenue to Oceano Campground. A half-mile loop trail circles Oceano Lagoon. Guiton Trail, keyed to an interpretive pamphlet which points out the importance of this marshland environment, begins at Oceano Campground

From a trailhead on Oso Flaco Lake Road, there's great dune hiking to a couple dune lakes, including Oso Flaco Lake. These lakes provide habitat and a rest stop for many species of birds.

Los Osos Oaks State Reserve
Oak Trail

> **Terrain:** Classic California oak woodland
> **Highlights:** Magnificent ancient oaks
> **Distance:** 1 to 2 miles round trip

Antiquarian California live oaks, estimated to be 600 to 800 years old, are the highlight of this state reserve in Los Osos Valley near San Luis Obispo. Two miles of trail meander through the the old oaks which have, during their long lifespan, contorted into some unusual shapes.

Botanists say the oak woodland is a culmination of thousands of years of plant succession that has transformed the area from sparsely vegetated sand dunes into a landscape of California live oaks. Though many of the oaks are quite large, some oaks growing on the crest of the dunes are dwarfed.

The oaks are full of bird life. Several species perch in the crown of the trees, others hunt bugs and grubs in the piles of leaves beneath the trees. The chaparral that makes up one-fourth of the reserve is home to quail and many more birds.

Those piles of sticks you see, some several feet high, are wood rat nests. Judging by all those nests, the rarely seen rodent may be the most common animal in the reserve.

Docent-led walks are sometimes scheduled on the weekeends. While walking in the reserve, stay on the trail; poison oak is abundant.

Directions to trailhead: From Highway 101 on the southern end of San Luis Obispo, exit on Los Osos Valley Road and travel eight miles to Los Osos Oaks State Reserve on the left side of the road.

The walk: The path crosses a bridge over a trickling creek, passes a plaque thanking, among others the California State Parks Foundation for preserving this place, then begins a clockwise loop through the reserve.

The main path winds through the old oaks, wanders near Los Osos Creek, then leads to an overlook of a still pastoral part of Los Osos Valley. At a couple of trail junctions, you have the opportunity to shorten or extend your walk.

Montaña de Oro State Park
Montaña De Oro Bluffs Trail

> **Terrain:** Dramatic coastal bluffs
> **Highlights:** Spring wildflowers—a "Mountain of Gold"
> **Distance:** 4 miles round trip
> **Degree of difficulty:** Easy

Atop the Montaña de Oro State Park bluffs grow fields of mustard and poppies, which give the park its "Mountain of Gold" name.

At the turn of the century, the greater portion of what is now the state park was part of the Spooner Ranch. The most popular beach in the park is Spooner's Cove; its isolation made it an ideal landing spot for contrabandistas during the Spanish era, and for bootleggers during Prohibition.

While walking the bluffs, you may see harbor seals venturing ashore or otters diving for food beyond the surf line. Bird-watchers delight at the pelicans, albatross, cormorants and crimson-billed black oyster catchers.

Inland areas of the park include Valencia Peak, which offers great Central Coast panoramas and Coon Canyon, where a stand of Bishop pine thrives. The park's campground occupies the bluffs above a small creek; the visitor center is the old Spooner ranch house.

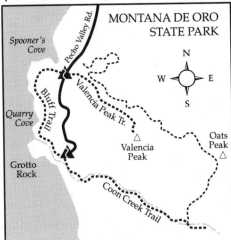

Directions to trailhead: From Highway 101, exit on Los Osos Road, continuing northwest for 12 miles until the road turns south to become Pecho Valley Road, which leads to Montaña de Oro State Park. There's parking at Spooner's Cove. The trail begins a hundred yard south of the turnoff for the campground on the west side of Pecho Valley Road. .

The walk: The path crosses a dry creek on a footbridge and leads up to the bluffs overlooking Spooner's Cove.

A half-mile from the trailhead, a short fork to the right leads to Coralina Cove, bedecked with sea-polished broken shells and beautiful beach pebbles. The crystal-clear tidepools are full of anemones, starfish, mussels and colorful snails.

Continuing on Bluffs Trail, you'll cross a wooden bridge. A mile from the trailhead is Quarry Cove, a fine tidepool site. The wide trail, lined with thistle and New Zealand spinach, eventually brings you to an overlook above some sea caves. Beyond is Grotto Rock.

You may return the same way, or cross Pecho Valley Road to the trailhead for Coon Creek Trail.

Footnotes: On fog-free days, the view of the Central Coast from Valencia Peak Trail (4 miles round trip) is inspiring. Coon Creek Trail (5 miles round trip) follows a year-round creek that winds through the Irish Hills.

Hikers who head north from Spooner Cove will encounter some fine dunes and great beach-walking. You can travel all the way to the Morro Bay sand spit (see Morro Bay state park walk). I highly recommend this walk!

Morro Bay State Park
Sand Spit Trail

> **Terrain:** Sand dunes, bay shoreline
> **Highlights:** Views of Morro Rock, Morro Bay
> **Distance:** 4 miles one-way
> **Degree of difficulty:** Easy to moderate

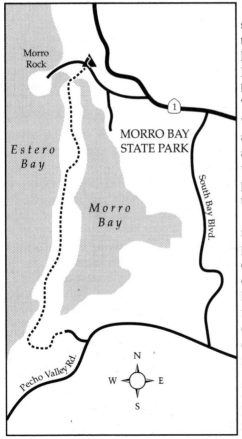

Dominating the seascape of Morro Bay is the "Gibraltar of the Pacific," 576-foot-high Morro Rock, first sighted by Juan Cabrillo in 1542. The 50-million-year-old volcanic peak was used as a rock quarry as late as 1969, but is now a wildlife preserve and part of the state park system.

Atop Morro Rock roosts the endangered peregrine falcon, the quickest and most prized of falcons. The falcons have staged a comeback from the devastating effects of DDT which caused them to lay fragile eggs.

On the inland side of Morro Bay is the state park, which includes a golf course, marina and superb nature museum.

Morro Bay is made possible by a long, narrow sand spit—one of Central California's special environments. Walkers stride the sand dunes and ridges that separate Morro Bay from the inland side and Estero Bay on the ocean side. Atop some of the higher dunes (about 80 feet above sea level), you'll be treated to good vistas of the bay, Morro Rock, and nearby mountains.

Heather, salt grass and coyote bush are among the hardy plants surviving in the harsh wind-lashed environment of the three-mile-long sand spit. Silver lupine, sea rocket and evening primrose add some seasonal color.

Bird-watchers may spot the snowy plover, which lays its eggs in the sand. On the muddy flats of the spit's bay side, willets, curlews and sandpipers feed.

Scientists say that a very high percentage of all sea life along the Central Coast originates in Morro Bay Estuary. The triangular-shaped marsh, lined with eel grass and pickleweed, is an important spawning and nursery habitat for such fish as the California halibut and sand perch. Beneath the surface of the bay are oysters, clams, worms, snails, crabs and shrimp.

To learn more about the bay's ecology, animal and plant life, visit the Morro Bay Museum of Natural History, which is located in Morro Bay State Park. Exhibits are well done and the panoramic view of the bay is superb.

A key element to this walk can be the Bay Taxi, a water-taxi service between the town of Morro Bay and the north end of the sand spit. The taxi operates May through September, Thursday through Monday, out of Virg's Landing (805) 772-1222.

Directions to trailhead: Assuming the Bay Taxi is running, this walk begins in the town of Morro Bay at 1215 Embarcadero.

Another way to reach the sand spit is to rent a canoe from the small marina located close to the Morro Bay Museum of Natural History. The shallow waters of the bay are a great place to practice your J-stroke.

If you want to arrange a car shuttle or begin the hike at the south end of the sand spit, here's how to reach the south trailhead: From Highway 101 in San Luis Obispo, exit on Los Osos Valley Road and head west through the town of Los Osos. One block after the road curves left to become Pecho Road, turn right on Monarch Lane. Drive to the end of this road and park.

The walk: From the end of the sand spit, where the Clam Taxi lands, walk south along the bay. The shoreline is silty, salty, and quite a contrast to the sandy dunes you'll be crossing further south.

A mile of bay-side walking brings you to Houseboat Cove. Across the bay from the cove is the Morro Bay Museum of Natural History. Continue another few hundred yards past the cove, then climb over the dunes to the ocean side of the sand spit. Walk south along surf's edge, which is littered with clam shells and sand dollars. After about 2½ miles of travel, as the dunes on your left begin to recede, walk up a valley toward the top of the dunes.

You'll see a large shell mound in the center of the valley, a massive artifact left by the Chumash. They piled clams, cockles, snails and even land game in these kitchen middens. (Inspect this shell mound and the others on the spit with care; they are protected archaeological sites.) The bountiful marsh is so full of bird, land, and aquatic life that it's easy to imagine a large population of Chumash here; the men hunting rabbits in the dunes, the beautiful baskets of the women overflowing with shellfish.

From the top of the dunes, you'll get a good view for Morro Bay and spit's end at Shark's Inlet. Across the bay are the Morros, a series of extinct volcanoes that includes the famous Morro Rock. Rising behind the Morros are the Santa Lucia Mountains that stretch to Big Sur and beyond. This viewpoint is a good place to turn around and return to the trailhead at the north end of the spit.

Foot notes: Black Mountain, a volcanic plug like famed Morro Rock, can be climbed via a 3-mile round trip trail that begins at the Morro Bay State Park campground. From the mountain's 640-foot summit, you can see the Morro Bay Estuary, the sand spit, and the hills of nearby Montana de Oro State Park.

Pt. Lobos State Reserve
Cypress Grove and North Shore Trails

Length: ¾ mile for Cypress Grove Trail; 3 miles or more for
  North Shore Trail
Terrain: Pine and cypress woodland, coastal bluffs
Highlights: Some call it "the greatest meeting of land and water
  in the world"
Degree of difficulty: Easy

At Point Lobos, the Monterey cypress makes a last stand. Botanists
believe that during Pleistocene times, some half-million years ago,
when the climate was wetter and cooler than it is now, huge forests of
cypress grew along the coast—indeed, throughout North America.
When the world's climate warmed, the cypress retreated to a few
damp spots. Nowadays, the grove at Point Lobos and another across
Carmel Bay at Cypress Point are the only two native stands in existence.

The Monterey cypress, with the help of humans, can cross hot and
dry regions and become established in cool areas elsewhere. In fact,
this rare conifer is easily grown from seed and has been successfully
distributed all over the world, so it's puzzling why the trees' natural
range is so restricted.

Cypress Grove Trail, a ¾-mile loop, visits Allan Memorial Grove,

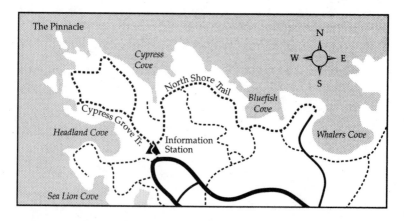

which honors A.M. Allan, who, in the early years of this century, helped preserve Point Lobos from resort developers. When Point Lobos became a reserve in 1933, Allan's family gave the cypress grove to the state.

The trail passes near The Pinnacle, northernmost point in the reserve. Winds off the Pacific really batter this point and the exposed trees. To combat the wind, the trees adopt a survival response called buttressing: a narrow part of the trunk faces the wind while the trunk grows thicker on the other side in order to brace itself. The wind-sculpted trunks and wind-shaped foliage give the cypress their fantastic shapes.

Cypress Grove Trail offers great tree-framed views of Carmel Bay and Monterey peninsula. Offshore are the rocky islands off Sea Lion Point. The Spaniards called the domain of these creatures *Punto de los Lobos Marinos*—Point of the Sea Wolves. You'll probably hear the barking of the sea lions before you see them.

North Shore Trail meanders through groves of Monterey pine, less celebrated than the Monterey cypress, but nearly as rare. This fog-loving, three-needled pine grows only in the reserve and two other areas along the California coast.

The trail also gives a bird's-eye-view of Guillemot Island. A variety of birds nest atop this large offshore rock and others. Pigeon guillemots, cormorants and gulls are some of the birds you might see.

As you hike by Whalers Cove, you'll probably see divers entering the Point Lobos Underwater Reserve, America's first such reserve set aside in 1960. Divers explore the 100-foot high kelp forests in Whalers and Blue Fish Cove. Mineral rich waters from the nearby 1,000-foot deep Carmel Submarine Canyon upwell to join the more shallow waters of the coves.

The reserve has an excellent interpretive program. Docent-led walks explore the trails and tidepools. Ask rangers or visit the park's information station for scheduled nature walks.

Directions to trailhead: Point Lobos State Reserve is located three miles south of Carmel just off Highway 1. There is a state park day use fee. Both Cypress Grove Trail and North Shore Trail depart from the northwest end of Cypress Grove parking area.

Carmel River State Beach
Carmel River Beach Trail

Terrain: Sandbar, river mouth, lagoon
Highlights: Wild ocean side of quaint Carmel, bird sanctuary
Distance: 2 miles round trip
Degree of difficulty: Easy

Carmel River, which arises high on the eastern slopes of the Santa Lucia Mountains and empties into the sea just south of Carmel, is a river of many moods. Some of its forks, swollen by winter and spring rains, can be capricious, frothy waterways as they course through the Ventana Wilderness.

Tamed by Los Padres Dam on the northern boundary of the national forest, the river's descent through Carmel Valley is relatively peaceful. At its mouth, too, the Carmel River has differing moods and appearances. About May, a sandbar forms, turning the river mouth into a tranquil lagoon. During winter, the river bursts through the berm and rushes to the sea. Steelhead trout swim upriver to spawn.

At the north end of Carmel River State Beach is a brackish lagoon, where shorebirds feed. Carmel River Lagoon and Wetlands Natural

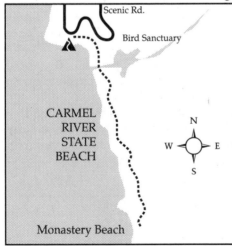

Reserve is here, and even the most casual bird-watcher will be impressed by the abundance of waterfowl. Ducks, mallards and coots patrol the lagoon. Egrets and herons stand amongst the reeds. Hawks hover overhead. Bring your binoculars.

This walk explores the river mouth, then travels the length of Carmel River State Beach to a point just north of Point Lobos named Monastery Beach, for the Carmelito Monastery located just across Highway 1 from the shore.

Directions to trailhead: During the summer and autumn months, the sandy berm at the Carmel River mouth provides a fine path between river and sea. At this time of year, you can start this walk at the north end of Carmel River State Beach. From Highway 1, just south of the town of Carmel, turn west on Rio Road. When you reach Santa Lucia Street, turn left, then proceed five more blocks to Carmelo Street. Turn left and follow this road to the beach.

You can also start at the south end of Carmel River State Beach, easily accessible from Highway 1.

The walk: Follow the shoreline down coast over the sandy berm. In places, the route is rocky, the domain of nervous crabs, who scatter at your approach. You'll surely notice the iceplant-lined path above the beach; save this path for the return trip.

After rounding a minor point and passing some wind-bent Monterey cypress, you'll arrive at Monastery Beach—also known as San José Creek Beach, for the creek that empties onto the northern end of the beach. With the chimes from the nearby monastery ringing in your ears, you might be lulled into thinking that Monastery Beach is a tranquil place, but it's not; the surf is rough and the beach drops sharply off into the sea. Even the most experienced swimmers should be ultracautious.

For a little bit different return route, take the state beach service road, which farther north becomes a trail. This dirt road/trail, just before reaching the lagoon, climbs a small hill where a large cross is implanted. The cross was erected by the Carmel Mission in 1944, and is similar to the one put here by the 1769 Portolá expedition in order to signal the Spanish ship that was to resupply them. Unfortunately, the expedition did not realize how close it was to its intended destination—Monterey Bay—and turned back south.

From the cross, follow a path down slope and intersect another path that leads along the south bank of the Carmel River. Follow the berm and beach back to the trailhead.

Natural Bridges State Beach
Monarch Trail

> **Terrain:** Beach, lagoon, eucalyptus grove
> **Highlights:** Largest concentration of monarch butterflies, superb tidepool exploration
> **Distance:** ¾ mile round trip
> **Degree of difficulty:** Easy

Until October 1989, when the devastating Loma Prieta Earthquake shook Santa Cruz, it was easy to see why the beach here was named Natural Bridges. Alas, this strong temblor doomed the last remaining natural bridge.

While its offshore bridges are but a memory, this park on the outskirts of Santa Cruz nevertheless offers plenty of other natural attractions. A eucalyptus grove in the center of the park hosts the largest concentration of monarch butterflies in America. The park has an extensive interpretive program from October through March, when the monarchs winter at the grove.

Another park highlight is a superb rocky tidepool area, habitat for mussels, limpets, barnacles and sea urchins. After you explore the park, visit nearby Long Marine Laboratory, located just up-coast at the end of Delaware Avenue. University of California Santa Cruz faculty and students use the research facility, which studies coastal ecology. The Lab's Marine Aquarium is open to the public by docent tours 1 to 4 p.m. Tuesday through Sunday.

Directions to trailhead: Natural Bridges State Beach is located off Highway 1 in Santa Cruz at 2531 W. Cliff Drive. Follow the signs from Highway 1.

The walk: Signed Monarch Trail begins near the park's small interpretive center. Soon the trail splits; the leftward fork leads to a monarch observation platform. Sometimes on cold mornings, the butterflies look like small, brown, fluttering leaves. As the sun warms the tropical insects, the "leaves" come to life bobbing and darting. During spring and summer the monarchs—easily the country's most recognized butterfly—leave their coastal California birthplace and disperse across America. Winters, however, are spent on the frost-free California coast—from Santa Cruz to Southern California to northern Baja. As many as 200,000 monarchs cluster in the state park on a "good" butterfly year.

The other branch of the trail is a self-guided nature trail. It ends in a grove of Monterey pine.

When you head back to the visitor center, detour down to the beach. Just up the beach is Secret Lagoon, the domain of ducks and great blue herons. Farther up the beach is one of the Central Coast's truly superb tidepool areas.

Wilder Ranch State Historic Park
Old Landing Cove Trail

Terrain: Coastal bluffs, both wild and cultivated
Highlights: Historic dairy ranch, dramatic bluffs, more brussels
  Sprouts than you've ever seen in your life
Distance: 2 miles round trip
Degree of difficulty: Easy

At Wilder Ranch State Historic Park, located on the coast just north of Santa Cruz, you get the feeling that no one stone has gone unpreserved.

The brussels sprouts fields are in an agricultural preserve, the former Wilder Ranch is in a cultural preserve, and Wilder Beach is now a natural preserve for the benefit of nesting snowy plovers. All these preserves are found within Wilder Ranch State Historic Park, which in turn preserves some 4,000 acres of beach, bluffs, and inland canyons.

Rancho del Matadero was started here by Mission Santa Cruz in 1791. The Wilder family operated what was by all accounts a very

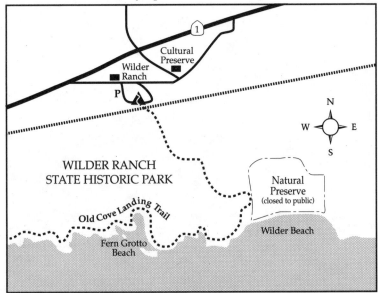

successful and innovative dairy for nearly 100 years. The California Department of Parks and Recreation acquired the land in 1974.

The Wilder's ranch buildings, barn, gardens and Victorian house still stand, and are open to public tours. The parks department is slowly restoring the area to reflect its historic use as a dairy.

In addition to the guided historic walks, the park boasts Old Landing Cove Trail, a bluff-top path that as its name suggests, leads to a historic cove. From the 1850s to the 1890s, schooners dropped anchor in this cove to load lumber. Observant hikers can spot iron rings, which supported landing chutes, still embedded in the cliffs.

Brussels sprouts fans will see more of this vegetable than they ever dreamed possible; fully twelve percent of our nation's production is grown in the state park.

Directions to trailhead: From Santa Cruz, head north on Coast Highway four miles to the signed turnoff for Wilder Ranch State Park on the ocean side of the highway. Follow the park road to its end at the large parking lot, where the signed trail begins.

The walk: The path, an old ranch road, heads coastward. Signs warn you not to head left to Wilder Beach (where the snowy plovers dwell) and discourage you from heading right, where pesticides are used on the fields of brussels sprouts.

The trail offers a bird's-eye-view of the surf surging into a sea cave, then turns north and follows the cliff edge.

Old Landing Cove is smaller than you imagine, and you wonder how the coastal schooners of old managed to maneuver into such small confines. If it's low tide, you might see harbor seals resting atop the flat rocks located offshore.

One more natural attraction at the cove: a fern-filled sea cave. The ferns are watered by an underground spring.

The trail dead-ends at the cove, so you must return the way you came.

Año Nuevo State Reserve
Año Nuevo Trail

Terrain: Sand dunes
Highlights: Huge population of elephant seals, guided walks.
Distance: 3 miles round trip
Degree of difficulty: Easy to moderate

One of the best new year's resolutions a walker could make is to plan a winter trip to Año Nuevo State Reserve. Here you'll be treated to a wildlife drama that attracts visitors from all over the world—a close-up look at the largest mainland population of elephant seals.

From December through April, a colony of the huge creatures visits Año Nuevo Island and Point in order to breed and bear young. To protect them (and the humans who hike out to see them), the reserve is open only through naturalist-guided tours during these months.

Slaughtered for their oil-rich blubber, the elephant seal population numbered fewer than one hundred by the turn of the century. Placed under government protection, the huge mammals rebounded rapidly

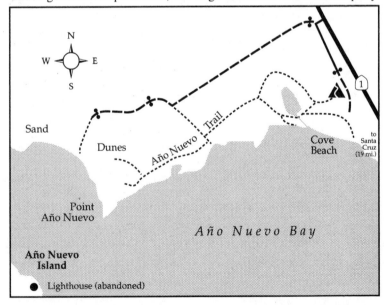

from the brink of extinction. Año Nuevo State Reserve was created in 1958 to protect the seals.

Male elephant seals, some reaching lengths of 16 feet and weighing three tons, arrive in December and begin battling for dominance. Only a very small percentage of males actually get to inseminate a female; most remain lifelong bachelors. The females, relatively svelte at 1,200 to 2,000 pounds, come ashore in January and join the harems of the dominant males.

La Punta de Año Nuevo (The Point of the New Year) was named by the Spanish explorer Sebastian Vizcaíno on January 3, 1603. It's one of the oldest place names in California.

The Año Nuevo area has hosted a variety of enterprises. From the 1850s to 1920, redwood cut from the slopes of the nearby Santa Cruz Mountains was shipped from Año Nuevo Bay. A dairy industry flourished on the coastal bluffs. The reserve's visitor center is a restored century-old dairy barn.

While the elephant seals are clearly the main attraction when they come ashore during the winter to breed and during the spring and summer to molt, the reserve is even fascinating when the big creatures are not in residence; in fact, Año Nuevo is a year-round destination.

Joining the elephant seals on Año Nuevo Island are Steller sea lions, California sea lions and harbor seals. Seals inhabit Año Nuevo year-round. Viewing is great in the spring and summer months—on the beaches. Autumn brings one- to-three year-old "yearling" seals ashore to rest on the beaches.

Reservations/information: Año Nuevo Point, where the elephant seals reside, is open only to visitors on guided walks, conducted by state park volunteer naturalists, from December through March.

Guided walks are conducted daily and consist of a 2½-hour, three-mile long walk. Advance reservations for the guided walks are strongly recommended. Reservations can be made through MISTIX, the state park system's reservation contractor by calling 1-800-444-PARK. Credit card payment is accepted.

From April through November, acccess to the Año Nuevo Point Wildlife Protection Area is by permit only. Permits are issued free of charge daily at the reserve, on a first-come-first-served basis.

Directions to trailhead: Año Nuevo State Reserve is located just west of Highway 1, 22 miles north of Santa Cruz and 30 miles south of Half Moon Bay.

McNee Ranch State Park
Montara Mountain Trail

> **Terrain:** Coastal scrub-covered Montara Mountain, far northern
>   extension of Santa Cruz Mountains
> **Highlights:** Fabulous coastal vistas from Half Moon Bay to
>   Golden Gate
> **Distance:** 7½ miles round trip; 2,000-foot elevation gain
> **Degree of difficulty:** Moderate to strenuous

Not even a sign welcomes you to McNee Ranch State Park, located
on the San Mateo County coast 25 miles south of San Francisco.

But what the park lacks in signs and facilities, it makes up in grand
views and wide open spaces. And oh, what a view! The coastline from
Half Moon Bay to the Golden Gate National Recreation Area is at
your feet.

The panoramic view is a hiker's reward for the rigorous ascent of
Montara Mountain, whose slopes form the bulk of the state park.
Montara Mountain, geologists say, is a 90-million-year-old chunk of

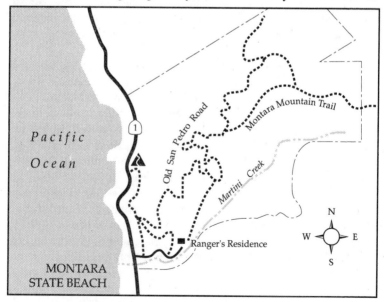

granite (largely quartz diorite) that forms the northernmost extension of the Santa Cruz Mountains.

Alas, what is a beautiful park to hikers is an ideal location for a multi-lane highway to the California Department of Transportation. Caltrans wants to build a Highway 1 bypass through the park to replace the existing landslide-prone stretch of highway known as the Devil's Slide that begins about two miles south of Pacifica.

Caltrans and its building plans have been fiercely contested by environmentalists, who fear the highway bypass would destroy the ambiance of the park and lead to further development in the area. The two sides have been battling it out in court for several years.

At the moment, it's not cement, but the coastal scrub community—ceanothus, sage and monkeyflower—that predominates on the mountain. The park also boasts several flower-strewn grasslands. Meandering down Montara Mountain is willow- and alder-lined Martini Creek, which forms the southern boundary of the state park.

The park's trail system includes footpaths as well as Old San Pedro Road, a dirt road that's popular with mountain bikers. Little hiker symbols keep walkers on the trail, but since all routes climb Montara Mountain and more or less meet at the top, don't be overly concerned about staying on the "right" trail.

Hikers will note that the nearest spot for provisions is the hamlet of Montara, where there's a cafe and grocery store. Good accommodations for a hiker on a budget are found in the Montara Lighthouse Hostel. The thirty-bed hostel, which is located right next to a working lighthouse, has kitchen facilities, a volleyball court, and even an outdoor hot tub.

Directions to trailhead: Take Highway 1 to Montara and park in the fair-sized lot at the north end of Montara State Beach. Walk carefully 150 yards up-coast and cross the highway. The unsigned trail begins at a pipe gate across a fire road on the inland side of Coast Highway.

The walk: Head up the fire road a short distance and join the trail on your left, which swings north, up-coast, over a seasonally flowered grassy slope. The path drops to join a dirt road, then begins ascending once more.

As you climb, you pass two benches, strategically placed for you to catch your breath. The dirt road eventually swings south, but you join a footpath and ascend to a saddle. Two trails lead left to the peak and terrific views.

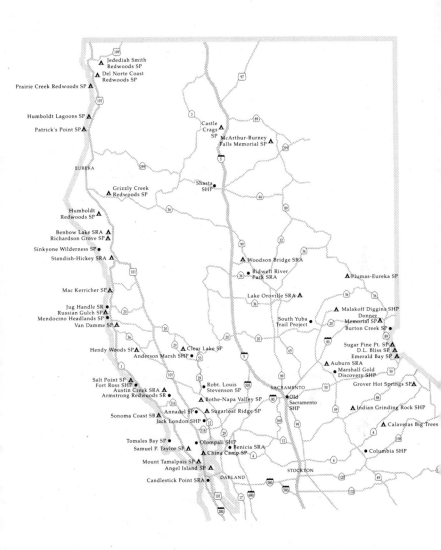

Jedediah Smith
Redwoods SP
Del Norte Coast
Redwoods SP
Prairie Creek Redwoods SP

Humboldt Lagoons SP

Patrick's Point SP

Castle
Crags
SP
McArthur-Burney
Falls Memorial SP

EUREKA

Grizzly Creek
Redwoods SP
Shasta
SHP

Humboldt
Redwoods SP

Benbow Lake SRA
Richardson Grove SP

Sinkyone Wilderness SP

Standish-Hickey SRA

Woodson Bridge SRA

Bidwell River
Park SRA

Plumas-Eureka SP

Mac Kerricher SP

Lake Oroville SRA

Jug Handle SR
Russian Gulch SP
Mendocino Headlands SP
Van Damme SP

Malakoff Diggins SHP
Donner
Memorial SP
Burton Creek SP

South Yuba
Trail Project

Sugar Pine Pt. SP
D.L. Bliss SP
Emerald Bay SP

Hendy Woods SP
Anderson Marsh SHP

Clear Lake SP

Auburn SRA
Marshall Gold
Discovery SHP

Grover Hot Springs SP

Salt Point SP
Fort Ross SHP
Austin Creek SRA
Armstrong Redwoods SR

Robt. Louis
Stevenson SP

SACRAMENTO

Indian Grinding Rock SHP

Bothe-Napa Valley SP

Old
Sacramento
SHP

Annadel SP
Sonoma Coast SB
Jack London SHP

Sugarloaf Ridge SP

Calaveras Big Trees

Tomales Bay SP
Samuel P. Taylor SP

Olompali SHP

Columbia SHP

Benicia SRA

Mount Tamalpais SP
Angel Island SP

China Camp SP

STOCKTON

Candlestick Point SRA

OAKLAND

Northern California

Northern California Mountains

The High Sierra stretches along the eastern edge of California. The rugged "Range of Light" is a magnificent backdrop for Lake Tahoe—and the state parks along its shores—Emerald Bay, D.L. Bliss, and Sugar Pine Point. A reminder of just how rugged the Sierra can be is found at Donner Lake, where a state park remembers the ill-fated journey and encampment of the pioneers of the Donner Party.

In the Sierra foothills lies the Gold Country, where the fabled Mother Lode lured hundreds of thousands of settlers to California. Highway 49 links former gold rush towns and a number of state parks that pay tribute to that era: Marshall Gold Discovery, Empire Mine, Malakoff Diggins. These parks preserve tunnels, trails, mines and mountains made famous by the forty-niners.

Also on the western slope of the Sierra Nevada are the famed giant sequoia groves of Calaveras Big Trees State Park. The "Big" in the park name is no exaggeration; sequoias are the largest living things on earth.

The environment that contributes to the making of fine wine—rolling hills, fertile valleys, warm days and cool nights—also adds up to some beautiful countryside, known to visitors from around the world as "California's Wine Country."Several inviting state parks are nestled in the land of the grape. It's easy to see why famed writer Jack London found inspiration at his Beauty Ranch, now preserved as Jack London State Historic Park. Robert Louis Stevenson was similarly inspired by the environs around Mt. Saint Helena; today a state park honoring the author preserves these mountain slopes.

In that "other wine country" north of Napa-Sonoma, Lake County, walkers can gain insight into Native American life at Anderson Marsh State Historic Park and take in (or jump in) California's largest body of water at Clear Lake State Park.

Jack London State Historic Park

Beauty Ranch, Lake, Mountain Trails

> **Terrain:** Vineyards, forests, meadows
> **Highlights:** A literary pilgrimage, grand vistas of the Valley of the Moon
> **Distance:** To lake is 2 miles round trip; to top of Sonoma Mountain is 8¼ miles round trip with 1,800-foot elevation gain
> **Degree of difficulty:** Moderate
> **Precautions:** Poison oak; don't stray onto nearby private property

There have been few more colorful, individualistic, and, ultimately more tragic figures in American literature than Jack London. Born in San Francisco in 1876, London struggled to release himself from the stifling burdens of illegitimacy and poverty.

His quest led him on a succession of rugged adventures in far-flung locales. He was an oyster pirate in San Francisco Bay, a gold prospector in the frozen Klondike, a sailor in the South Seas. He drew largely on his rough-and-tumble experiences throughout his prolific career as a writer of novels, short stories, and magazine articles.

London, who by most accounts was the most successful writer of his time—in terms of financial earnings, fame and popularity—is today best-known for his outdoor adventure stories. *White Fang, The*

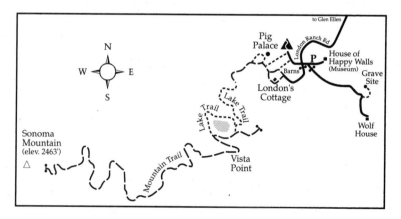

Call of the Wild, and *To Build a Fire,* his most popular works, have stereotyped the writer as one who depicts the theme of the individual's struggle to survive, using nature's harshness as a backdrop. But London's message was more complex than that, yet through time it's been largely ignored.

A passionate humanist, London was deeply committed to the cause of socialism. In his day, before the Russian Revolution skewed the promise of utopian socialism, London viewed socialism as the way to restore human dignity and respect for the individual. He raged against the oppressive social conditions of the Industrial Age in *The People of the Abyss, Martin Eden,* and *The Iron Heel.*

London's life was a mass of contradictions. He was a wealthy socialist, a he-man who was plagued with ill health, an imaginative writer who feared he would one day run out of ideas. He and his wife Charmian lived in the bucolic setting of Glen Ellen, far from the crowded city conditions he decried.

London first purchased land in the Sonoma Valley in 1905, and continued to add to his holdings until he owned 1,350 acres. As he described the setting: ". . . there are great redwoods on it . . . also there are great firs, tanbark oaks, live oaks, white oaks, black oaks, madrone and manzanita galore. There are canyons, several streams of water, many springs. . . . I have been riding all over these hills, looking for just such a place, and I must say that I have never seen anything like it."

The Jack London Ranch is now the site of Jack London State Historic Park, established in 1960 in accordance with the wishes of his wife.

Among the attractions to be found in the park are the House of Happy Walls Museum, built by Charmian London as a memorial to her husband's life and work and the remains of the Wolf House mansion, suspiciously burned to the ground shortly before the Londons were scheduled to move in.

Before or after this walk, be sure to make the 1½-mile pilgrimage to Jack London's gravesite and to the Wolf House ruins.

This excursion lets you meander through the main part of what Jack London called his "Beauty Ranch," visits a small reservoir, then offers energetic hikers the chance to tackle Sonoma Mountain, located just outside the park boundary.

Directions to trailhead: From Santa Rosa head east, from Sonoma head north on Highway 12. Take the signed turnoff (Arnold Drive) a mile to the hamlet of Glen Ellen. Turn right on Jack London Ranch

Road and proceed 1¼ miles to the state park. To visit the museum, turn left; for trailhead parking, angle right.

The walk: The path ascends a hundred yards southwest through a eucalyptus grove to a trail map and picnic area. Proceed straight ahead, past an old barn to a dirt road, where you go right.

A side trail leads to the cottage where London worked in his final years. The dirt road forks. You head right along a vineyard, meandering past "Pig Palace," London's hog pen deluxe, and assorted silos.

About a half-mile from the trailhead, you'll crest a hill and get your first great view of the Valley of the Moon. The trail soon splits: equestrians go left, hikers go right on a narrow footpath through a forest of Douglas fir, bay laurel and madrone that ascends past some good-sized redwoods.

Lake Trail loops around the London's little lake, where the couple swam and enjoyed entertaining friends. This is a good turnaround point for families with young children.

Sonoma Mountain-bound hikers will join the dirt road, Mountain Trail, which curves east to Mays Clearing, another fine vista point offering Valley of the Moon panoramas.

Mountain Trail climbs steadily, crosses two forks of fern-lined Graham Creek, and ascends to what was once Jack London's hunting camp (Deer Camp), tucked in a grove of redwoods. It's marked "Rest Area" on the park map.

Mountain Trail resumes climbing, steeper now, beneath big black oaks, for another mile, ascending to the headwaters of Middle Graham Creek and up to the park boundary.

The park map shows the path ending here; actually, it continues another quarter-mile to the crest of Sonoma Mountain's east ridge. Enjoy the superb views from this, the park's summit. (The actual mountaintop, eighty feet higher in elevation than the east summit, is forested with antennae and microwave relays and is located another quarter-mile to the west.)

Annadel State Park

Warren Richardson, Steve's S Trails

Terrain: Rolling hills, meadows
Highlights: Fishing in Lake Ilsanjo, great picnicking
Distance: To Lake Ilsanjo is 5 miles round trip with 500-foot elevation gain; circling the lake adds an additional 2 miles
Degree of difficulty: Moderate
Precautions: Early-rising hikers and anglers note the park's rather late (9 a.m.) opening time; plenty of poison oak in park.

Thirty-five miles of hiking trail plus good black bass and bluegill fishing are the highlights of Annadel State Park located an hour's drive north of San Francisco .

Tucked away in the heart of the park, Lake Ilsanjo, where the fish bite and hikers hike, is a pleasant destination for day hike. You can bring meal worms to tempt the bluegill to bite, or purple plastic worms for the bass, or simply bring your own picnic and let the fish feed themselves.

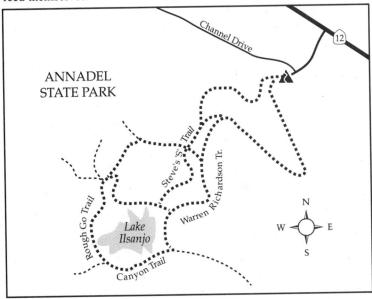

The lake's Spanish-sounding name does not date from the days of the ranchos and rancheros, as one might guess; it's actually a composite formed from the first names of two former landowners, Ilsa and Joe Coney, who built the lake in 1956.

It was not the tranquil shores of Lake Ilsanjo, but the rocky hills around it that brought the first humans to the area. Pomo and Wappo gathered obsidian, using the shiny black rock to fashion knife blades, arrowheads and spearheads.

White settlers, too, came for the rocks. Basalt was quarried here at the turn of the century to build San Francisco; after the great 1906 earthquake, the rock was used to rebuild the city. Also quarried, for city streets, was cobblestone, though in no time such paving fell into disfavor with drivers of the new horseless carriages.

Once part of the 1837 Mexican land grant, Rancho Los Guilicos, the Annadel area was owned by a series of farmers and gentlemen ranchers. Annadel became a state park in 1971.

A favorite way to Lake Ilsanjo is via Warren Richardson Trail, a wide path that honors a prominent Sonoma County cattle rancher and avid horseman with a love for trails. Warren Richardson Trail winds through a cool forest and crosses an open meadow on the way to the lake. For a fun return trip, loop back on steep, fern- and fir-lined Steve's S Trail.

Directions to trailhead: From Highway 101 in Santa Rosa, exit on Highway 12 (toward Sonoma) and follow it east through town. Turn right on Montgomery Drive, then right again on Channel Drive and follow it a mile into the park. The park office (where you'll find water, maps for sale) is at the entrance; trailhead parking is a mile farther down the road.

The walk: From the parking lot, join the trail leading south, which in no time at all delivers you to a dirt road—Warren Richardson Trail. You'll pause to view an interpretive display about how the natives used acorns, then spot Steve's S Trail (your return route) on the right.

Three-fourths of a mile of easy walking from the trailhead brings you to a hairpin turn and a junction with Two Quarry Trail. Swing northwest on Warren Richardson Trail and begin ascending through a forest of redwoods and Douglas fir. Sword ferns seem to point the way uphill.

The dirt road turns south again, passes a junction with Louis Trail, then begins descending. You get your first glimpse of Lake Ilsanjo. Emerging from the woods, you cross a meadow to the lakeshore.

To circle the lake, continue on Warren Richardson Trail, then join Rough Go Trail and Middle Steve's S Trail. Parts of the lakeshore are carpeted with blue-eyed grass. Sticking above the grass is mule ear (one look at this plant's protruding leaves will confirm how it got its name). In spring, mule ear sprouts yellow, sunflower-like blossoms.

Your return route joins Steve's S Trail, which skirts the east end of the meadow as it begins to ascend. Topping a hill, the path joins up with the North Burma Trail for a brief descent; then Steve's S Trail forks left and descends through a Douglas fir forest. A mile's descent deposits you on Warren Richardson Trail, very close to where you began this hike.

Foot notes: Cobblestone Trail passes through an area quarried for cobblestone. More evidence of quarrying can be seen along Orchard Trail.

While most first-time visitors enter Annadel through the main (Channel Drive) entrance, the park has two more entry points, with accompanying hikes. From Spring Lake County Park, on the state park's northwest boundary, you can pick up the usually cool and pleasant Spring Creek Trail, then join Rough Go and Canyon Trails for 5½-mile loop trip to Lake Ilsanjo. From the Lawndale Road entry on the park's southeast side, you can join Lawndale Trail for the four-mile round trip hike to Ledson Marsh, a favorite bird-watching spot.

Sugarloaf Ridge State Park
Bald Mountain, Vista, Gray Pine, Meadow Trails

> **Terrain:** Maycamas Mountains between Sonoma and Napa Valleys; oak woodland
> **Highlights:** Napa Valley views, spring wildflowers
> **Distance:** 6-mile loop through park with 700-foot elevation gain; shorter and longer loops possible
> **Degree of difficulty:** Moderate

Depending on time, energy, and inclination, the hiker can fashion several four- to eight-mile loops through Sugarloaf Ridge State Park. For a good introduction to local flora, join the ¾-mile Creekside Nature Trail. Numbered posts along the trail correspond to park brochure nature descriptions.

Directions to trailhead: From Highway 101 in Santa Rosa, exit on Highway 12 and travel east 11 miles to Adobe Canyon Road. Turn

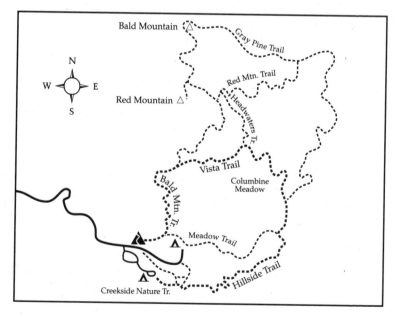

left and follow it four miles to the hikers' parking lot a bit before road's end.

The walk: From the east end of the parking lot, hit the trail which leads into a meadow and soon splits. Join Lower Bald Mountain Trail, which crosses a meadow, then ascends through an oak and madrone woodland. After a mile's brisk climb, the path intersects paved Bald Mountain Trail. A strategically placed bench allows you to catch your breath and to gaze out over the park

Proceed right on the road, ascending steeply a quarter-mile to signed Vista Trail. The intrepid will continue marching up the road, past the turnoff to Red Mountain (2,548 feet) to the summit of Bald Mountain (2,729 feet). From Bald Mountain, enjoy the view of the Napa Valley below, Mt. Saint Helena above. On especially clear days, the panorama includes the High Sierra and San Francisco Bay.

Those forsaking the peak, will join Vista Trail, which drops into a couple of ravines watered by seasonal Sonoma Creek tributaries. Vista Trail serves up promised vistas of Sugarloaf Ridge, then descends through Columbine Meadow. Cross Sonoma Creek, join Gray Pine Trail and cross a meadow. Bordering the meadow is quite a mixture of trees: maples, black oaks, alder and bay.

At a signed trail junction, you can select Meadow Trail, which crosses a meadow and returns you to trailhead.

A less direct way back is to join Hillside Trail which climbs above Sonoma Creek and gives you another perspective —a northern view—of the state park, then descends to join Creekside Nature Trail near the campground and trailhead.

Foot notes: Bordering Sugarloaf Ridge on the northwest is Hood Mountain Regional Park. Ascend the 2,730-foot mountain for great Sonoma County views. From the state park, ascend Goodspeed Trail (8 miles round trip) into the county park and onto the summit. Another fine climb of Hood Mountain begins in the county park; begin on Santa Rosa Creek Trail meandering with the lush creekbed, then join Hood Mountain Trail for the long, steep pull to the summit.

Bothe-Napa Valley State Park
Redwood Trail Ritchey Canyon Trail

Terrain: Redwood lined canyon, volcanic cliffs
Highlights: Napa Valley views, wildflowers
Distance: 6½ miles round trip with 1,200-foot elevation gain;
   longer, shorter options possible
Degree of difficulty: Easy to moderate
Precautions: Stay on trail to avoid poison oak

It's a great place to unwind and uncork. At least that's what most visitors figure when they discover Bothe-Napa Valley State Park in the heart of the wine country.

First-time visitors to this park typically arrive by accident, not design; they've just completed a tour of one of the renowned Napa Valley wineries and are looking for a place to picnic and sample a recent purchase.

But if it's the park's proximity to wineries (just down the road are Beringer Vineyards, Charles Krug Winery and a dozen more) that first

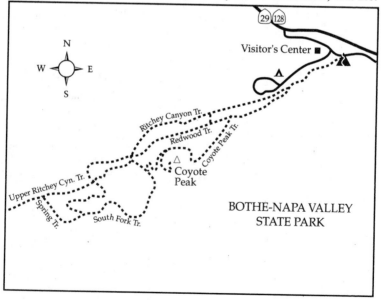

lures travelers, it's the park's beauty that brings them back: Year-round Ritchey Creek shaded by redwoods and Douglas fir, plus inspiring wine country views from Coyote Peak. The park is a particularly pleasant refuge in summer, because it stays cool when Napa Valley temperatures soar into the 90s.

Directions to trailhead: Bothe-Napa Valley State Park is located on the side of Highway 29 in the Napa Valley, five miles north of St. Helena, four miles south of Calistoga. Leave your car by the visitor center or at the horse trailer parking area just past the campground road turnoff where the trail begins.

The walk: The trail, which travels west beneath big leaf maple, madrone and oaks soon crosses a paved road and begins paralleling the road to the campground, as well as Ritchey Creek.

Beneath the tall Douglas fir and redwoods grows a tangle of ferns, bay laurel and wild grape. Half-a-mile along, you'll pass a trail on your right leading to the campground. A mile out, the forest thins and you intersect Coyote Peak Trail on your left.

Recently reworked and rerouted Coyote Peak Trail climbs high and dry terrain and offers good views of Upper Ritchey Canyon, plus glimpses of the wine country and mighty Mt. Saint Helena.

As the path steepens, you'll pass more big redwoods and fir. About 1½ miles along, you cross Ritchey Creek (usually an easy crossing except when rains swell the creek). This is a good turnaround point for the leg-weary or families with small children.

The trail continues up-canyon, crossing Ritchey Creek again and linking up with Upper Ritchey Canyon Trail. After passing a junction with Spring Trail, you climb above the forest into a brushy environment of manzanita and scrub oak, then dip back into the redwoods.

Three miles from the trailhead, your path forks. The main trail angles left, then climbs south to the park boundary.

A better bet is the right fork, which leads over an old bridge to an 1885 homestead site, where plum and apple trees grow in a picnic-perfect clearing.

Return the same way, or take a slightly longer route back via either Spring Trail or Coyote Peak Trail.

Robert Louis Stevenson State Park

Stevenson Memorial Trail

Terrain: Dramatic, knobcone pine-dotted slopes of Mt. Saint Helena

Highlights: Step into California's literary history—the secluded canyon where author Robert Louis Stevenson honeymooned. Enjoy awesome views of Napa Valley, High Sierra, San Francisco Bay

Distance: 2 miles round trip to Stevenson Memorial; 10 miles round trip with 1,300-foot elevation gain to summit of Mt. Saint Helena

Degree of difficulty: Moderately strenuous

Precautions: Dress for cold temperatures, high winds; occasionally, snow closes trail to peak. Very hot and dry in summer

You can see the imposing mountain towering above the wineries. Mt. Saint Helena is a landmark, a wild backdrop behind the neat cultivated vineyards of Napa Valley.

The best view of the wine country is from the top of 4,343-foot Mt. Saint Helena, reached by a five-mile trail that winds through stands of knobcone pine to deliver summit panoramas of not only Napa Valley but the High Sierra and San Francisco Bay as well.

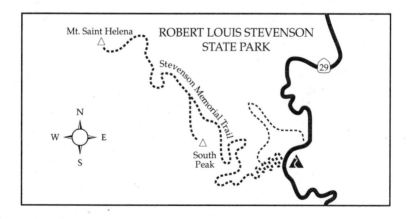

While winter is not the most popular of seasons for touring the wine country, it is the best time for looking down at it from the top of Mt. Saint Helena. Crisp, clear winter days mean breathtaking views from the summit. Local Sierra Club members schedule an annual New Year's Day hike up the mountain—surely an invigorating way to celebrate the year past and welcome the year ahead.

Most of the summit and broad shoulders of Mt. Saint Helena are protected by Robert Louis Stevenson State Park. Stevenson, best remembered for his imaginative novels, *Dr. Jekyll and Mr. Hyde* and *Treasure Island,* honeymooned in a cabin tucked in one of Mt. Saint Helena's ravines in the summer of 1880.

Quite the world traveler, Stevenson, constantly seeking relief from chronic tuberculosis, globe-trotted from Switzerland to the south of France to Samoa. The native Scot followed his heart to California to marry an American woman, Fanny Osbourne.

Short of money, the newlyweds honeymooned in the abandoned mining camp of Silverado, moving into an old cabin and using hay for a bed. While so encamped, Stevenson filled a diary with local color and later penned an account of his experience, *The Silverado Squatters,* which introduced him to American readers.

Stevenson filled his notebooks with descriptions of the many colorful Napa Valley denizens—from stage drivers to winemakers—he met. Perhaps the biggest influence upon Stevens during his stay on Mt. Saint Helena was the mountain itself; it became the model for Spyglass Hill in his novel *Treasure Island.*

Today you can take a short (one mile) hike into California literary history by joining the trail leading to the secluded site of the Stevensons' honeymoon. Wrote Stevenson: "At sunrise, and again later at night, the scent of sweet bays filled the canyon." A memorial in the form of an open book commemorates the author's stay on the mountain and marks the site of his cabin.

Travelers interested in learning more about Robert Louis Stevenson and his work should head for the Silverado Museum in St. Helena, located seven miles south of Calistoga. The museum features books, letters, and other memorabilia of Stevenson's life.

Stevenson Memorial Trail is particularly enjoyable for the first interesting mile as it winds through the forest to the memorial. The next four miles of trail—a well-graded fire road leading to the summit—are frankly a bit monotonous; however, the grand vistas, becoming better and better as you climb, more than compensate.

Directions to trailhead: From downtown Calistoga, at the junction of Highways 128 and 29, head north on the latter road. Highway 29 ascends 8¼ miles to a summit, where you'll find parking at turnouts on both sides of the highway for Robert Louis Stevenson State Park. The trail departs from the west side of the highway. Hint: The not-very-well-signed state park is easy to miss. If you find yourself rapidly descending on Highway 29, you overshot the summit and the state park. Carefully turn around and return to the summit.

The walk: Just above the parking lot is picnic area. During Stevenson's day, a stage stop and the Toll House Hotel were located here. The Stevensons came down the hill from their honeymoon cabin to buy provisions.

Signed Stevenson Memorial Trail switchbacks up a shady slope forested with oak, madrone, bay and Douglas fir. A pleasant mile's walk brings you face-to-face with the granite Stevenson memorial, itself something of a historical curiosity, having been erected by "The Club Women of Napa County" in 1911.

To continue to the peak, scramble up a badly eroded hundred-yard-long stretch of trail to the fire road and turn left. The road soon brings you to a hairpin turn and the first grand view en route. You can admire part of the Napa Valley and surrounding ridges, San Francisco high-rises, as well as two distinct and aptly named nearby peaks: Turk's Head to the west and Red Hill to the south.

The road continues climbing moderately, but doggedly, up the mountain. Wind-battered, but unbowed, knobcone pine dot the middle slopes of Mt. Saint Helena. Three miles from the trailhead, you'll pass under some power lines, and another half-mile's travel brings you to a junction with a spur trail leading ⅜-mile to Mt. Saint Helena's South Peak.

Half-a-mile from the summit, the road passes through a forest of sugar pine and Douglas fir, then begins the final climb to the peak. Various transmitters, communication facilities and a fire lookout clutter the summit, but don't block the view. Vistas include the Sonoma County coast to the west, Santa Rosa due south, San Francisco and the Bay to the southwest, the High Sierra north of Yosemite to the east. On the clearest of days, you might be able to glimpse Mt. Shasta, nearly 200 miles to the northeast.

Anderson Marsh State Historic Park

Cache Creek, Anderson Flats, Ridge, Marsh Trails

> **Terrain:** Oak-dotted grasslands, tule marsh
> **Highlights:** Exploring pioneer and Pomo heritages
> **Distance:** 2 to 3 miles round trip
> **Degree of difficulty:** Easy

One of the most populous Native American groups in California, the Pomo occupied the Anderson Marsh area as far back as 10,000 years ago. The Pomo, known as some of the best basket-makers on the continent, found an ample supply of raw material in the marsh. Pomo elders construct a village in the park every year.

Anderson Marsh is also a nature preserve, which protects the habitat of a tule marsh, itself an integral part of the Clear Lake ecosystem. Anderson Marsh is a remnant (about 8 percent) of a once-vast tule marsh that nourishes Clear Lake, California's largest natural lake.

Two trails lead along the wetter parts of the park—Cache Creek and the marsh. Two other trails—Ridge (which ascends through an oak woodland) and Anderson Flats (which crosses a grassland) explore drier parts of the park. It's less than a mile's walk to the reconstructed Pomo village.

Directions to trailhead: Anderson Marsh SHP is located just off Highway 53 between the hamlet of Lower Lake and the town of Clear

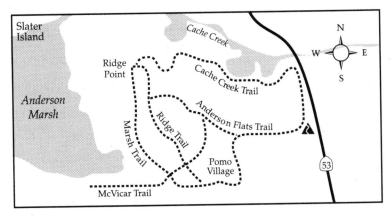

181

Lake. The park is a short distance north of Lower Lake and the Highway 29/53 junction.

Leave your car in the lot by the visitor center or, if the park gate is closed, in a turnout across the highway from the park entrance.

The park is open Wednesday through Sunday, 9 a.m. to 5 p.m.

The walk: Head west through the meadow along the park's southern boundary fence. The flat path through the Anderson pastureland forks: Anderson Flats Trail (a possible return route) is on your right, but you bear left, angling with the fence line to what is (sometimes) the site of a reconstructed Pomo village.

The path ascends through a blue oak woodland, passes a junction with Ridge Trail, then turns left to an interpretive display about bald eagles that drop in on the marsh during winter months. (Those seeking an up-close look at the marsh, will join McVicar Trail that heads into the Audubon Sanctuary. Hope you brought your binoculars to spot the abundant bird life!)

Otherwise, join Marsh Trail, which offers a good view of the marsh as it descends from the oak woodland toward the marsh. A bit more than a mile from the start, you'll top a low ridge and meet up with Cache Creek Trail. Atop this ridge, amidst plenty of poison oak, are Pomo grinding holes and petroglyphs. For a moment, you're able to imagine Pomo life, at least until you look into the distance and spot the vacation homes fringing the marsh.

The quick way back—a straight line across the meadow— is Anderson Flats Trail. A more interesting return is along Cache Creek, Clear Lake's main outlet, and a watercourse that eventually empties into the Sacramento River.

Cache Creek Trail meanders across meadowland, then turns east to follow the cottonwood-lined creek. The path nears the highway, then veers right and returns to the ranch house.

Clear Lake State Park
Dorn Nature Trail

Terrain: Oak-dotted slopes above lake.
Highlights: California's largest natural lake, the "Bass Capital of the West"
Distance: 1½-mile loop
Degree of difficulty: Easy

Clear Lake is the largest lake located entirely within the state. (Tahoe is a larger lake, but it's partly in Nevada.)

The lake is located in southern Lake County, in that "other" wine country, located immediately north of Napa and Sonoma counties, and about a hundred miles north of San Francisco. Around the lake are mountains, and beyond the mountains a fruited plain of vineyards, walnut groves and, as locals boast, "the world's largest Bartlett pear growing area."

Clear Lake, earth scientists estimate, is 2.5 million years old; some

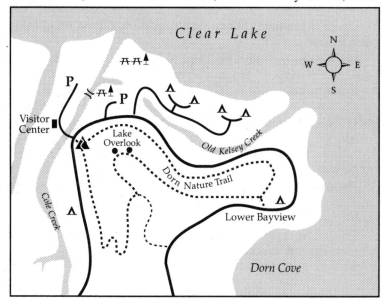

claim it's the oldest lake in North America. At the very least, it's considerably older that such 5,000-year-old "infants" such as Lakes Tahoe and Superior.

Clear Lake is a natural lake, meaning that it has a set-in-nature feeling, and gives an altogether more tranquil vibe than state mega-reservoirs such as Folsom Lake or Lake Oroville.

Clear Lake State Park offers much-needed public access to the lake and preserves about two miles of lakeshore. Swimming, water skiing and hiking are popular at the park, but fishing is as big as the lake itself. "Wall to wall" catfish, bluegill, crappie and black bass lure fishermen to the lake.

Located on the lake's south shore, the state park includes some terrific lakeshore campsites at Kelsey Creek Campground. A modern visitor center features exhibits about the lake, as well as Native America lore, and local flora and fauna.

Dorn Nature Trail samples the slopes above Clear Lake and offers fine Lake County vistas.

Directions to trailhead: From Highway 29 in Kelseyville (just south of Lakeport) turn east on signed Soda Bay Road and follow the signs to Clear Lake State Park.

Leave your car in the day use parking area near the visitor center.

The walk: From the visitor center, walk back up the day use access road to the main park road; here you'll see signed Dorn Nature Trail. The path joining Dorn Nature Trail from the left is the return leg of the loop.

The path ascends into a woodland of California buckeye and valley oak, switchbacks a bit, and soon serves up the first view of the lake.

A quarter-mile climb brings you to the crest of a minor ridge and a junction with a side trail splitting to the right and leading to Upper Bayview Campground. Stay left and continue on Dorn Trail to an overlook.

A bit farther down the trail, a second overlook offers another vista of the lake, as well as towering Mount Konocti.

Three-quarters of a mile out, about halfway through this walk, the path descends and passes a right-forking trail leading to Lower Bayview Campground.

The descent continues over fern-covered slopes, contours west, then drops to the park road back at the trailhead.

Calaveras Big Trees State Park
South Grove Trail

> **Terrain:** Forested slopes, watershed of Big Trees Creek.
> **Highlights:** Magnificent Sierra redwood groves
> **Distance:** 5 miles round trip; 400-foot elevation gain
> **Degree of difficulty:** Moderate
> **Precautions:** Snow closes the road to South Grove; call the
> park for latest road and weather conditions.

The "Big Trees" in the park name is a tip-off: two groves of giant Sequoia redwoods are the highlights of Calaveras Big Trees State Park. The trees became world famous in the 1850s, thanks in part to some circus-style promoters, who chopped down "Discovery Tree" and took it on tour. Another set of profiteers stripped the bark off the "Mother of the Forest" and exhibited the "reassembled" tree in New York and in England's famed Crystal Palace.

Fortunately, for the trees, anyway, most of the truly curious came to visit the Sierra redwoods rather than expecting the trees to "visit"

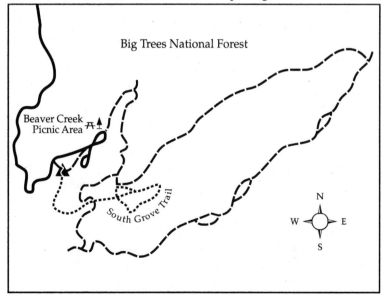

them. Scientists, celebrities, and thousands of just plain fascinated folks made their way to Calaveras County, often staying in the Mammoth Grove Hotel built close to the big trees.

For a time, scientists believed the giant sequoias in North Grove were the only ones on earth. With the discovery of other, greater groves in the Yosemite-Sequoia National Park areas, the Calaveras Big Trees, as a tourist attractio, declined somewhat in importance.

The biggest trees are truly big—250 to 300 feet high and 25 to 30 feet across. And they're ancient—2,000 to 3,000 years old. The trees are relics from a warmer and wetter clime and time, the Mesozoic Era, some 180 million years ago, when dinosaurs roamed the earth. Once much more numerous, the big trees survive now only in 75 groves on the western slope of the High Sierra.

The park has some great campgrounds and picnic areas, as well as an opportunity for trout fishing and a dip in the Stanislaus River. Most visitors, however, come to see the big trees, particularly those found in North Grove. A gentle one-mile trail meanders through the grove, leading to such grand sequoia specimens as Abraham Lincoln, Siamese Twins, Empire State and Father of the Forest.

Much, much less visited is the park's more remote South Grove, which offers a chance for solitude among the giants. The grove is protected in a "Natural Preserve," the highest category of environmental protection offered by the state park system.

Interpretive pamphlets for both South Grove and North Grove trails are available for a small donation at their respective trailheads or at the park's museum and visitor center.

Directions to trailhead: The park is located off Highway 4, four miles northeast of Arnold, and some 21 miles from Angels Camp and the junction with Highway 49. Once in the park, continue nine miles along the scenic park road (Walter W. Smith Memorial Parkway) to South Grove trailhead.

The walk: South Grove Trail soon crosses Beaver Creek on a footbridge and reaches a junction with Bradley Trail. (This 2½-mile-long path loops through land logged in the early 1950s. After the loggers left, park caretaker Owen Bradley planted Sequoia seedlings and today about 150 young Sierra redwoods thrive in Bradley Grove, a testament to forest regeneration and to the future.)

South Grove Trail climbs moderately through tall sugar and ponderosa pines and rises out of the Beaver Creek drainage. After crossing a fire road, the path meanders upstream alongside Big Trees Creek.

Bear right at the trail junction and continue hiking among the Sierra redwoods, incense cedar and occasional big leaf maple. Just past a large hollow redwood lying across the creek, you'll reach another junction. You can bear left to complete the loop trail, but better yet, head right to visit Agassiz Tree, largest in the park. One of the more curious Sierra redwoods encountered en route is aptly named Chimney Tree; its insides were long ago consumed by fire, forming a "chimney" in a still-living tree.

Agassiz Tree, one of the "Top Ten" Sierra redwoods in size, honors nineteenth-century naturalist Louis Agassiz, last of the scientific creationists and a pioneer in Ice Age theory and plant and animal classification.

While the trail ends here at this biggest of the big trees, the adventurous can continue another mile along Big Trees Creek and get up-close looks at other magnificent South Grove specimens: The Moody Group, named for a nineteenth-century evangelist, storied Old Goliath, felled by a windstorm in 1861, and three mammoth trees called The Portals.

Retrace your steps back to loop trail junction, this time branching right and descending back to the trailhead.

Foot notes: Besides the easy loops through the North Grove and the above-described loop through the South Grove, the park has two more trails of note. Four-mile-long River Trail connects North Grove with the Stanislaus River. Lava Bluff View Trail loops around bold outcroppings of lava that rise above the surrounding forest.

Grover Hot Springs State Park
Burnside Trail

> **Terrain:** Alpine meadows, east side of Sierra Nevada
> **Highlights:** Hidden lake, soothing soak in hot springs
> **Distance:** To waterfall is 3 miles round trip; to Burnside Lake is
>   10 miles round trip with 2,100-foot elevation gain
> **Degree of difficulty:** Moderate to strenuous

Nothing like a soothing soak in a hot spring after a long day on the trail. For the High Sierra visitor who wants to take a hike and "take the cure" in the same day, Grover Hot Springs State Park, located a bit south of Lake Tahoe, is the perfect destination.

Don't expect a Baden-Baden-style, deluxe Euro-resort; Grover Hot Springs offers your basic soak, nothing more, nothing less. Bathers can sit in one hot pool (102° to 105°F) fed by six mineral springs, and one cool pool. The two pools and the changing rooms are the extent of the state park facilities.

Tucked in Hot Springs Valley, surrounded on three sides by Sierra Nevada peaks, Grover Hot Springs offers a soak in a setting as soothing as its waters. The granite peaks, including 10,023-foot Hawkins Peak to the northwest and 9,419-foot Markleeville Peak to the southwest, form an inspiring backdrop to an area that's been attracting visitors since the 1850s.

Easy family hikes include a nature trail called Transition Walk that

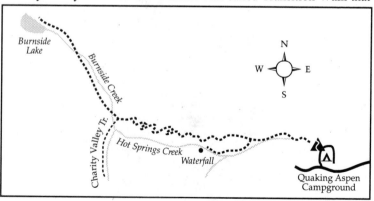

loops around the park's alpine meadow and a three-mile round trip walk to a waterfall on Hot Springs Creek.

A more ambitious jaunt for hikers in good condition is the hike to Burnside Lake located in the adjacent Toiyabe National Forest. Burnside Trail crosses the state park, then ascends through a pine forest to the alpine lake.

Directions to trailhead: From Highway 89 in Markleeville (a half-hour drive from South Lake Tahoe), turn west on Hot Springs Road and travel 3½ miles to Grover Hot Springs State Park. Park at the pool (then walk a footpath and the park road to the trailhead) or proceed past the park entrance station to the overflow parking area and the signed trailhead at the north end of Quaking Aspen Campground.

If you want to make the trip to Burnside Lake a one-way trip, you can drive to the lake. From the signed turnoff on Highway 88, drive 5½ miles down bumpy, dirt Burnside Road to road's end at the lake.

The walk: The path parallels Hot Springs Creek, a year-round watercourse that flows through the park's large meadow. Some of the catchable trout planted in the creek are caught by campers for their suppers, though serious anglers head for nearby Carson River.

The quaking aspen fringing the meadow are particularly showy in autumn, when the fluttering leaves turn orange and gold.

A short mile's walk from the trailhead brings you to a signed junction. (The trail to the waterfall branches left, leading along Hot Springs Creek. Some minor rock climbing leads to an overlook above the small, but vigorous falls.)

Burnside Trail enters the forest and ascends a mile to another junction, this one with Charity Valley Trail, which heads south along Charity Valley Creek. Soon thereafter, Burnside Trail crosses Burnside Creek and climbs northwest, switchbacking up steep Jeffrey pine- and white fir-cloaked slopes. Near the top, you'll get a grand, over-the-shoulder view of Hot Springs Valley.

The last mile of this hike resembles the first mile—a walk through meadowland. The meadow below Burnside Lake is much wetter than the one in the state park, however, so take care to stay on the trail; you won't get your boots so wet, and you'll help protect the fragile meadow ecology.

Boulders perched above the lakeshore suggest fine picnic spots, and inspiring places from which to contemplate pretty Burnside Lake.

Indian Grinding Rock State Historic Park

South Nature Trail

> **Terrain:** Pine and oak woodland
> **Highlights:** Grinding rocks—mortar cups the Miwok called
>   *chaw' se*
> **Distance:** ½ mile to 1 mile round trip
> **Degree of difficulty:** Easy

The grinding rock—a 173-foot length of bedrock with 1,185 mortar cups is something to behold. If you let your imagination go a bit, you can conjure a whole village at work.

The Miwok gathered acorns when they ripened in autumn and stored them in large granaries. The acorns were cracked and shelled, then ground with stone pestles in the mortar holes, or *chaw' se,* into flour. The acorn meal was then cooked on hot rocks.

Evidence of the Miwok, whose ancestral territory centered on the

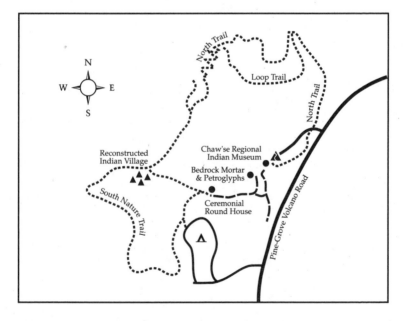

western slope of the Sierra Nevada, and ranged over to the San Francisco Bay area, has been discovered in numerous locales—and in such state parks as China Camp and Olompali—but here around the grinding rock, in the Sierra foothills, it's easiest to imagine their way of life.

Miwok crafts are on display in the park's excellent Chaw'se Regional Indian Museum. On the grounds are replicas of the Miwok's sturdy barkhouses and a roundhouse, a traditional ceremonial gathering spot of old as well as a meeting place for several different Native American groups today.

Two short trails explore the park. North Trail (one mile round trip) begins near the Museum. It follows a low ridge and loops back to the reconstructed Miwok village. At the village, you can join South Nature Trail or return to the museum via a more direct route past the ceremonial roundhouse.

South Nature Trail (a one-half mile loop) is a self-guided interpretive path keyed to a park pamphlet. As you tour meadowland, oak woods, plus stands of sugar pine and ponderosa pine, you'll learn how the Miwok collected and used the bountiful local vegetation.

Directions to trailhead: From Highway 49 in Jackson, head east nine miles to the hamlet of Pine Cove. Turn left and travel 1½ miles to Indian Grinding Rock State Historic Park. There's ample parking near the museum/visitor center.

Marshall Gold Discovery
State Historic Park

Discovery, Monument Trails

> **Terrain:** Bank of American River, historic downtown Coloma
> **Highlights:** Discovery site that started Gold Rush, James
>   Marshall Monument
> **Distance:** 1½-mile loop
> **Degree of difficulty:** Easy

It was here in 1848 James Marshall discovered gold; a year later, the world discovered California. Marshall, a carpenter, was constructing a sawmill in partnership with John Sutter when he spotted some golden flecks in the American River. He went to Sutter's Fort to share his news with his employer. The two tried to keep the gold news secret but word leaked out and the world rushed in.

The population of the hamlet of Coloma swelled to 10,000 in 1849. Two years later, the gold gave out and most of the miners left. Coloma, birthplace of the Gold Rush, is a tiny village within the boundaries of Marshall Gold Discovery State Historic Park. Several historic buildings line Highway 49, as well as narrow back streets.

Park highlights include an operating replica of Sutter's Mill and the Gold Discovery Museum, with its mining exhibits and videos telling the story of Marshall's discovery. A walking tour takes in a number of forty-niner-era buildings, as well as structures dating from later in the nineteenth century. Step into the Wah Hop Store, a Chinese general store. Visit Marshall Cabin, where Marshall, who benefited little from his great discovery, died bitter and penniless.

Other walks into history include a stroll down Main Street Coloma and a visit to the Pioneer Cemetery and Coloma Winery.

Monument Trail climbs to James Marshall Monument, where a bigger-than-life figure holds a bigger-than-life gold nugget and points to the spot where he made his discovery.

Monroe Ridge Trail, completed in 1993, extends 2.3 miles from North Beach picnic area to the Marshall Monument; if you want a little more of a workout than that offered by the historical walk, this is the trail to take.

The trail honors a pioneering African-American family who first settled here during the Gold Rush era. Family matriarch Nancy Gooch was brought to California as a slave but was soon freed when California entered the Union as a free state. She earned her living by doing laundry and domestic chores for miners and earned enough to purchase the freedom of her son Andrew Monroe and his wife Sara Ellen, who were still enslaved in Missouri.

The Monroes had a successful fruit orchard, prospered, and began buying land. Some of the family holdings included the famed gold discovery site, which the parks department purchased from the Monroe family in the 1940s.

Monroe Ridge Trail travels from the Marshall Monument to a vista point to the Monroe fruit orchard. Pick up a park trails map/interpretive pamphlet, which has some fascinating historical details; the map's east-west orientation can be confusing to hikers, however.

Directions to trailhead: Marshall Gold Discovery State Historic Park is located on Highway 49 in the town of Coloma, some 6½ miles

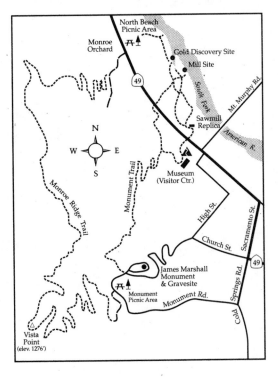

north of Placerville on Highway 50; some 17 miles south of Auburn and Highway 49's junction with Interstate 80.

On the southern outskirts of Coloma, Highway 49 bends sharply east; you should bear south here onto Springs Road and in a short distance turn right on Monument Road, following it to a parking area near the Marshall Monument, which occupies the top of a hill. Walk back down the hill along the road a short ways to the signed trailhead on your right.

The walk: Monroe Trail (a fire road for a short distance) leads first to an old spring house, surrounded by ferns. You then begin a stiff half-mile northern ascent via a series of switchbacks that brings you to Vista Point. Rest a moment at a picnic table and admire the vista—the hamlet of Coloma and the South Fork of the American River.

The path descends gently, following the ridgetop, then more abruptly as it switchbacks down to the old Monroe fruit orchard. Stop at the brass plaque honoring the Monroe family, then carefully cross Highway 49 to the North Beach Picnic Area. Cross the parking lot and join the riverside path which leads to the gold discovery site and mill site, then to the sawmill replica.

Cross the highway again to the park visitor center and join signed Monument Trail. A half-mile climb over forested slopes brings you to the top of a hill and to James Marshall Monument, built in 1890. The trailhead is just below the monument.

John A. Sutter

James W. Marshall

South Yuba River Project

Independence Trail

Terrain: Steep banks of South Yuba River, dramatic river canyon

Highlights: Wheelchair accessible trail; world's longest single-span covered bridge

Distance: 2 miles round trip; longer walks possible.

Degree of difficulty: Easy

Wheelchair access to the forest primeval has fortunately become more common over the years, but longer, truly challenging trails for the physically disabled, re-main in short supply.

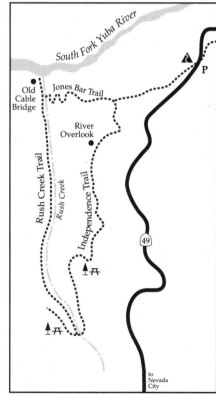

So it was with much delight that I recently dis-covered the South Yuba Independence Trail, which offers delightful passage through California's Gold Country for adventurers of all abilities.

Today's Independence Trail had its origins as the Excelsior Canal, built in 1859 to carry water from the South Yuba to hydraulic gold mining operations in Smartsville, 25 miles away. While the five-foot wide aqueduct crossed very steep country, it followed the con-tours of hillsides and thus was almost completely level.

This relative flatness of the trail, combined with some ingenious bridgework,

195

adds up to what was an admirable engineering feat for its time, as well as a terrific trail today. Particularly impressive are the wooden flumes that bridge steep ravines.

Volunteer efforts, spearheaded by activist John Olmsted and the nonprofit group Sequoya Challenge, rebuilt crumbling wooden flumes and transformed the long-abandoned water ditch into a scenic, wheelchair-accessible trail. The California Department of Parks and Recreation, as well as volunteer groups, have ambitious plans to complete a full ten miles of whole access trail along the South Yuba River. For an update on trail conditions, call: (916) 272-3459.

Independence Trail is a major, but by no means the only, highlight of a state park-in-the-making called the South Yuba River Project. Other highlights include the world's largest single-span covered bridge, and miles of dramatic canyon of the South Yuba River.

The project is an exciting—and large—undertaking for the state park system. When completed, the park will extend some 20 miles from Malakoff Diggins State Historic Park to the confluence of the South and main forks of the Yuba River.

The South Yuba River itself has been studied and proposed for "Wild and Scenic River" status, a designation that would give further protection to the river ecosystem.

A trail extends along parts of the twenty-mile stretch of river. One length of trail begins at the park visitor center and famed covered bridge, reached by driving eight miles north on Pleasant Valley Road from Highway 20.

Directions to trailhead: The main entrance to the Independence Trail is just off Highway 49, seven miles north of Nevada City, and one mile past the Yuba River crossing.

The walk: From the signed trailhead, the path uses an underpass to dip under Highway 49, then begins contouring along the south bluff of the river. You can walk in the old water ditch or on a parallel path above it.

The pleasant path crosses ravines by way of several wooden flumes. A bit more than a mile of woodsy walking brings you to Flume 28 over Rush Creek. Here you'll find a vista point, fishing platform, picnic deck and an outhouse.

Independence Trail continues another half-mile (as a wheelchair accessible route) to Jones Ravine. From the ravine, a hiking trail continues westward.

Empire Mine State Historic Park

Hardrock Trail

> **Terrain:** Sierra foothills
> **Highlights:** Tour one of California's oldest and richest gold
>   mines
> **Distance:** 2 to 3 miles round trip
> **Degree of difficulty:** Easy to moderate

Empire Mine, one of California's richest, produced more than six million ounces of gold during its hundred years of operation. The gold mine, along with 784 acres of gold country, is preserved in Empire Mine State Historic Park.

Shortly after the great gold rush of 1849, logger George Roberts discovered an outcropping of gold-bearing quartz about where today's visitors park their cars. Miners swarmed these hills to lay claim to the riches below. Trouble was, the gold was way below the surface, which pretty well thwarted most of the low-tech, low-budget prospectors. The miners dug 20- to 40-foot "coyote holes," tunneled and blasted, only to see their efforts fall victim to cave-ins or floods.

Around 1851 George Roberts and his fellow gold-seekers sold their claims to a consortium that consolidated them and dubbed the operation the Empire Mine. San Francisco businessman William Bourn and his son William, Jr., took over in 1870 and, after investing more

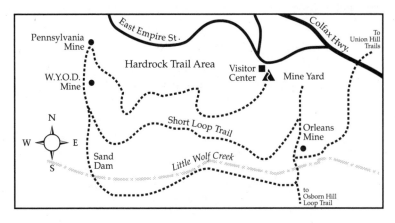

money and digging deeper than many thought possible, eventually turned a profit in the 1880s and beyond.

Much of the Empire's success can be attributed to the experienced hard-rock miners from Cornwall, England who came here. By some accounts, the 1890 population of Grass Valley was 85 percent Cornish.

Park visitors can get a look at the main mine shaft from an observation platform. At the visitor center are interpretive exhibits and gold samples displayed in an open vault.

The advantages of owning a gold mine are evident when one takes a look at the Empire Cottage, an English manor-style home designed by famed San Francisco architect Willis Polk for William Bourn, Jr., in 1898. Quite a "cottage!"

Join one of the park's scheduled tours of the Empire Cottage and/or Empire Mine. Or take a 16-stop walking tour on your own past structures, building foundations and mining machinery.

After your walk through history, hit the trail. The park has ten miles of pathways—above ground that is. Below you, the earth is honeycombed with some 367 miles of tunnels, some nearly a mile deep.

Across the highway from the visitor center is the Union Hill section of the park. This part of the park is wooded (sugar pine, ponderosa pine, incense cedar and Douglas fir), along with some oaks and big leaf maple. A few fruit trees—apple, pear, cherry—are reminders of early settlers in the area.

Three trails, one to three miles long, explore Union Hill. Along Pipeline Trail are remains of a waterpipe that carried water from a reservoir to the north and generated power to operate mining machinery. Indian Ridge Trail is a historic pathway used by the Nisenan tribe of Maidu. Union Hill Trail skirts the fringe of the fast-growing community of Grass Valley.

Two-mile long Hardrock Trail is a 20-stop interpretive trail that visits mines, machinery, a mule corral, a stamp mill and much more. Pick up the park's "Walking Trails of Empire Mine" brochure to get all the details of the complexities of hard-rock mining.

Osborn Hill Loop Trail, a mile-long side trail splitting off from Hardrock Trail, ascends to a couple more mine sites and offers a great view of the Sacramento Valley.

Directions to trailhead: Empire Mine State Historic Park is located in Grass Valley, just east of Highway 49 on East Empire Street. Follow the signs from the highway to the park.

Malakoff Diggins State Historic Park
Diggins Loop Trail

Terrain: Colorful cliffs, forested slopes
Highlights: Site of world's largest hydraulic gold mine, a historic walking tour through old North Bloomfield
Distance: 3-mile loop down into giant mining pit; 600-foot elevation loss, then gain
Degree of difficulty: Easy to moderate
Precautions: Trails are passable but not particularly well maintained; check on conditions at park office

Bordered by colorful cliffs, the Malakoff mine pit is more than a mile long, a half-mile wide and nearly 600 feet deep. In the right light, it resembles a Bryce Canyon in miniature.

Malakoff Diggins State Historic Park is the site of what was once the world's largest hydraulic gold mine. As the story goes, an Irish prospector thought he discovered gold by the Yuba River; despite his best efforts at subterfuge, he was unable to keep his secret from his

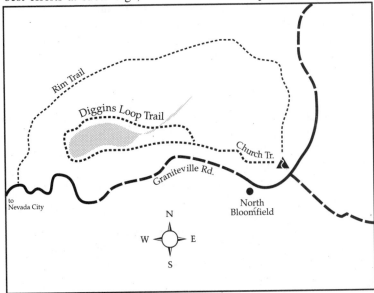

fellow miners in the nearby town of Nevada City, 16 miles away. The miners tried their luck, found nothing, and declared the site a "humbug," a name that stuck to the adjacent hamlet and creek.

Several years later, when gold was really discovered, residents of Humbug deemed the name inappropriate and unrespectable so they changed it to Bloomfield. Alas, Bloomfield already existed farther south in California so the town's name changed again—this time to North Bloomfield.

The change in the town's name, accompanied by a change in technology—hydraulic mining—led to a dramatic change in fortune. Spraying vast amounts of water under high pressure onto the gold-laden gravels of the Malakoff area, the miners created quite a pit—and profit—for the mine owners. During its operation, between 1866 and 1884, some 41 million cubic yards of earth was excavated, yielding several million dollars worth of gold.

The amount of erosion and subsequent environmental damage caused by hydraulic mining was astonishing. Debris dumped into the Yuba River was carried all the way to the Central Valley; silt clogged up the river and caused floods, leading to loss of life and property. Silt was flushed all the way to San Francisco Bay. Navigation of the Sacramento River was imperiled.

In one of the great landmark cases in early conservation history, Woodruff (a Central Valley property owner) vs. the North Bloomfield Gravel Mining Company, Judge Lorenzo Sawyer issued a permanent injunction in 1884 against dumping tailings into the Yuba River. Other injunctions soon followed, all but ending hydraulic mining.

You can learn more about hydraulic mining and the life of a miner at the state park's excellent museum. On summer weekends, rangers lead tours of the park's historic sites and the restored buildings—drug store, general store, Skidmore House, livery stable and more—of North Bloomfield.

Tour the small mining town on your own with the pamphlet "A Walking Tour of North Bloomfield." Pick up a copy at the park office.

The state park has thirty sites for camping and three replica miners' cabins, complete with potbellied stoves, for rent. Bring your own bedding and cookware. Call the park for reservations.

Walkers can choose from a variety of pathways. Rim Trail is a fairly level 3½ mile jaunt overlooking the great mining pit. The path offers close-up views of the spectacular erosion, both human-caused and natural, that shaped this land.

You'll pass grassy flats bedecked with lupine, buttercups and other wildflowers, thickets of manzanita, as well as slopes forested with sugar and ponderosa pine. Highlighting the trail are panoramas of the pit and its surrounding colorful cliffs.

Directions to trailhead: Malakoff Diggins State Historic Park is located 16 miles northeast of Nevada City on North Bloomfield Road.

The walk: From the park's picnic area, join signed Church Trail to the cemetery. Pick up the signed trail to the Diggins below the cemetery and descend rapidly through mixed forest to a trail junction. Diggins Loop Trail splits; the south (left) loop descends through a diverse environment of brush and conifers. A side trail leads a short distance to California Historical Landmark #852, which commemorates the North Bloomfield Mining and Gravel Company.

Another side trail leads to the dark and dank Hiller Tunnel, a quarter-mile spur (you need a flashlight to explore this). The tunnel is a segment of a much larger drainage tunnel that sent lots of muck and sediment down Humbug Creek and then on down to the South Yuba River.

Diggins Loop Trail circles Diggins Pond, which at first looks lifeless, but it's not. Watch for sandpipers at water's edge. Cattails crowd the shoreline in places, while just above the lakeshore slopes grow alder and willows.

Diggins Trail, somewhat overgrown with brush, continues its loop around the north side of the pond then reaches a junction with the Church Trail, which you'll join and return to the trailhead.

Foot notes: The park's Humbug Trail descends 2½ miles along Humbug Creek to the Yuba River where there are some U.S. Bureau of Land Management campsites.

Plumas-Eureka State Park
Eureka Peak Loop Trail

> **Terrain:** Granite peaks, pine and fir forest
> **Highlights:** Gold mining history, Sierra vistas
> **Distance:** 6 miles round trip; 1,800-foot elevation gain; if ski
>   lift road open, 3 miles round trip with 1,000-foot gain
> **Degree of difficulty:** Moderate
> **Precautions:** Don't venture into any open mine shafts

Most California gold discoveries began with a flash in the pan; this one began with a hike.

The year was 1851. An exploratory party of miners dispatched two members to climb Eureka Peak. The two found a quartz outcropping, rich in gold, silver and lead. "Gold Mountain" the miners promptly dubbed the peak. Their discovery became known as the Eureka Chimney, a mammoth deposit of ore-bearing rock that would yield more than two million dollars in gold in a fourteen-year period.

From 1872 through 1890, the highly efficient British firm, Sierra Buttes Mining Company worked Eureka Peak and extracted many more millions of dollars worth of gold from the mountain. Seventy shafts were sunk into the peak, and more than seventy miles of tunnels were constructed in the area.

Hard-rock mining was hard work, but the miners knew how to have fun as well. Winter fun for the miners centered on sport skiing, with Eureka Peak serving as a popular downhill run. Hitting the slopes in 1870, the well-equipped skier strapped on twelve-foot long, four-inch wide wooden skis. All skiers carried their favorite "dope"—various concoctions of tallow, turpentine, pine pitch and castor oil—that they applied to their skis.

Eureka Peak has another claim to fame: it may have been the site of the first-ever ski lift. One of the mines had a series of gravity-powered trams which carried ore down in buckets. The miners hopped aboard, caught a lift up the slope, then skied down.

Today Plumas-Eureka (the name comes from an early mine) State Park emphasizes hard-rock mining history with a museum and several historic structures. You can visit a blacksmith shop, a stable, a stamp mill, the Moriarity House (a typical residence of a miner's family, circa 1890), and miners' bunkhouse, now the park museum/visitor center.

The trail to Eureka Peak begins at the park's ski area, which features a ski lift operated on winter weekends. Cross-country skiing is particularly popular on the state park's trails. For the hiker, the route to Eureka Lake and Eureka Peak offers grand High Sierra views. The peak's reflection in the deep blue waters of the lake is a majestic sight.

Directions to trailhead: From the visitor center, follow the park road (County Road A-14) a mile through the historic hamlet of Johnsville to road's end at the Ski Area. From the parking lot, a dirt fire road ascends to Eureka Lake where Eureka Peak Loop Trail begins. Monday through Thursday, vehicles are permitted to travel the road between the ski area and the lake; beginning your hike at the lake effectively halves the six-mile distance. Friday through Sunday, only foot-traffic is permitted on the dirt road.

The walk: You'll get an up-close look a the ski lift and ski bowl as you ascend the fire road. The mostly westward-traveling road bends briefly east just before it reaches Eureka Lake.

The road ends at the lake and you join the trail, which crosses over Eureka Lake's earth fill dam, dips in and out of a ravine, then begins a steep ascent of a white pine- and red fir-forested Eureka Peak.

A long half-mile ascent brings you to a junction, where you veer left, ascending to False Peak (sometimes called North Peak, 7,286 feet). Truly the best views are from Eureka's "False" Peak. Look for Beckwourth Peak to the east, the pointed Sierra Buttes to the southeast and snow-topped Mt. Lassen (10,457 feet) to the northwest.

Continue past wind-bowed pine and hemlock, circling around the south side of the actual Eureka Peak, and following the trail as it abruptly drops off the peak and descends steeply back to the loop trail junction. Retrace your steps back to Eureka Lake and the trailhead.

Washoe Meadows State Park
Washoe Meadows Trail

> **Terrain:** Broad meadowland
> **Highlights:** Small part of Washoe native lands
> **Distance:** 2 to 4 miles round trip
> **Degree of difficulty:** Easy

Washoe Meadows State Park, located on the outskirts of South Lake Tahoe, is a completely undeveloped park. Like Burton Creek State Park on the other end of the lake, its use—even its whereabouts—is virtually unknown except by locals.

Lake Tahoe has long been the center of Washoe territory. The lake and environs are the geographical, indeed, spiritual focus of the tribe. As tribal elders put it: "We did not travel here from another place. We have been on this land since the beginning and have always lived here." In fact, anthropological evidence suggests at least ten thousand years of Washoe occupation.

During an 1844 expedition, Captain John C. Frémont reported meeting a peaceful people, who used snow shoes and caught rabbits with nets. A flood of miners and settlers (ironically, often arriving via Washoe hunting trails) displaced and devastated the Washoe people.

Washoe ancestral land centered around *Da ow a ga* (Lake Tahoe), sacred giver of life; the land included fertile valleys, the desert, and snow-covered mountains. And, it included meadows as well—so it's altogether fitting that a park be named after this long-neglected group of Native Americans.

The meadow's trail system is not waymarked, so try to stay oriented. Fortunately because it's a meadow, you can see where you're going, where you've come from.

Directions to trailhead: Best place to start your walk is at the trailhead off Lake Tahoe Boulevard. Follow Lake Tahoe Boulevard 0.4 mile past its intersection with Sawmill Road. You'll see a gated dirt road on your left. Park nearby and walk down this dirt road.

The park also extends 1½ miles along Sawmill Road, which leads to Highway 50; entering the park from this direction, however, can be confusing for first-time visitors.

D.L. Bliss and Emerald Bay State Parks
Rubicon Trail

Terrain: Pine- and fir-cloaked slopes above Lake Tahoe
Highlights: Grand views of the "Lake in the Sky," including Emerald Bay and Fannette Island. Cold-water swimming for the hardy. Tour the Norse castle, Vikingsholm
Distance: To Old Lighthouse is ¾ mile round trip; to Emerald Point is 6 miles round trip; to Vikingsholm is 9 miles round trip
Degree of difficulty: Moderate
Precautions: Winter snows close the state parks

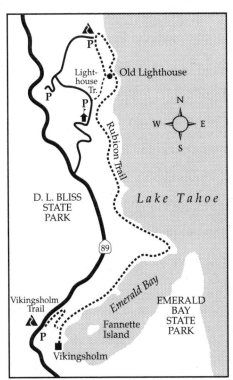

Adjoining state parks D.L. Bliss and Emerald Bay protect six miles of Lake Tahoe's shore. Rubicon Trail, a superb shoreline pathway, contours over shady slopes, linking the two parks and offering grand views of what Native Americans called the "Lake in the Sky."

Even if the parks themselves weren't so splendidly scenic, they would still attract lots of visitors because they offer something in short supply around Lake Tahoe: public access to the lake.

For the tree-loving hiker, Rubicon Trail offers plenty of arboreal companionship. You get the

Christmas spirit when you wander through stands of red and white fir. Joining the stately firs are ponderosa pine, Jeffrey pine and incense cedar. "Leaf peekers" or homesick New Englanders will enjoy how autumn colors Tahoe's aspen and maple trees.

Not all park flora is a hundred feet high. Monkeyflower, columbine, lupine and leopard lily are among the wildflowers splashing spring and summer color on park slopes.

Most park visitors come not to see flora's handiwork, but Lora's handiwork—Lora Knight, that is. In 1928, Knight commissioned the Swede Lennart Palme to build her a ninth-century Norse castle. A year later, Vikingsholm—turrets, towers and 38 rooms—was completed. Knight, a Santa Barbaran, spent summers in her authentically furnished fortress until her death in 1945.

During the summer months, guides give tours of Vikingsholm. (Tours are conducted 10 a.m. to 4 p.m., daily, every half-hour, through Labor Day, then only on the weekends for a few more weeks.

Even if you can't schedule a tour, the two-mile round trip hike on Vikingsholm Trail (a road closed to vehicle traffic) to view the curious structure is well worth the effort. Just looking at the exterior of the castle (not a single tree was disturbed when it was constructed) in its lakeside setting is impressive.

Another reward at trail's end is Emerald Bay itself, one of Tahoe's best beaches. Swimmers can brave the bay's chilly waters, which warm only to the low 60s F. even in midsummer.

Directions to trailhead: From South Lake Tahoe, drive 11 miles north on Highway 89 to the D.L. Bliss State Park entrance. If you're coming from Tahoe City, you'll drive sixteen miles south on 89 to the park entrance. Follow the park road 2½ miles to its end at the parking area for Calawee Cove Beach.

To reach the trailhead for Vikingsholm from South Lake Tahoe, drive north nine miles on Highway 89 to the Vikingsholm Overlook, a large parking area on your right. If you're coming from Tahoe City, drive 18 miles south on 89.

Emerald Bay/Vikingsholm is also the terminus for the Rubicon Trail, described below.

The walk: Sunbathers hit the beach while hikers choose between two paths—an upper and lower trail—looping south. Take either; they rejoin in a bit more than a quarter-mile at the Old Lighthouse.

The short spur trail leading to the lighthouse is hardly worth the effort; the lighthouse looks more like an outhouse. Surely at one time

the lighthouse must have offered quite a view of the lake, but these days conifers screen out the scene.

Rubicon Trail climbs gently south, soon offering much better views of Lake Tahoe, then ascending into a white fir forest. Emerging from the trees, the path begins a one-mile descent to the lakeshore, then meanders lakeside to Emerald Point. Here the trail splits: one branch visits Emerald Point, the other bypasses the point. The trails soon rejoin, you cross the boundary from D.L. Bliss State Park into Emerald Bay State Park, and you hike another half-mile among pine, fir and incense cedar to the park's Boat Camp. This camp is an ideal lakeside picnic spot.

For its last mile, Rubicon Trail sticks close to shore with only a single foray inland to climb around Parson Rock. Vikingsholm is your turnaround point, unless you've arranged to have transportation waiting for you at Vikingsholm parking lot, a one-mile ascent up Vikingsholm Trail.

Sugar Pine Point State Park

General Creek Trail

> **Terrain:** Lush mountain meadows ringed by aspen and
>   lodgepole pine
> **Highlights:** Creekside picnicking, escape from Tahoe crowds,
>   jump-off place for longer treks into Desolation Wilderness
> **Distance:** 4½ mile loop with 300-foot elevation gain; to Lily
>   Pond is 6½ miles round trip with 500-foot gain; to Duck Lake
>   is 14 miles round trip and to Lost Lake is 14½ miles with
>   1,300-foot gain
> **Degree of difficulty:** Moderate to strenuous

Sugar Pine Point names a forested promontory above the western
shore of Lake Tahoe, and a park that offers ten terrific miles of trail.

While the state park has about two miles of lakefront, most of the
park—and the best hiking—is inland along General Creek. Trails lead
along the creek through a forested valley to the state park boundary,

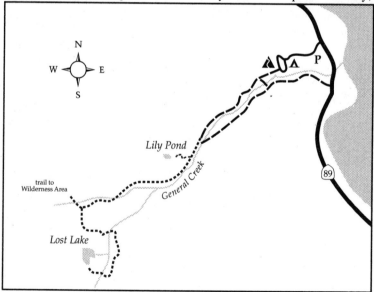

then into El Dorado National Forest. The park is often used by long-distance hikers to gain access to the northerly part of the Desolation Wilderness, as well as to intersect the Pacific Crest Trail and other paths leading into the High Sierra backcountry west of Lake Tahoe.

Trees are one attraction of a hike through the state park. Besides the sugar pine, look for Jeffrey pine and stately white fir. In autumn, the black cottonwood and quaking aspen are something to behold.

Directions to trailhead: From Tahoe City, drive nine miles south on Highway 89 to Sugar Pine Point State Park. The state park is located some eighteen miles north of the community of South Lake Tahoe. Once inside the park, rangers recommend that hikers park in the campground overflow lot near the entrance to General Creek Campground. The trail, a dirt road closed to vehicles, begins at Camp-site 150.

The walk: The wide path leads west along the north bank of General Creek. At a signed junction you'll spot a trail leading down to a bridge crossing the creek. This bridge and another two miles farther along General Creek Trail, allow a pleasant loop trip.

The trail meanders through well-spaced stands of Jeffrey and lodge-pole pine and across meadowland seasonally sprinkled with lupine and aster. Those granite boulders you see looking so out of place in the sylvan scene were left behind ages ago by a retreating glacier. Hikers with an interest in geology will enjoy glimpses of the two large lateral moraines that border the valley of General Creek.

A bit more than two miles along, when you reach a second foot-bridge, you can loop back to the trailhead via a path on the opposite side of General Creek.

Soon after passing this bridge, General Creek Trail dwindles to a footpath and another half-mile's travel brings you to a signed junction with a side trail leading to Lily Pond; it's a ¾-mile, heart-pounding ascent to the little pond.

General Creek Trail continues meandering above the creek. About 3½ miles from the trailhead, you'll exit the state park and enter El Dorado National Forest. After more meandering, the trail crosses General Creek (no bridge this time), turns south, then east, and after a mile crosses the creek fed by Lost Lake and Duck Lake.

Now the trail turns south again and climbs to shallow Duck Lake, ringed by lodgepole pine. Lost Lake, another quarter-mile along the trail, is a bit more dramatic than neighboring Duck.

Burton Creek State Park
Burton Creek Trail

> **Terrain:** Forest and meadows
> **Highlights:** Two natural preserves, virtually unknown and undeveloped park
> **Distance:** 2 to 8 miles round trip
> **Degree of difficulty:** Moderate

Lake Tahoe's secret state park is Burton Creek, more than 2,000 acres of forest and meadowland, located just across the highway from the tiny, but well-known lakeshore campground at Tahoe State Recreation Area. (The Tahoe SRA entry kiosk is a good place to ask question about Burton Creek.)

The park has a lot of potential to be a favorite of trail users—cross-country skiers, mountain bicyclists, hikers—as soon as access problems are resolved and some signs are erected.

Bisecting the park, from its northwest to its southwest corners, is Burton Creek. The creek has been dammed, but two natural preserves have been established in the creek corridor. Above the dam is Antone Meadows Natural Preserve; from the dam to the highway is Burton Creek Natural Preserve.

The park is completely undeveloped except for some six miles of dirt roads. Chief users of the trail system are cross-country skiers. During the winter, Tahoe Nordic Center grooms the park trails. (To reach the center, take Village Road off Highway 28.)

The hiking is strictly improvisational; wander the dirt roads for as long or short a hike as you please. Aiding your navigation of the tangle of roads somewhat are the numbers posted at road junctions. Keep track of those numbers!

A section of the new Tahoe Rim Trail leads through the western part of the park. Best walking is along Burton Creek and through the surrounding meadows.

The park has two entrances from Tahoe City. The Bunker Drive entrance has parking; the Tamarack Lodge entrance has both access and parking problems.

Donner Memorial State Park
Lakeshore Interpretive Trail

> **Distance:** 2½ miles round trip
> **Terrain:** Wooded High Sierra basin
> **Highlights:** Donner Lake, bizarre chapter in California history
> **Degree of difficulty:** Easy
> **Precautions:** As the Donner Party discovered, heavy snowfall
> sometimes occurs December through April

It's the dark side of the California dream, one of the most gruesome stories of the Old West: The Donner Party.

In April, 1846, a group of Midwestern families left Independence, Missouri, bound for California. Their wagon train rolled over the Great Plains and through the Rockies, but was seriously delayed when a "shortcut" leading southwest was anything but. A breakdown in civilized behavior followed: the emigrants quarreled constantly; one man killed another; an old man was left on the trail to die.

An early and severe snowstorm that prevented passage over the

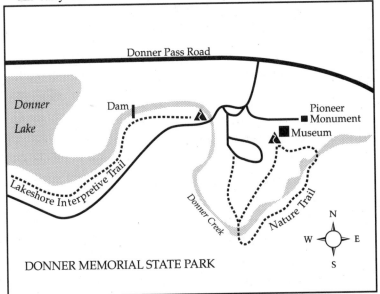

DONNER MEMORIAL STATE PARK

211

High Sierra forced the ill-fated party to spend the winter near present-day Truckee. Forty-one of the 89 would-be settlers perished. When their provisions and oxen were consumed, the emigrants finally cannibalized their dead friends and relatives.

Today, Donner Memorial State Park is located where many members of the Donner Party spent their final days. Rangers report that about two hundred thousand visitors, most very curious about the cannibalism aspect of the Donner story, stop at the state park each year.

The state park's surprise is that it displays not only the dark side of human nature, but the beautiful side of Mother Nature. Anything but gruesome, the state park and surrounding Sierra Nevada is a major recreation center, featuring camping, hiking, fishing and boating. In winter, the Truckee-Donner area is a favorite for downhill and cross-country skiing.

Experienced High Sierra hikers and backpackers who have visited the range's spectacular alpine lakes will probably disagree with local Truckee boosters that 3-mile long, ¾-mile wide Donner Lake is the "Gem of the Sierra;" still, it's a mellow place for a hike, a picnic or a little trout fishing. The state park, located on the east side of the lake, has 2½ miles of lake frontage.

Outside the park visitor center is the tall Pioneer Monument; its base measures 22 feet high, the height of the snow during that terrible winter of 1846-47.

Inside the park visitor center is the Emigrant Trail Museum, which depicts the demise of the Donner Party, plus some of the more positive aspects of the region's history. The museum also offers a nice introduction to the natural history of the Sierra Nevada.

To see some of this natural history for yourself, take a hike. One of the most dramatic (and obvious) workings of nature is the evidence left behind of recent glaciation. The great sheet of ice that slid through the region thousands of years ago left behind huge boulders and other rock debris.

Jeffrey pine and white fir cloak park slopes; the woods are home to deer, squirrels, chipmunks and raccoons.

The state park doesn't have an extensive trail system, but does offer two enjoyable family hikes. When snow covers the park, rangers link park roads and trails into a good beginners' cross-country ski route.

Serious hikers will want to tackle more difficult trails in the surrounding Tahoe National Forest. A nearby section of the Pacific Crest Trail passes by Donner Peak and Donner Pass, and offers grand views of Donner Lake.

The park's Nature Trail (½-mile round trip) begins just south of the museum. It meanders by a pine and fir forest to Donner Creek. An interpretive booklet, explaining flora and fauna, is available at the museum.

Lakeshore Interpretive Trail (2½ miles round trip) is even more educational. Eighteen trailside exhibits illustrate the history of the Emigrant Trail and tell of the area's geology and ecology, Washoe culture, and the local recreational possibilities. The path leads to, and along, Donner Lake. At trail's end at the lake is some fine picnicking.

Directions to trailhead: Donner Memorial State Park is located south of Interstate 80, and west of Truckee. From downtown Truckee, follow Donner Pass Road two miles to a stop sign. Turn left and follow the signs into the park. Truckee itself is located 33 miles west of Reno, thirteen miles from Lake Tahoe.

McArthur Burney Falls Memorial State Park

Falls, Burney Creek, Rim Trails

> **Terrain:** Pit River country of evergreen forest, volcanic peaks
> **Highlights:** Spectacular Burney Falls, lava geology; Lake Britton
> **Distance:** 3½ miles round trip
> **Degree of difficulty:** Easy to moderate

President Theodore Roosevelt proclaimed Burney Falls "the eighth wonder of the world." High praise indeed, for the twin, thundering 129-foot falls, accompanied by numerous plumes of water, is a spectacular sight.

Burney Falls is protected by McArthur Burney Falls Memorial State Park, one of the more off-the-beaten track units of the California state park system. The park is sometimes described as being located in "Pit River Country," "the Shasta-Cascade Wonderland," or "halfway between Mt. Shasta and Lassen Peak." Geologists describe the park's location as on the edge of the Modoc Plateau or on the far south end of the Cascade Range.

Volcanic action was the dominant force shaping the landscape in this part of California. This vulcanism is evident not only around nearby Shasta and Lassen Peaks, but in more subtle ways in the state park itself.

Sometimes water percolates through the porous surface of the lava rock and is trapped in huge subterranean rivers and reservoirs. One of these underground aquifers feeds Burney Creek—and in turn, Burney Falls. The falls flows all year even though a half-mile above the falls, Burney Creek is often absolutely dry.

· Present-day park flora illustrates the aftereffects of vulcanism, too. Notice the scarcity of bushes—what botanists call "understory"— beneath the trees. This lack of ground cover is due to the composition of the ground itself; what moisture falls onto the porous basalt rock percolates deep into the ground and is thus unavailable to many shallow-rooted plants that would normally grow in this type of climate and ecosystem.

Several Native American groups, particularly the Ilmawi, had villages near the present-day park. They dug deep pits nearby in order to trap big game. Nineteenth-century explorers and settlers referred to these people as Pit River Indians. The falls was considered a "power spot" by the native people.

To some turn-of-the-century Californians, the falls was a power spot too—for hydroelectric power that is. One dam, Pit River Number Three, resulted in the formation of Lake Britton, located a mile down-canyon from Burney Falls. For a time, the falls was threatened by dam builders but their preservation was assured in 1922 when Frank McArthur donated the falls, along with some surrounding land, to the state park system. The park honors McArthur's pioneer parents, John and Catherine McArthur.

Park trails serve up several different views of the falls and the 200 million gallons of water that tumble into Burney Creek Gorge. A one-mile nature trail with 24 stops introduces visitors to geological and

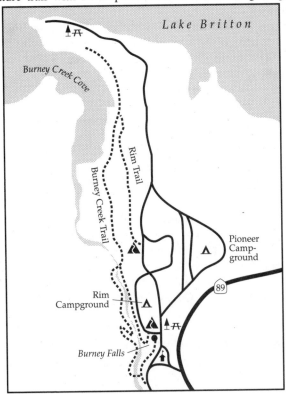

botanical features. Pick up an interpretive pamphlet at the park visitor center or at the camp store.

Directions to trailhead: The state park is located off Highway 89, eleven miles north of the town of Burney. Falls Trail begins at a viewpoint on the west side of the park entrance, opposite a little camp store.

The walk: Follow Falls Trail, paved for a couple hundred yards, switchbacks down toward the falls. Falls Trail is also the park's nature trail, with a number of interpreted stops en route.

Most park visitors aren't hikers, so most venture only as far as the base of the falls. The spray from the falls is terrific natural air-conditioning; it's always quite cool in the canyon, even on a summer's day.

I recommend following Falls Trail along the east side of Burney Creek to the first footbridge over Burney Creek, then heading up-creek along the west side of Falls Trail. After you ascend the gorge wall and get an eye-level-view of the falls, retrace your steps.

Burney Creek elbows west then north, while you continue due north on Burney Creek Trail into a mixed forest of ponderosa pine, incense cedar and Douglas fir. A mile's walk brings you to a signed junction: Burney Creek Trail continues north to its end at a peninsula separating Burney Creek Cove from the main body of Lake Britton. You'll find a boat launch facility at the cove, a sandy beach and swimming area on the lake.

From the junction, Rim Trail ascends moderately up the rim of Burney Creek Canyon, then skirts the park's campground before petering out just short of the viewpoint where you began this walk.

Castle Crags State Park

Crags Trail

Terrain: Pine- and fir-forested slopes, granite peaks
Highlights: Inspiring spires of the crags; vistas of Mt. Shasta
Distance: 5½ miles round trip with 2,200-foot elevation gain
Degree of difficulty: Not that long a hike, but strenuous
   because of elevation gain

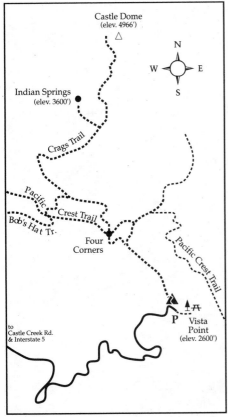

Soaring above the upper Sacramento River Valley are the sky-scraping spires of granite called the Castle Crags. From the lofty ramparts, the hiker can look down on a forested slopes and up at magnificent snow-covered Mt. Shasta.

The Castle Crags were formed in much the same manner as nearby Mt. Shasta and the other peaks of the Cascade Range— by volcanic activity some 200 million years ago. For the last million years, the Crags have been subjected to the forces of wind, rain, ice and even some small glaciers, which have shaped the granite into its distinctive shapes. Rising beside the spikey peaks is a round one, Castle Dome, which many mountaineers liken to Yosemite's Half Dome.

In 1855, the territory below the Crags was the site of a struggle between local native people and settlers. The locals, armed only with bows and arrows, were driven from their land in a one-sided battle that was chronicled by Joaquin Miller, "poet of the High Sierra."

Mining—first gold, later mercury and chromite—and logging, were the chief industries around the Crags for a hundred years. During the 1920s and 1930s, conservationists worked to protect the Castle Crags; they circulated photographs of the scenic spot and promoted the idea of a comprehensive California state park system.

Crags Trail, with its steep elevation gain, is a real workout. Rewarding your effort are postcard-views of the Crags and of Mt. Shasta. The trail crosses Kettlebelly Ridge, part of the old California-Oregon Toll Road used by settlers on their way west.

Directions to trailhead: Castle Crags State Park is located some 25 miles north of Lake Shasta (6 miles south of Dunsmuir) off Interstate 5. Take the Castella exit and follow signs to the park. Follow the entrance road to the Vista Point parking area. The signed trail begins just down the road from the Point.

The walk: From the signed trailhead, the trail climbs west through a mixed forest of pine, fir and cedar. After a short time, you'll pass a junction with Root Creek Trail, a mile-long path leading through the forest to its namesake creek. A little more climbing brings you to a four-way intersection. Here you meet the famous Pacific Crest Trail, seven miles of which leads through the state park. Your quiet contemplation of the notion of walking 2,000 miles from Mexico to Washington will undoubtedly be interrupted by the sizzle of electricity passing through the high-voltage lines above the trail junction.

You continue on Crags Trail on an ever-more-earnest ascent for another half-mile to a short connector trail known as Bob's Hat Trail which drops a quarter-mile back to PCT. (Keep this trail in mind as a return trip option.)

Crags Trail turns north, and in another half-mile splits again. The left fork goes to Indian Springs, where cold water bubbles from the depths of the Crags. Your path climbs even more steeply, winding among boulders and over flat rocks. Trees become more sparse with the gain in elevation, opening up ever-grander views. Trail's end is at the base of roundish Castle Dome.

You can climb rocks to your heart's content around here, but use caution and don't exceed your abilities.

Northern California Redwoods

Long considered the "gems" of the state park system, the redwood parks preserve both small and large groves of California's official state tree. The coastal redwoods were a rallying point during the 1920s, and in earlier decades, for such conservation groups as the Save-the-Redwoods League; concern over the fate of the redwoods helped launch the state park movement.

The famed *Sequoia sempervirens* grow in a long belt on the western side of the Coast Range from Big Sur to the Oregon border. The characteristic long, lingering fogs and heavy winter rains found in this belt provide the ideal climatic conditions for the coastal redwoods.

The best old-growth redwoods remain in Del Norte, Humboldt and Mendocino counties. Along Highway 101, Prairie Creek, Jedediah Smith and Del Norte state parks lie between the Pacific and the Klamath Range; these parks are included, in loose confederation with Redwood National Park.

Jedediah Smith features the 5,000-acre National Tribute Grove. At Prairie Creek, the redwoods are sprinkled with open meadows, roamed by the unusual Roosevelt elk.

A hundred miles south of these far-north redwoods is another string of state parks along the South Fork of the Eel River. Largest is Humboldt Redwoods State Park, bisected by the Avenue of the Giants, the famed 33-mile long scenic highway. Heart of the park is the Rockefeller Forest, the most impressive ancient redwoods left on earth.

Armstrong Redwoods State Reserve/
Austin Creek State Recreation Area

Gilliam Creek, Austin Creek Trails

Terrain: Maple-shaded creeks, oak- and fir-forested slopes
Highlights: Contrasting environments of cool redwood groves
  and open slopes seasonally sprinkled with wildflowers
Distance: 4-mile loop with 800-foot elevation gain or 8-mile
  loop with 1,000-foot elevation gain. Longer options possible
Degree of difficulty: Moderate to strenuous
Precautions: Note you lose elevation first; very steep return to
  trailhead

Armstrong Redwoods State Reserve/Austin Creek State Recreation
Area is one place on the map, but two distinct environments on the
ground.

Armstrong Redwoods is a 700-acre tall tree preserve, a cool and
dark forest. Austin Creek, in contrast, offers open sun-drenched,
grassy hillsides dotted with oaks.

Both parks are a welcome respite from the Russian River resort
traffic and all those wine country tourists in the flatlands below.

Both parks offer good hiking: a gentle saunter through Armstrong
Redwoods, moderate to vigorous hike through the Austin Creek
foothills.Armstrong Redwoods is a place to cool off in the summer;
it's so shady and shadowy that Native Americas considered it a "dark
hole" and avoided it. Austin Creek's exposed slopes are a bit too hot
in summer; hiking here is far more pleasant in spring and fall.

Armstrong Redwoods was set aside as a preserve by mega-logger
Colonel James Armstrong, surely one of the few nineteenth-century
timber barons who recognized both the beauty, and the board feet in
California's redwood groves. The park has some excellent picnic
grounds and features the Redwood Forest Theater, a 1,200-seat outdoor amphitheater, a popular site for concerts and plays.

Best hike through the redwoods is the self-guided nature trail. As
you wander among the virgin trees past interpretive displays, you'll
visit the 310-foot Parson Jones tree and the old (1,400-plus years)
Colonel Armstrong tree. After you walk the short mile along Fife

Creek to the picnic area, you can loop back to the trailhead via East Ridge Trail.

Austin Creek's twenty miles of trail for the most part follow creeks—East Austin, as well as Gilliam, Schoolhouse and Fife—through an environment of alder, big leaf maple and Oregon ash. Paths also traverse slopes forested with Douglas fir, oak and madrone.

Three backcountry camps—Tom King, Manning Flat and Gilliam Creek—suggest Austin Creek State Recreation would be an ideal location for a weekend getaway or a family backpacking trip.

This walk offers short (four-mile) and longer (nine-mile) loops that head down Gilliam Creek and ascend back to the trailhead along Austin Creek.

Whichever loop you choose, it's downhill first, uphill last; save some energy for the return trip.

Directions to trailhead: From Highway 101, four miles north of Santa Rosa, exit on River Road and drive west some 16 miles to Guerneville. Turn north on Armstrong Woods Road and drive two miles to Armstrong Redwoods State Reserve. Continue up the steep park road to a fork; the main park road continues to Bullfrog Pond, but you veer left to parking for the signed Gilliam Creek Trail.

The walk: Descend north into mixed forest of oak, Douglas fir and

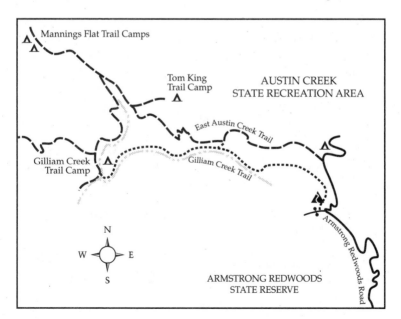

redwood. A half-mile out, you'll climb a bit and see some coastward views of the multiple ridges rolling to the west.

The trails turns west and descends through woods, then grassland, to Schoolhouse Creek, about a mile from the trailhead. You'll cross a fork of the creek as well as Schoolhouse Creek itself as you descend another mile to a trail junction located near the meeting of waters of Gilliam and Schoolhouse creeks.

Those opting for the four-mile hike will go right at this trail junction, cross Schoolhouse Creek, then follow the banks of Gilliam upcreek a short distance to meet Austin Creek Trail (a fire road). You'll hike the fire road back toward the trailhead.

Those in the mood for a longer hike will continue following Gilliam Creek, crossing and recrossing the creek a couple of times as the path leads past ferns, flowers (in spring), cascading water and quiet pools.

Three miles out you cross Gilliam Creek for the last time, then climb gently above the north bank of the creek, and descend again. A short side trail leads to Gilliam Creek Camp.

Near the confluence of Gilliam and East Austin creeks, you'll ford the latter and climb briefly, but steeply, to meet a fire road. Turn right on the fire road, which climbs gradually north through a forest of oak, madrone and fir.

Five miles out, you descend to cross East Austin Creek and meet East Austin Creek Trail. To visit Manning Flat Trail Camp, head left to the shady camp perched on the west bank of the creek.)

Turn right on the road, which follows its namesake East Austin Creek and soon passes a great swimming hole. All too soon, you think (especially on a hot day), your path begins and earnest half-mile ascent, passes the side trail leading to Tom King Trail Camp, and leaves Austin Creek behind.

Next comes a half-mile descent and meeting with the short spur connecting to Gilliam Creek Trail. One way back to the trailhead is to take the spur, then retrace your steps on the Gilliam Creek Trail. It's a stiff climb back.

An equally stiff climb (some choice, huh?) is to continue on East Austin Creek Trail. The killer climb toward Bullfrog Pond Campground is a long mile, with a thousand foot elevation gain.

When you reach the paved park road (carefully, walk on the shoulder) a half-mile, then pick up a short footpath on your right that leads back to the trailhead.

Hendy Woods State Park
Gentle Giants, Discovery, Navarro River Trails

> **Terrain:** Virgin redwoods forest, wooded banks of Navarro River
> **Highlights:** Interpretive trails, kayaking, swimming, steelhead fishing
> **Distance:** 3 miles round trip
> **Degree of difficulty:** Easy
> **Precautions:** Plentiful poison oak

Drive inland a bit from the forever-foggy Mendocino County Coast and you'll find sunny meadows, a pastoral valley of apple orchards, vineyards and farm houses, plus tall redwoods that escaped the logger's ax.

Hendy Woods, a twenty-mile drive from the coast, is warmer, and has an altogether different vibe than the other coastal redwood parks.

The land now comprising the state park was purchased a century ago by Joseph Hendy, who later sold his land to the Masonite Corporation; the corporation, in cooperation with the Save-the-Redwoods League, donated 405 acres to the state park system in 1958.

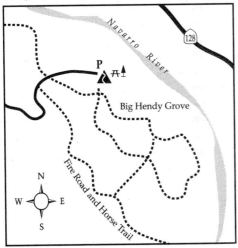

While Hendy Woods, with two old-growth redwood groves, is rightly categorized as a "redwood park," some locals are quick to point out that it could also be considered a "wine country park." Anderson Valley, where the park is situated, is an emerging wine-making center.

Getting to the park is part of the fun: Highway 128, winds from Cloverdale on Highway 101 to the Mendocino Coast, following the Navarro River. Along the way are farmhouses, apple orchards, sheep, cows, vineyards, and the drowsy hamlets of Yorkville, Boonville, and Philo.

The Navarro River which runs the length of the park, offers swimming (wading, really) in summer, canoeing and kayaking during late winter and early spring. Redwoods grow tall along the banks of the Navarro.

Hikers will enjoy the half-mile Discovery Trail, plus another nature trail, wheelchair accessible, that explores the redwoods.

This walk begins with a loop or two through the redwoods, then continues along the Navarro River.

Directions to trailhead: From Highway 1, about ten miles south of Mendocino, turn inland on Highway 128 and travel twenty miles to Philo Greenwood Road. Turn right and drive a half-mile to the entrance of Hendy Woods State Park. Follow the park road 1¾-miles to its end at the picnic area.

(If you're traveling Highway 128 northwest from Cloverdale-Highway 101, you'll proceed some eight miles past Boonville to the state park turnoff.)

Those New Age hikers staying at Shenoa Retreat or those folks staying at one of the other private resorts might want to begin this walk from the vicinity of Shenoa Retreat, located off Ray's Road, 2½ miles from Highway 128. However, this area is private property; unless you're a guest at one of these facilities, you should start your walk at the state park.

The walk: From the picnic area, follow the path into the redwoods. You'll wind through the old growth redwoods and their neighboring trees—madrone, Douglas fir, bay laurel and more. Join the two-looped Discovery Trail, then take a right-forking trail that ascends to a gravel fire road.

After crossing a creek, travel through an area filled with impressive redwoods. You'll pass two signed "Horse Trails" that lead down to some inviting swimming holes on the Navarro River.

Your turnaround point, about 1½ miles from the trailhead, could be at the state park boundary or a mile farther near Shenoa Retreat on the far outskirts of Philo.

Standish-Hickey State Recreation Area
Big Tree, Mill Creek Trails

Terrain: Redwood-Douglas fir forest, towering bluffs of Eel River
Highlights: Miles Standish Tree, grand river views
Distance: 2-mile loop via Big Tree Trail; 6-mile loop via Mill Creek Trail
Precautions: Main park trails accessible only during summer

The redwood groves (mostly second-growth) are pleasant enough, but it's not the trees that attract visitors year after year, it's the river.

The Eel River, that is. Occupying both banks of the Eel's South Fork, the recreation area offers a swimming hole, a three campgrounds, steelhead and salmon fishing in winter, and some good hiking.

The park's premier arboreal attraction is the Captain Miles Standish Tree, a scarred 225-foot tall, 13-feet-in-diameter giant, estimated to be 1,200 years old. The tree honors one of the early Pilgrims; his descen-

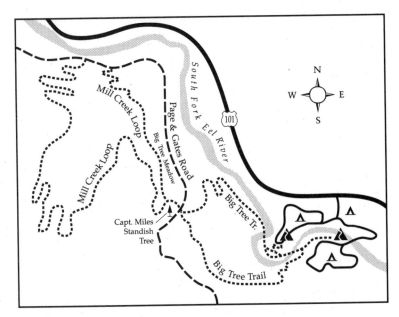

dants, the Standish family, along with the Hickey family, donated much of the acreage to form the park.

Because the rain-swollen Eel River floods so often, its banks, bottom and swimming holes change each year. All the park's Eel-spanning footbridges are removed during the winter, effectively making most of the trail system inaccessible. In fact, sometimes high water knocks out the bridge in late spring and early summer as well.

Standish-Hickey's three-mile round trip Lookout Trail offers a pretty good look down at the Eel, but I prefer the more intimate view of the park offered by two loop trails—Big Tree and Mill Creek.

Directions to the trailhead: From Highway 101, a mile north of Leggett, take the Standish-Hickey State Recreation Area exit. Once inside the park, continue straight past the entrance station, taking the very steep road down to the seasonal bridge across the Eel River and over to Redwood Campground. Bear right after campsite #108 to the day use parking lot.

The walk: Join signed Big Tree Trail for a short distance to a fork and bear left. The path soon leaves the banks of the Eel and begins a mellow ascent through the redwoods.

A mile out, the trail passes a junction with the other leg of Big Tree Trail, crosses Page & Gates Logging Road, and arrives at the impressive Captain Miles Standish Tree. While admiring the redwood, you can choose whether to return via the other branch of Big Tree Trail and complete your hike, or join Mill Creek Loop Trail.

The latter path crosses meadowland and ascends through the woods to a slightly scary-looking landslide area above Mill Creek. The trail descends to cross the creek, then climbs again, traveling along a ridge, then descending again toward the Eel River.

The path meets Page & Gates Road, very close to the mouth of Mill Creek where it flows into the Eel River. Go right on the road for a short distance. Follow the trail signs which take you back into the creekbed for a short detour around the now-unsafe bridge over Mill Creek, then resume walking on Mill Creek Loop Trail, which ascends a bit at first before leveling out through lovely Big Tree Meadow.

Back at Miles Standish Tree, you'll join Big Tree Trail's left fork on the other side of Page & Gates Road, descending to the river and crossing Cabin Meadow. When you reach the banks of the Eel, near the park's swimming area, you'll cross a little log bridge, follow the trail over the opposite gravel bar to a second wooden bridge to Redwood Campground and the trailhead.

Richardson Grove State Park

Lookout Point, Tan Oak Springs,
Durphy Creek Trails

> **Terrain:** Cool, shady redwood groves
> **Highlights:** Redwoods, tranquil Durphy Creek
> **Distance:** 4 miles round trip
> **Degree of difficulty:** Moderate

You can't miss viewing the redwoods in Richardson Grove State Park; the highway lobby had Highway 101 built right through the heart of the park.

But if you really want to experience the magic and majesty of "The Grove," as it's affectionately known, you must get off the highway and hit the trail. Fortunately, Richardson Grove has some fine footpaths that visit quiet redwood groves and Eel River beaches.

The park, acquired in the 1920s, is named for California's twenty-fifth governor, William Friend Richardson, though it's any park lover's guess why; the ultra-conservative Richardson was completely unsympathetic to the state park system, then in its infancy, and vetoed all expenditure bills.

Start your visit to Richardson Grove with a look at the natural history exhibits and history displays at the visitor center. Check out the arboreal curiosities: a walk-through tree, and a dawn redwood, the

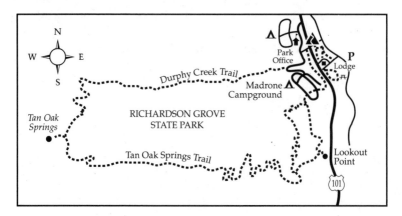

coastal redwood's Chinese cousin, located in the group camp. The park features a full schedule of interpretive programs during the summer months.

This loop trip offers a enjoyable jaunt through the redwoods growing above the South Fork of the Eel River. The Eel's frequent floods in years past have deposited thick layers of rich soil—ideal for growing especially tall redwoods.

Directions to trailhead: From Highway 101, eight miles south of Garberville, take the Richardson Grove State Park exit.

Once inside the park, getting to either of the trailheads is a bit tricky, unless you happened to have reserved a site in Madrone Campground. If you're not camping, best bet is to park at the picnic ground near the visitor center, follow the short path to the Highway 101 underpass, emerging on the other side and picking up the path leading to and through Madrone Campground.

The walk: From the signed trailhead in Madrone Campground, begin your climb to Lookout Point Trail, which almost immediately forks. Stay left and begin ascending thorough redwoods and Douglas fir to Lookout Point. The so-so vista is of the Eel River Canyon and Highway 101.

From the lookout, the path steepens. You briefly join the trail to Hartsook Inn before meeting up with Tan Oak Springs Trail and switchbacking up a forested ridge.

After cresting the ridge, about 1½ miles from the trailhead, the path descends a short distance to Tan Oak Springs. The cattail- and tule-surrounded spring isn't much to behold, but it's a nice place to take a breather.

Past the spring, the trail continues descending to the south bank of Durphy Creek, then levels off to follow the creek eastward on a more level course through the redwoods.

The trail ends at the park road, where you'll turn left to return to the trailhead.

Benbow Lake State Recreation Area
Pioneer Meadow, Pratt Mill Trails

> **Terrain:** Wooded and grass banks of Eel River
> **Highlights:** Canoeing, swimming in Benbow Lake
> **Distance:** 2½ mile loop with 400-foot elevation gain
> **Degree of difficulty:** Easy to moderate

Benbow Lake is a summer-only attraction: the Eel River is dammed from Memorial Day to Labor Day, creating a lake that's very popular with swimmers and canoeists. During this time, park staff offers guided "canoe hikes"—fun and educational excursions on the lake.

In the 1920s, the Pratt family constructed a steam-driven sawmill on one side of the Eel River, while the Benbow family constructed a hotel-resort. Fortunately, not all the scenery went through the mill, so that in 1926 when the large Tudor-style Benbow Inn opened for business, its setting on the South Fork of the Eel River was still beautiful.

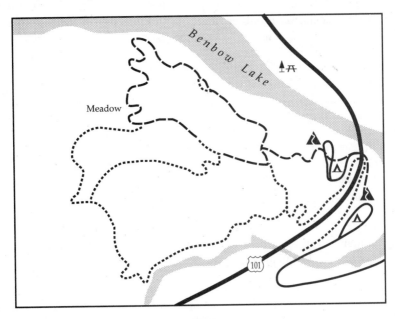

Hollywood celebs frequented the inn back then, as did Herbert Hoover and Eleanor Roosevelt.

Walter Benbow and his family built the dam across the Eel in 1932. The resulting lake was an immediate attraction. The dam also generated power for a time and was sold to PG&E in 1947. The utility generated electricity a few more years before turning the dam over to the Department of Parks and Recreation.

Benbow Lake Recreation Area today consists of 1,200 acres of riverfront, meadows and redwood groves. The park, fast becoming a cultural center, hosts a summer arts festival, a Shakespeare festival, and concerts.

A couple of trails sample the recreation area, offering the walker some great views of the lake. If a 2½-mile hike isn't enough exercise, try swimming or canoeing on the lake or tackling the park's par exercise course, located along the picnic area.

Directions to trailhead: From Highway 101, two miles south of Garberville, take the Benbow exit, following the frontage road to the park. Turn into the campground and drive to its north end. The trail leaves from campsite 73. During the off-season, when the upper campground loop is closed, you'll have to begin this walk at campsite 11 and hike an extra quarter-mile.

The walk: From campsite 73, join Pratt Mill Trail and begin ascending through redwoods. The path dips into, then switchbacks out of, a ravine and, a half-mile from the trailhead, comes to a junction. Go left to meet Pioneer Trail, which ascends west for a quarter-mile to a junction with Ridge Trail; this path loops a mile (rejoining Pioneer Trail) to a peak for great views of South Fork country.

Pioneer Trail levels out a bit, passes the other branch of Ridge Trail, then descends to oak-shaded Pioneer Meadow. The path continues descending, offering views of Benbow Lake, to a junction with Pratt Mill Trail (an old road).

Bear right and hike along the lakeshore a quarter-mile to a short side trail leading to Pratt Mill. A rusted boiler located (somewhat curiously) among tall redwoods marks the site of the old mill.

Your trail continues southeast, ascending briefly to a lookout high above Benbow Lake, the Inn, and the park's picnic area. A bit more climbing brings you back to close the loop and a left turn returns you to campsite 73 and the trailhead.

Humboldt Redwoods State Park
Bull Creek Flats Loop Trail

Terrain: Old-growth redwoods on banks of Bull Creek
Highlights: Rockefeller Forest—largest remaining and most magnificent redwood forest
Distance: 8½-mile loop
Degree of difficulty: Moderate
Precautions: Seasonally installed footbridge over Eel River makes loop trip easiest in summer. Trails open all year, but don't attempt crossing Eel in times of high water

Famed Avenue of the Giants offers a good look at Humboldt County's redwoods. More than a dozen short paths meander through Avenue-adjacent groves named for the rich and famous.

The 32-mile parkway, the parallel scenic alternate to Highway 101, runs the length of Humboldt Redwoods State Park. This park was one of California's first to be preserved when the state park system was established in the 1920s. Today it protects about one-eighth of all remaining old-growth coast redwoods.

Just off the Avenue of the Giants in Weott is the park visitor center. Stop to pick up maps, inquire about trail conditions and check out the nature exhibits, including an excellent one about the importance of ancient forests.

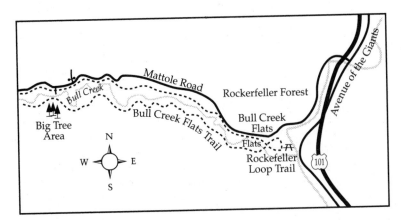

The matchless old-growth forest along Bull Creek was an early cause célèbre with early California conservationists, who struggled to save the redwoods from the mill. Out of this struggle to save Humboldt County's tall trees came the formation of the Save-the-Redwoods League in 1918.

Thanks to John D. Rockefeller, Jr., quietly funnelling $2 million to the league, matching state funds, conservationists were able to purchase some 10,000 acres along Bull Creek from the Pacific Lumber Company in 1930.

Today the Bull Creek backcountry forms the heart of the park. Thriving along this creek is more than a redwood grove; it's truly a forest. The Rockefeller Forest is, without resorting to too many superlatives, the most impressive stand of redwoods in the world.

A five-mile long road winds through the Bull Creek area, as do several hiking trails. My favorite is the route along Bull Creek itself. This path offers curiosities (Flatiron Tree, Giant Tree and more), as well as swimming in and sunning beside Bull Creek. And, of course, there are the spectacular redwoods—explored by a trail that not only stretches the legs, but the imagination as well.

Directions to trailhead: From the north-central part of the Avenue of the Giants, four miles north of the park visitor center and just south of the hamlet of Redcrest, turn west on Mattole Road and drive 1½ miles to the parking area for the Rockefeller Forest Loop Trail. (If you want to make this a one-way hike and make car shuttle arrangements, a second trailhead is located at the Big Trees parking area, another three miles west on Mattole Road.

The walk: Begin your walk on the right branch of the Rockefeller Loop (a very pleasant family hike in its own right) and follow it for a short quarter-mile or so to a junction, bearing right onto Bull Creek Flats Loop Trail. The path heads up-creek, along a path crowded in places by rushes and horsetail. A mile out, the trail breaks into a clearing, a half-mile farther crosses a tributary creek on a bridge; another mile more, a log bench beckons you to take a break.

About a mile from the Big Trees parking area, the path climbs to closely parallel Mattole Road. After crossing a couple side creeks on wooden bridges, you arrive at the parking lot.

From here, cross the bridge over Bull Creek and follow the signs to the oddly shaped Flatiron Tree and to Giant Tree. The Giant is not the world's tallest redwood, but it is the biggest—the champion by virtue of its combined height, diameter and crown size.

Leaving behind the Giant Tree, the path travels through a fern-filled forest, crosses Squaw Creek on a bridge, and soon passes a junction with the right-forking Johnson Camp Trail. Not only do the ancient trees towering above make you feel small, their fallen cousins, which require a 75-yard zig and a 75-yard zag by trail to get around, are also humbling to the hiker.

The trail enters and exits a hollow, hike-through log, then meanders a bit, north and south, with Bull Creek. A mile-and-a-half from the Big Trees area, the path plunges into the fern-filled canyon of Connick Creek, emerging to travel past awesome redwoods, including the so-called Giant Braid, a trio of redwoods twisted together.

For the most part, as you hike along, you'll hear but not see Bull Creek; that is until a half-mile or so from the Rockefeller Loop, when the path drops close to the creek. The trail explores some more magnificent redwoods on the flats above the creek.

Your redwood journey ends when you cross Bull Creek on a seasonal bridge, and reconnect with Rockefeller Loop Trail for the short walk back to the parking area.

Foot notes: If you're pressed for time, both ends of the above-described Bull Creek Flats Loop Trail have shorter, inviting explorations. You can easily walk from the Big Trees parking area to Giant Tree, then stroll along Bull Creek. The half-mile Rockefeller Forest Loop Trail is a gem.

From the Avenue of the Giants, there's easy access to a many short trails into the redwoods. Favorites include Children's Forest Loop Trail, Founders Grove Trail, Drury-Chaney Trail, Franklin K. Lane Grove Trail.

If you want to climb above the redwoods for a grand view, take Grasshopper Peak Trail from the Garden Club of America parking lot. The hike is a strenuous twelve-mile round trip to a lookout; grand views are your reward for the climb.

Also beginning at the superb 5,000-acre Garden Club of America Grove is two-mile round trip Canoe Creek Trail.

Grizzly Creek Redwoods State Park
Memorial, Baird Trails

> **Terrain:** Redwood-lined banks of Van Duzen River
> **Highlights:** Old-growth redwood groves, remote park
> **Distance:** 1½ miles round trip; longer hikes possible
> **Degree of difficulty:** Easy

One of the smallest of California's coast redwoods state parks, Grizzly Creek is also farthest from the coast—nearly 30 miles. Its location far from Highway 101/Avenue of The Giants tourist route, means few visitors discover the park's 300-foot redwoods or the six short trails that visit them.

The park is tucked in the Van Duzen River Valley, where Grizzly Creek meets the Van Duzen River. This locale may be remote, but filmmaker George Lucas found one of the park's virgin redwood groves so appealing he used the location in his Star Wars sequel, *Return of the Jedi.*

The park is located on Highway 36, a remote byway that links such out-of-the-way places as Mad River, Forest Glen, Wildwood, and Beegum as it winds through the forest from Highway 101 to Interstate 5. So remote is this road, that it's difficult to believe that until 1918, before the completion of 101, this little road was the major route of travel between San Francisco and Eureka.

Before the age of motoring, the "highway" was a stage route; a stagestop was located at what is now the the park's campground.

Worth a stop is Cheatham Grove, a stand of virgin redwoods located three miles west of the main part of the state park. A short loop trail explores the grove where six wonderful environmental campsites are located. (They offer a tranquility not found at the adequate, but not particularly restful Grizzly Creek Campground, located right next to Highway 36.)

The park's fern-lined trails meander among the old-growth and second-growth redwoods. A nature trail interprets local flora.

During summer, the low water level permits installation of a footbridge across the Van Duzen River. The bridge gives access to 1¼-mile long Memorial Trail which loops through the forest. From

Devil's Elbow, a bend in the river, hikers get a good view of the river and the park.

Directions to trailhead: From Highway 101 in Alton, exit on Highway 36 and drive 17 miles east to Grizzly Creek State Park. Turn right past the entrance station and park in the picnic area lot.

The walk: Cross the Van Duzen River on the summer bridge and follow a dirt road for a short distance to Memorial Trail on your left.

Memorial Trail heads into the redwoods—a drier, less fern-filled forest than those found closer to the coast, and drier even than other groves in the park. After a quarter-mile, the path splits: Go right, meandering into a tan oak, maple and bay laurel woodland.

At the eastern end of Memorial Trail, take the short Baird Trail looping through the old-growth redwood forest thriving on the banks of the Van Duzen River.

After you've enjoyed the redwoods, finish Memorial Loop Trail, which returns you to the picnic area.

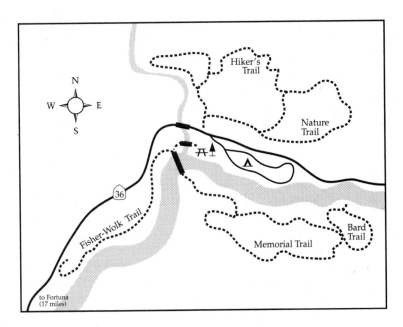

Prairie Creek Redwoods State Park

Fern Canyon, James Irvine, Clintonia,
Miners Ridge Trails

Terrain: Fern-filled canyon, redwood forest, wild beach
Highlights: Awesome fern canyon, wilderness beach, watching
  Roosevelt elk
Distance: Loop through Fern Canyon 1 mile round trip; via
  Gold Bluffs, Gold Bluffs Beach is 6½ miles round trip with
  500-foot elevation gain
Degree of difficulty: Easy to moderate

Dim and quiet, wrapped in mist and silence, the redwoods roof a moist and mysterious world. Park trails meander over lush ground and the walker is treated to the cool feeling and fragrance of wood and water.

A couple beautiful "fern canyons" are found along the North Coast, but the Fern Canyon in Prairie Creek Redwoods State Park is undoubtedly the most awe-inspiring. Five-finger, deer, lady, sword, and chain ferns smother the precipitous walls of the canyon. Bright yellow monkeyflowers abound, as well as fairy lanterns, those creamy white, or greenish, bell-shaped flowers that hang in clusters. Ferns are descendants of an ancient group of plants which were much more numerous 200 million years ago. Ferns have roots and stems similar to flowering plants, but are considered to be a primitive form of plant life because they reproduce by spores, not seeds.

Gold Bluffs was named in 1850 when prospectors found some gold flakes in the beach sand. The discovery caused a minor gold rush. A tent city sprang up on the beach but little gold was extracted.

Gold Bluffs Beach is a beauty—eleven miles of wild, driftwood-littered shore, backed by extensive dunes. Sand verbena, bush lupine, and wild strawberry splash color on the sand.

This walk explores some of the highlights of Prairie Creek Redwoods State Park—Fern Canyon, magnificent redwood groves, and Gold Bluffs Beach.

Directions to trailhead: From Highway 101, three miles north of Orick, turn west on Davison Road. The dirt, washboard road (suitable only for vehicles under 24 feet in length) descends logged slopes and through second-growth redwoods to the beach. The road heads north along Gold Bluffs Beach. One and a half miles past the campground, the road dead-ends at the Fern Canyon Trailhead.

The walk: The path leads along the pebbled floor of Fern Canyon. In the wettest places, the route follows wooden planks across Home Creek. With sword and five-finger ferns pointing the way, you pass through marshy areas covered with wetlands grass and dotted with a bit of skunk cabbage. Lurking about are Pacific giant salamanders.

A half-mile from the trailhead, the path climbs out of the canyon to intersect James Irvine Trail, named for a man who contributed much to the formation of redwood parks.

The James Irvine Trail crosses to the south side of the canyon and proceeds southeast with Home Creek. The trail reaches the upper neck of Fern Canyon and junctions with Clintonia Trail. (James Irvine Trail continues ascending through dense redwood forest to a trailhead near the park visitor center.) Clintonia Trail leads a mile through virgin redwood groves to a junction with Miners Ridge Trail. Bear right.

Part of Miners Ridge Trail is an old logging road, once used by mule-drawn wagons. The trail was also a pack train route for the Gold Bluffs miners. You'll descend with Squashan Creek to the ocean.

It's a 1½-mile beach walk along Gold Bluffs Beach back to the trailhead.

Lucky walkers might catch a glimpse of the herd of Roosevelt elk that roam the park. These graceful animals look like a cross between a South American llama and a deer and convince walkers that they have indeed entered an enchanted land.

Foot notes: Revelation Trail for the blind invites both sighted and blind or otherwise disabled visitors to explore the giant redwoods and other flora in the state park.

Ossagon Trail (3½ miles round trip) de-

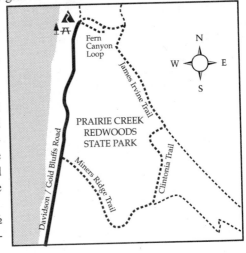

scends from a trailhead on Highway 101 to Gold Bluffs Beach. This expansive wilderness beach is a terrific walk, wherever you join it.

From the north end of the park's Beach Road, the three-mile long Beach Trail is a great way to go.

West Ridge Trail, which extends north-south over the backbone of the state park can be joined from Zig Zag Trails #1 and #2 and linked with Prairie Creek Trail for a grand (12-mile loop) tour, or for shorter hikes.

Del Norte Coast Redwoods State Park

Last Chance Trail

Terrain: Steep coastal slopes
Highlights: Redwood forest, hiking on old Redwood Highway
Distance: From Enderts Beach Road to Highway 101 is 7 miles
    one way; shorter and longer round trip hikes possible
Degree of difficulty: Moderate

Del Norte Coast Redwoods State Park delivers the scenery in its name: an impressive coastline, as well as magnificent old-growth redwoods. The combination of redwoods—and a mixed forest of Sitka spruce, Douglas fir and red alder—along with the coast, adds up to a walk to remember.

The majority of the state park is located on the ocean side of Highway 101; in fact, what is now a splendid hiking trail used to be the Redwood Highway (101). The old highway was abandoned in 1935 for its present route. Part of the old road is on the National Register of Historic Places.

Don't think you're lost if you see Redwood National Park signs (easy to recognize because the agency seems to be the last proponent of the metric system in America), instead of Del Norte Coast Red-

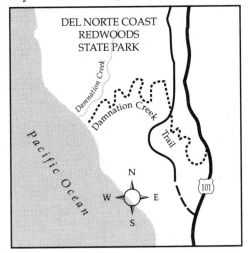

woods State Park signs. The national park service has jurisdiction over the Enderts Beach trailhead; however, more than two-thirds of Last Chance Trail is on state park land.

Directions to trailhead: From Highway 101, about two miles south of Crescent City, turn west on Enderts Beach Road and wind 2½ miles to road's end at Crescent Beach Overlook and the beginning of Last Chance Trail.

The walk: As you hike south on the old coast highway, you'll get grand views behind you of the Crescent City coastline and in a short while will be treated to good views south of Enderts Beach. A quarter-mile from the trailhead, a short side trail on the right offers the opportunity to descend to this pocket beach.

Last Chance Trail drops into Nickel Creek Canyon, where another side trail leads to a walk-in campground. A half-mile out, Last Chance Trail begins a very steep climb of a bit more than a mile, ascending through old-growth redwoods. Two miles along, you top out and begin a descent, entering Del Norte Coast Redwoods State Park.

Three miles along are the magnificent redwoods thriving in the headwaters of Damnation Creek. Another mile of travel and a short descent brings you to a ford of Damnation Creek. (This is a good turn-around point; it's an eight-mile round trip hike, by the time you get back to the trailhead.)

Those hikers continuing with Last Chance Trail will cross (use caution, the log "bridges" are slippery) Damnation Creek and travel another mile through the forest. The path nears Highway 101 at mile 5, junctions with Damnation Creek Trail at the 6-mile mark, leads through some more redwood forest primeval and reaches Highway 101 seven miles from the trailhead.

Foot notes: From the campground, a ¾-mile long nature trail loops through the redwood forest. Mill Creek Trail (2.6 miles) meanders creek-side. Hobbs Wall Trail leads through second-growth redwoods and passes abandoned logging cables and machinery.

Damnation Creek Trail, a historic Yurok path, descends steeply 2½ miles through dense redwood forest to a hidden beach; it connects with Last Chance Trail.

Check out the California Coastal Trail, which continues south from Del Norte Coast Redwoods State Park through other state and national redwood park lands.

Jedediah Smith Redwoods State Park
Boy Scout Trail

> **Terrain:** Redwood forest primeval
> **Highlights:** Old-growth redwoods, waterfall
> **Distance:** 7½ miles round trip to Fern Falls
> **Degree of difficulty:** Moderate

Northernmost of California's redwood state parks, Jedediah Smith beckons the hiker with both a redwood forest primeval and the banks of the Smith River, the state's only major river without a dam.

The park honors mountain man/pathfinder Jedediah Smith, credited with discovering (for west-bound travelers) the Rocky Mountains pass through which most California- and Oregon-bound emigrants traveled.

Smith was also the first to journey (by land, anyway) to what was to become the west coast of the continental United States—from San Diego to just short of the Canadian border. The Smith River was named for the dogged adventurer, who crossed the wild watercourse in 1828.

Centerpiece of the state park is Stout Memorial Grove. Among the magnificent 5,000 acres of nearby National Tribute Grove is one of the world's largest: Stout Tree, named not for its considerable girth, as

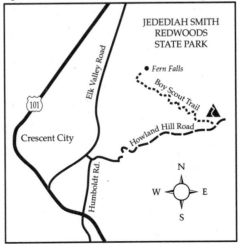

you might suspect, but for Frank D. Stout, whose family donated the grove to the Save-the-Redwoods League.

Another towering redwood is Boy Scout Tree, visited by a trail constructed by the scouts of Crescent City's Troop 10 in the 1930s.

Directions to trailhead: From Highway 101, at the south end of Crescent City, turn east on Elk Valley Road. After a mile and a half, fork right on Howland Hill Road and continue east about four more miles to the signed trailhead located on the north side of the road.

The walk: Stroll the fern-lined path, the 300-foot tall trees towering above you. After a mile, the trail follows a redwood-topped ridge, with tall sword ferns pointing the way.

About two miles along, the path descends a series of wooden steps to a lush, lovely creek. Another mile of quiet forest walking brings you to a fork: the right branch goes to Boy Scout Tree while the other leads to Fern Falls.

Northern California Coast

Extending almost 400 miles from San Francisco to the Oregon border, California's North Coast is a land of rugged shores and pounding surf.

San Francisco is known as a city of walkers; favorite destinations of weekend walkers include China Camp, Angel Island, and Mt. Tamalpais state parks, which offer great vistas of the bay and the city.

North Coast state parks pay tribute to a variety of cultures: Chinese fishermen at China Camp, the Russian outpost at Fort Ross. Olompali State Historic Park celebrates thousands of years of uniquely Californian history from ancestors of the Miwok people to Spanish missionaries to the Grateful Dead rock band.

Few coastal locales are as photographed as the town of Mendocino and its bold headlands. The state park-protected-headlands are laced with pathways that offer postcard views of wave tunnels and tidepools, sea stacks and blowholes.

Accenting the coast is a variety of flora, from the towering Sitka spruce at Patrick's Point State Park to the delicate blossoms in Kruse Rhododendron State Preserve. Five-finger and bird's foot, lady and licorice—these are some of the colorful names of the ferns growing in Van Damme State Park's well-named Fern Canyon.

Wildest of the north coast parks is Sinkyone Wilderness State Park, part of California's "Lost Coast," where the hearty explorer discovers dense forests, prairies and black sand beaches.

Candlestick Point
State Recreation Area
Candlestick Point Trail

Terrain: Windblown San Francisco Bay
Highlights: Walking, picnicking near Candlestick Park
Distance: 2 miles round trip
Degree of difficulty: Easy

To San Francisco baseball and football fans, Candlestick Park is the windy home stadium of their beloved Giants and Forty-Niners.

In the shadow of "The Stick," is a state recreation area that beckons other sports-minded visitors. Advanced board-sailers relish the challenge of the wind tunnel off the south shore of the park. Afternoon winds funnelling through Alemany Gap to the Bay often create rides to remember.

Kayakers like to put-in and take-out on the park's sandy beach. Fishermen enjoy the two fishing piers. Some of the best winter bird-

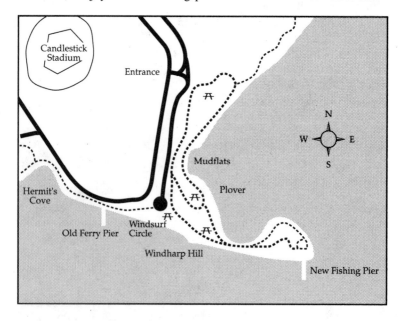

watching on the Bay is found at Candlestick Point. And there are plenty of facilities for picnics and barbecues.

For the walker, a multi-use trail extends a mile or so along the shoreline from the fishing pier to the picnic areas.

Expect a windy walk. Those infamous winds that have long plagued outfielders, turning even routine fly balls into a challenge to catch, once even blowing a pitcher off the mound, can really slow down a walker.

Directions to trailhead: From Highway 101, south of San Francisco, take the Candlestick Park exit. Follow the Hunters Point Expressway around the stadium to the state recreation area. There's limited parking along the road, plentiful parking near the main picnic/day use area.

Angel Island State Park
Angel Island Loop Trail

Terrain: Rocky coves, forested ridges
Highlights: A 360-degree view of San Francisco Bay, plus
  historic military buildings
Distance: 5 miles round trip with 400-foot elevation gain
Degree of difficulty: Moderate

For an island barely a square mile in size, Angel Island has a diverse history. Over the last two centuries, the island has seen use as a pirate's supply station, a Mexican land grant, an Army artillery emplacement, and an Immigrant Detention Center. Now it's a state park, attracting hikers, history buffs, and islophiles of all persuasions.

A hundred years of U.S. military occupation began in 1863 when the first gun batteries were installed. The military used the island until 1962, when its Nike Missile Station was deactivated. During wartime periods, particularly during the Spanish-American War, Angel Island was one of the busiest outposts in America. The island served as a processing center for men about to be dispatched to the Philippines, and as a reception/quarantine center for soldiers who returned with tropical diseases.

Not all of the island's attractions are historical. Rocky coves and sandy beaches, grassy slopes and forested ridges, plus a fine trail network, add up to a walker's delight. Perimeter Road takes the walker on a five-mile tour of the island and offers a different bay view from every turn. From atop Mt. Livermore, a terrific 360-degree panorama unfolds of San Franciso Bay and the Golden Gate.

Directions to trailhead: For information about ferry service to island from Tiburon, call Tiburon Ferry at (415) 435-2131. There is limited ferry service from San Francisco via Red and White Fleet; call (415) 546-2896. The ferries land at Ayala Cove on the northwest side of the island.

Park your car—for a fee—in one of Tiburon's parking lots near the waterfront, or attempt to find some of the scarce free parking.

The walk: When you disembark, head for the park visitor center, located in a white building that once served as bachelor quarters for unmarried officers assigned to the U.S. Quarantine Station that operated here from 1892 to 1949. At that time, Ayala Cove was named Hospital Cove. At the visitor center, you can check out the interpretive exhibits and pick up a park map.

Walk uphill on the road to the left of the visitor center. You'll intersect Perimeter Road and the Sunset trailhead at the top of the hill.

Sunset Trail switchbacks up steep, coastal-scrub covered slopes, to

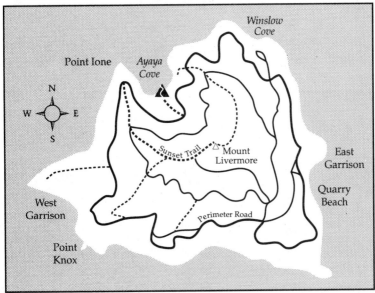

the top of 781-foot Mt. Caroline Livermore. Picnic tables have replaced the helicopter pad and radio antennae that once stood on the summit. Views of Ayala Cove, Tiburon, and the Golden Gate, are memorable.

Continuing right (west) on Perimeter Road, you'll soon overlook Camp Reynolds (West Garrison). A side road leads down to the island's first military fortifications. You can walk the parade ground and see the brick hospital built in 1908. Still standing are the chapel, mule barn, barracks, and several more structures. Some of the buildings are being restored.

Perimeter Road turns eastward, contouring around chaparral-covered slopes and offering a view down to Point Blunt. You may hear and see the seals gathered around the point. The road curves north and soon arrives at East Garrison, where a collection of utilitarian-looking buildings are a reminder of the many thousands of men who were processed here. East Garrison trained about 30,000 men a year for overseas duty. The hospital, barracks, mess hall, and officers' homes still stand.

Continue north. You'll soon come to the Immigration Station, the so called "Ellis Island of the West." From 1910 to 1940, 175,000 immigrants, mostly Asians, were (often rudely) processed. During World War II, German, Italian, and Japanese prisoners of war were confined here.

Perimeter Road rounds Pt. Campbell, northernmost part of the island, and you'll get a glimpse of the Richmond-San Rafael Bridge, and then a view of Tiburon, before the road descends to Ayala Cove.

Mount Tamalpais State Park
Railroad Grade, Fern Creek Trails

> **Terrain:** Deep canyons, steep slopes
> **Highlights:** Fantastic urban and natural panoramas
> **Distance:** Mountain Home Inn to East Peak summit is 6 miles
>   round trip with 1,300-foot elevation gain
> **Degree of difficulty:** Moderate

For more than century, Bay Area walkers and visitors from around the world have enjoyed rambling the slopes of Mount Tamalpais. Glorious panoramas of the Pacific coastline and San Francisco Bay were attracting walkers to the mountaintop well before Mount Tam was preserved as a state park in 1928. If you're lucky, perhaps you'll experience what some Bay Area walkers call "a Farallons Day"—one of those clear days when visibility is greater than 25 miles, thus allowing a glimpse of the sharp peaks of the Farallon Islands.

The Mount Tamalpais and Muir Woods Railroad, known as "the crookedest railroad in the world," was constructed in 1896; it brought

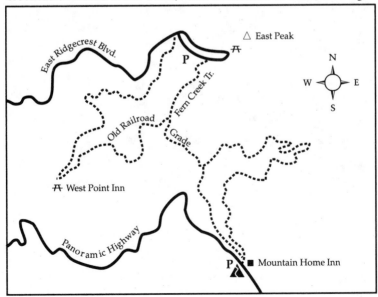

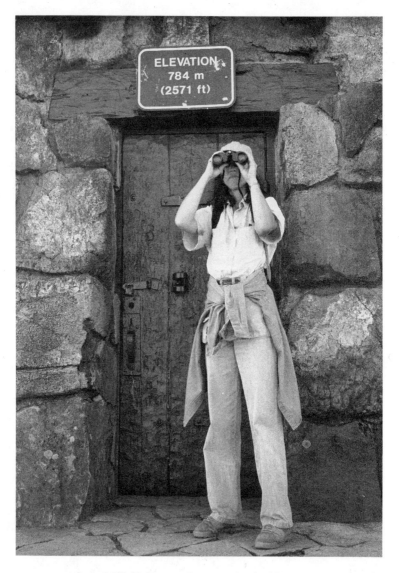

passengers from Mill Valley to the summit via 281 curves. Atop Mt. Tam, the Tavern of Tamalpais welcomed diners and dancers.

Redwood-lined creeks, stands of Douglas fir, and oak-dotted potreros are just a few of the great mountain's delightful environments. Thanks to the early trail-building efforts of the Tamalpais

Conservation Club, as well as later efforts by the CCC during the 1930s, more than fifty miles of trail explore the state park. These trails connect to two hundred more miles of trail that lead through the wooded watershed of the Marin Municipal Water District, and over to Muir Woods National Monument and Golden Gate National Recreation Area.

The top of Mt. Tam, with its fire lookout tower ringed with barbed wire, itself isn't quite as nice as the top-of-the-world views it offers. Motorists can drive to within 0.3 of a mile to the top, which often means a crowd at the summit.

Ah, but getting there is more than half the fun, particularly on trails like Railroad Grade and Fern Creek, which offer a little bit of everything: dense stands of laurel, open grassland, oak-dotted knolls, a canyon full of redwoods and ferns.

If you want to stay on the Railroad Grade all the way to the top of Mt. Tam, add 2½ miles to the ascent plus 2½ miles to the descent.

Directions to trailhead: From Highway 1 in Mill Valley, veer right on Panoramic Highway, ascending a few miles to Mountain Home Inn and a parking area. The trail begins across Panoramic Highway. A bus stops at Mountain Home Inn, so by all means consider the bus a way to the trailhead.

The walk: Begin your steady ascent (7 percent grade all the way) on the Old Railroad Grade. Occasional views open up among the brush.

Almost two miles out, you'll reach a junction with the east fork of Fern Canyon. Take this very steep shortcut a long half-mile to Ridecrest Boulevard just below the East Peak parking lot.

(Dogged railroad buffs will ignore such shortcuts and stay on the Railroad Grade which visits the West Point Inn, originally built by the railroad and now owned by the Marin Water District and run by the West Point Inn Association. Hikers may pause on the veranda and buy some liquid refreshment. You'll circle clockwise around West Point, heading north another two miles up the railroad grade).

Once you reach the summit parking lot and picnic area, catch your breath and join the 0.3-mile summit trail to the top of Mt. Tam.

Footnotes: The whole Railroad Grade Trail (8¼ miles one way) from Corte Madera to the summit makes an interesting, if long, day trip that appeals particularly to train buffs. Steep Ravine Trail (3 miles one way) from Pantoll to Stinson Beach is a favorite mountain path. If you use the bus stops in and around the state park, you can design some terrific one-way hikes up and down Mt. Tam.

China Camp State Park
Shoreline, Bay View Trails

Terrain: Woodland, meadows, coastal marsh around Bay.
Highlights: Preserves last Chinese fishing village on San
   Francisco Bay
Distance: 4½ miles round trip with 400-foot elevation gain.
Degree of difficulty: Moderate

On Point San Pedro Peninsula, only a few ramshackle buildings remain of the once-thriving shrimp fishing village of China Camp. During the last century, more than thirty such camps were established on the shores of San Francisco Bay.

The fishermen were mostly Chinese, primarily natives of the city of Canton. The fishermen staked nets on the shallow bay bottom, in order to capture the tiny grass shrimp. The shrimp were dried, then the meat separated from the shell. It was a labor-intensive process, but a ready market for the shrimp existed in China and Japan.

Competing fishermen helped push through legislation that banned

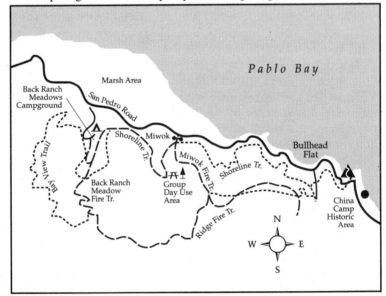

the use of bag nets, and in 1905, the export of dried shrimp was banned entirely, thus ending the San Francisco Bay shrimping business.

In 1977, the state acquired 1,500 acres of bay shore to form China Camp State Park. Some 1890s-era buildings still stand, and interpretive exhibits tell of the difficult life in this fishing village.

"The park's ridge separates the 1890s from the 1990s," explains long-time park ranger Patrick Robards. "While the view south sure has changed, the view down to China Camp on San Pablo Bay is almost exactly what it was at the end of the last century."

Shoreline Trail is a mellow path that meanders through the forest and grassland above the miles of marshland that border China Camp. For a grand tour of the park, follow Shoreline Trail 5½ miles to the west boundary of the park. An optional return route could be on Bay View Trail, which travels through redwoods and stands of bay through the higher (750 feet or so) elevations of the park. Views of upper San Francisco Bay are outstanding. Returning via Bay View and Ridge trails adds up to 6½ miles; all together that's a 12-mile tour of the park.

A more modest loop, described below, uses parts of Shoreline and Ridge trails, for a fine family outing.

Directions to trailhead: From Highway 101 in San Rafael, take the North San Pedro Road exit, and head east through a residential area to China Camp State Park. Leave your car in the lot above the China Camp Historic Area. Cross North San Pedro Road and join signed Shoreline Trail. You can also begin this hike at the parking area at Bullhead Flat, then walk up the park service road to join Shoreline Trail.

The walk: Shoreline Trail soon crosses the park service road, and comes to a signed intersection with Peacock Trail, which in turn, connects to Ridge Trail. Bear right to stay on Shoreline Trail.

As you follow San Pablo Bay from east to west, you'll stay at about a one hundred foot elevation. You'll get good views of the park's four distinct shoreline hills—Jake's Island, Turtle Back, Bullet Hill and Chicken Coop Hill. When bay waters were higher, these hills were islands.

Two miles out, you'll reach the dirt road leading to Miwok Meadows, a day use area. Ambitious hikers will continue on Shoreline Trail, while those opting for a shorter loop will join Miwok Fire Trail for the ascent to Ridge Trail.

Head east on Ridge Trail, enjoying a different, higher, perspective than Shoreline Trail. When you reach Peacock Trail, you'll turn left, descending briefly to Shoreline Trail, then back to the trailhead.

Three unsigned, short, spur trails lead south across Miwok Meadows to intersect with Miwok Trail. No matter which spur you take, bear right (west), on Miwok Trail. This path jogs south, becomes Back Ranch Trail, and soon leads to the park's walk-in campground.

From the camp, the trail switchbacks up slopes forested with oak, madrone, and bay.

At the intersection with Ridge Trail, you may proceed right (west), up to the former Nike Missile Station. Fine views of San Pablo Bay are yours from this viewpoint.

Heading east, Ridge Trail passes near the community of Glenwood. Two unsigned trails lead rightward into a residential area, but you'll stay left and begin a steep descent on Miwok Trail. This path intersects North San Pedro Road near Chicken Coop Hill.

Benicia State Recreation Area
Dillon Point Trail

Terrain: Marsh, bay shore
Highlights: Narrowest part of San Francisco Bay
Distance: 3 miles round trip
Degree of difficulty: Easy

"Where the waters meet" might be a good slogan for Benicia State Recreation Area.

Flowing from the east are no less than the combined waters of fourteen tributaries of the Sacramento and San Joaquin rivers; the waters surge through the Carniquez Strait, creating quite a spectacle. Nowhere else is San Francisco Bay more narrow than at Dillon Point in the state recreation area.

For the walker, Benicia offers a couple different bay-side strolls. The trail system is part of that ambitious path-in-the-making, the Bay Area Ridge Trail.

Most popular is 1½-mile-long walk out to Dillon Point on the park road. The road is open to vehicles (fee charged), but auto traffic is usually very light and far outnumbered by walkers, runners and cyclists. At Dillon Point is a popular fishing area where local anglers cast for starry flounder, sturgeon and striped bass.

Another path, beginning near the park entrance, features an exercise parcourse, so you can make your walk a real workout. Paths lead from the exercise trail through the adjacent marshland to water's edge. Bird-watching is particularly good in the marsh.

Directions to trailhead: From Highway 780, exit on Columbia Parkway and follow the signs to Benicia State Recreation Area.

Samuel P. Taylor State Park
Ridge Trail, Barnabe Trails

> **Terrain:** Steep grassy slopes, redwood-lined creeks
> **Highlights:** Historic retreat, viewful Barnabe Peak.
> **Distance:** 6 mile loop with 1,300-foot elevation gain
> **Degree of difficulty:** Moderate with some steep sections.

From Barnabe Peak, you get a fire lookout's view: Pt. Reyes, National Seashore, Mt. Tamalpais, and central Marin County.

Barnabe Peak honors explorer John C. Frémont's mule. Barnabe lived out his days as the Taylor family pet. The view from 1,466-foot Barnabe Peak is not as grand as that from Fremont Peak (see Fremont Peak State Park walk) but does provide an inspiring Marin County panorama. And the view is fairly unobstructed; Barnabe Peak, along with famed Mt. Tam are the only Marin County peaks with fire lookouts.

This loop trip offers a pleasant riverside stroll, plus a good workout to the peak.

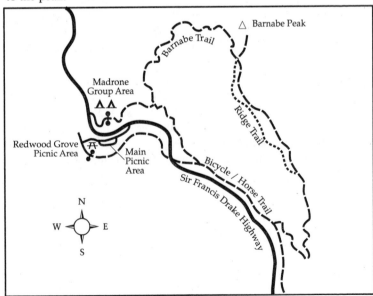

Don't miss visiting the park's anything-but-satanic Devil's Gulch, heavenly shaded by oak, madrone and Douglas fir, with slopes brightened in spring with milkmaids, Indian paintbrush and buttercups. With judicious use of the park map, you could add Devil's Gulch to your hike with a two mile or so extension, or simply visit it separately from the trailhead located off Sir Francis Drake Highway.

Directions to trailhead: From Highway 101 in San Rafael, exit on Sir Francis Drake Boulevard and travel some fifteen miles to the park. The park entrance is about two miles past the tiny hamlet of Lagunitas. Leave your car in the picnic area lot.

The walk: From the picnic area, cross the bridge over Lagunitas Creek and turn left onto the bike/horse trail. This wide, pleasant trail, the former railway bed of the North Pacific Coast Railroad, travels creekside in the shade of bay, maple and redwoods. It soon recrosses the creek, and crosses Sir Francis Drake Highway on a hiker/cyclist bridge.

The level path continues along the north bank of Lagunitas Creek, and is soon joined by a riding/hiking trail. A half-mile from this junction you'll come to another—with signed Ridge Trail. The riding/hiking trail, also known as Cross-Marin Trail, continues 13 more miles to Mount Tamalpais, but you go left, and begin a steady ascent on the aptly named Ridge Trail, gaining good vistas of central Marin County.

A bit more than a mile from the summit, the fire road you've been following offers a parallel trail alternative; the trail is your best bet for spring wildflower-watching while the road serves up better vistas. Both trail and road climb briskly, but not too steeply, to the summit.

Enjoy the views west of Bolinas Ridge and Golden Gate National Recreation Area, Mt. Tamalpais to the southeast.

Join Barnabe Trail for a steep descent of a bit over a mile to meet the park's horse trail. Detour a short distance to the right to visit Samuel P. Taylor's gravesite. Otherwise turn left, continue a short ways, and then turn right again on the path leading to Madrone Group Campground.

Follow the campground road out to the highway, cross it, and pick up North Creek Trail. Head left (south) back to the main picnic area.

Olompali State Historic Park
Olompali Trail

> **Terrain:** Grassy ridges, oak- and madrone-filled ravines
> **Highlights:** A walk through 4,000 years of California history,
>   spring wildflowers
> **Distance:** 2¾ miles round trip with 600-foot elevation gain
> **Degree of difficulty:** Easy to moderate

Olompali State Historic Park in Marin County, one of our newest state parks, embraces 4,000 years of a history that is uniquely Californian—from the Miwok of 2,000 B.C. to the Chosen Family Commune of the 1960s, from Spanish missionaries to the Grateful Dead.

For the hiker, Olompali offers a colorful history lesson and a great walk in the park.

"Not only do you get to walk through a couple thousand years of history, but you get a feel for what the land looked like when the Miwok lived here," explains state park ranger Fred Lew.

From what anthropologists surmise, the Coast Miwok lived in shelters made of sticks, tules and grass. They enjoyed lives, by all evidence, of abundance: they gathered acorns, hunted game in the mountains, fished from the shores of the nearby bay. Olompali (pronounced O-lum-pa-lee) was one of the largest villages in the area.

The arrival of Spanish missionaries and soldiers ended the Miwok's way of life, though at Olompali they made a valiant effort to adapt.

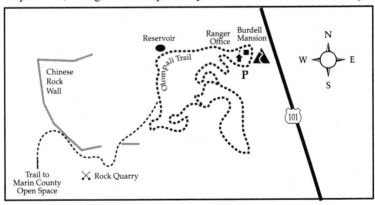

The Miwok learned to make adobe bricks at nearby missions and replaced their tule huts with adobe shelters. They planted crops, raised livestock. In 1843 Franciscan-educated Miwok leader Camillo Ynitia was given Olompali by the Mexican government; he was one of the very few native people to ever receive a land grant.

A decade later, Ynitia sold his land. By 1865, Rancho Olompali, as it was now known, belonged to San Francisco's first dentist Galen Burdell and his wife Mary. The Burdells raised cattle and developed a fabulous estate, complete with imposing mansion and a huge formal garden.

During the 1950s, University of San Francisco Jesuits used the property as a religious retreat. The Chosen Family Commune leased the estate in 1967. The Grateful Dead played here, and one of their album covers of that era features a view of the Olompali hills. After hosting a nude wedding ceremony and celebration that attracted nationwide media coverage, the commune disbanded when a fire destroyed much of the old Burdell mansion.

The state purchased the land in 1977 and opened Olompali State Historic Park in 1990.

With the aid of an interpretive booklet, you can take a walk through Olompali history. You'll see Camillo Ynitia's adobe, the ruins of the Burdell mansion, and what's left of Mary Burdell's grand garden, where daffodils, planted here more than a century ago, still bloom each year. A barn, a blacksmith shop, the ranch foreman's house and much more can be visited on this history walk.

Olompali is now more than a walk through a historic park. A recently completed 2½-mile trail extension allows hikers to ascend the eastern slope of 1,558-foot Mt. Burdell. The path connects the 700-acre park with another 2,000 acres of Marin County parkland.

Directions to trailhead: From Highway 101, a half hour's drive or so north of San Francisco, and three miles north of Novato, get in the left turn lane for San Antonio Creek Road. Make a U-turn and drive south to the park entrance.

The walk: Pick up the self-guided tour booklet to Olompali and begin your exploration of the park's historic structures. After wandering among the buildings and visiting what's left of the estate's once fabulous formal garden, hit the trail.

The trail's a loop, so it doesn't matter which way you want to hike it. Near the crest of the loop, you'll get glimpses of San Pablo Bay.

Tomales Bay State Park
Johnstone Trail

> **Terrain:** Wooded bluffs above Tomales Bay, meadows, carpets of springtime wildflowers
> **Highlights:** Sunny, sheltered beaches, Bishop pine forest
> **Distance:** Heart's Desire Beach to Jepson Memorial Grove is 3 miles round trip with 300-foot elevation gain; to Shell Beach is 8 miles round trip
> **Degree of difficulty:** Moderate

Two lovely trails, named for a professor and a planner, explore Tomales Bay State Park. Botanist Willis Jepson, founder of the School of Forestry at the University of California, Berkeley, and author of the authoritative *Manual of the Flowering Plants of California,* is honored by the Jepson Trail.

Conservationist Bruce Johnstone, Marin County planner, and his wife, Elsie, worked long and hard to preserve Tomales Bay and place part of it in a state park. Johnstone Trail leads bayside from Heart's Desire Beach to Shell Beach.

Bay area walkers have a little secret: When fog smothers Pt. Reyes and San Francisco Bay, try heading for Tomales Bay State Park. The park has a microclimate, and often has sunny days and pleasant temperatures when other neighboring coastal locales are damp and cold.

Directions to trailhead: From the town of Inverness, follow Sir Francis Drake Boulevard to Pierce Point Road. Turn right and drive a half-mile to the entrance to Tomales Bay State Park. Follow signs to the large parking lot at Heart's Desire Beach.

The walk: Near the trailhead are some interpretive displays that tell of clams and Bishop pine. Signed Johnstone Trail departs from the south end of Heart's Desire Beach and immediately climbs into a moss-draped forest of oak, bay, madrone, and wax myrtle.

A half-mile of travel brings you to Pebble Beach. At a trail junction, a short side trail goes straight down to Pebble Beach, but Johnstone Trail swings southwest and begins switchbacking up forested slopes. Some wetter areas of the coastal slope are dotted with ferns. The trail crosses a paved road and soon junctions.

If you want to continue to Shell Beach, you'll bear left with the Johnstone Trail. The trail detours around some private property, and contours over the coastal slope at an elevation of about 500 feet. The path leads through Bishop pine and a lush understory of salal and huckleberry bushes. After a few miles, the trail descends through madrone and oak forest to Shell Beach.

Walkers content with looping back to Heart's Desire Beach via Jepson Trail will continue straight at the above-mentioned junction. Bishop pine, along with its similar-looking piney cousins, the Monterey and knobcone, are known as fire pines, because they require the heat of fire to crack open their cones and release their seeds. Bishop pines are slow to propagate and are relatively rare in coastal California. (Another nice stand of Bishop pine is located in Montaña de Oro State Park in San Luis Obispo County.)

The surest way to distinguish a Bishop pine from its look-alike, the Monterey pine, is by counting the needles: Monterey pines have three needles to a bunch, Bishop pines have two needles to a cluster.

Some strategically placed benches allow walkers to savor the fine bay views afforded by the Jepson Trail, which descends gently to Heart's Desire Beach.

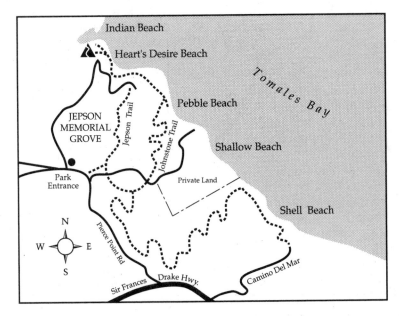

Sonoma Coast State Beaches
Sonoma Coast Trail

Terrain: Pastoral bluffs, ravines
Highlights: Hidden beaches, dramatic coastline
Distance: Blind Beach to Shell Beach is 4 miles round trip; to
  Wright's Beach is 6½ miles round trip.
Degree of difficulty: Easy to moderate

The names alone are intriguing: Blind Beach and Schoolhouse Beach, Arched Rock and Goat Rock, Penny Island and Bodega Head.

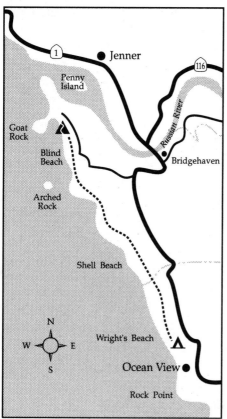

These colorfully named locales are some of the highlights of Sonoma Coast State Beach, thirteen miles of coastline stretching from the Russian River to Bodega Bay.

Sonoma Coast State Beach is not one beach, but many. You could easily overlook them, because most aren't visible from Highway 1. The beaches are tucked away in rocky coves, and hidden by tall bluffs.

Sonoma Coast Trail is a pretty blufftop route that connects some of these secret beaches. During spring, wildflowers brighten the bluff: blue lupine, Indian paintbrush and sea fig.

Sonoma Coast Trail begins on the bluffs above

Blind Beach, but the walker can also begin at Goat Rock, located a half-mile north of the trailhead. The rock is connected to the mainland by a causeway. During the 1920s, Goat Rock was quarried, and used to build a jetty at the mouth of the Russian River.

A mile north of the trailhead, and a half-mile north of Goat Rock is the mouth of the Russian River. The 110-mile- long river is one of the largest on the North Coast. At the river mouth, you can observe ospreys nesting in the treetops. The California brown pelican is one of several species of birds that breed and nest on Penny Island, located in the river mouth.

Directions to trailhead: From Highway 1, ten miles north of the town of Bodega Bay, turn west on Goat Rock Road. Signed Sonoma Coast Trail begins at a small parking lot on the left of the road. If you'd like to begin this walk at Goat Rock, continue to road's end at a large parking area.

The walk: Sonoma Coast Trail heads south along the edge of the bluffs. Soon, you'll step over a stile and head across a pasture. The trail climbs to a saddle on the shoulder of Peaked Hill (elevation 376 feet).

You then descend to the flat blufftops, and cross a bridge over a fern-lined ravine. It's a pastoral scene: grassy bluffs, a weathered old barn in the distance.

After crossing another ravine, the path reaches the Shell Beach parking area. A short trail descends the bluffs to Shell Beach. Another trail extends northwest, crosses the highway, and reaches redwood-shaded Pomo Canyon. Picnic tables and walk-in (environmental) campsites are located near the creek.

Sonoma Coast Trail continues south, detouring inland around a private home, then doubling back seaward. The trail plunges into Furlong Gulch, then switchbacks back up to the bluffs. You can may follow the trail or the beach to Wright's Beach Campground.

Fort Ross State Historic Park
Fort Ross Trail

Terrain: Rye grass- and wild barley-covered coastal terrace, a calm sheltered cove. Dramatic bluffs shaped by San Andreas Fault

Highlights: Reconstructed Fort Ross, largest Russian settlement on California coast; ocean views

Distance: To Fort Ross Cove is ½ mile round trip; to Reef Point Campground is 4 miles round trip; can extend your hike north along the park bluffs, or south along Sonoma County's "lost coast"

Degree of difficulty: Moderate

Precautions: Don't get stranded by the high tides that cover the Sonoma county beaches near Fort Ross

Fort Ross, the last remnant of czarist Russia's foothold in California, is today a walker's delight. Near the fort, sinuous Highway 1 suddenly straightens. You look out upon a handsome, windswept bluff, and spy a redwood stockade and Russian Orthodox chapel. For the first-time visitor, it's a startling sight.

Napoleon was beginning his 1812 invasion of Russia when Fort Ross—named for *Rossiya,* itself—was built. The fort's location ideally suited the purposes of the colony. The site was easily defensible. Tall trees, necessary for the fort's construction and the shipbuilding that would take place in the nearby cove, covered the coastal slopes. The waters were full of sea otters—an attraction for the Russian American Fur Company, which would soon hunt the animals to near-extinction. Wheat, potatoes, and vegetables were grown on the coastal terrace, and shipped to Russian settlements in Alaska. All in all, the fort was nearly self-sufficient.

Thanks to the state's replication and restoration efforts, the fort's building brings back the flavor of the Russian's foray into North America. The high stockade, built entirely of hand-hewn redwood timber, looks particularly formidable.

Also of interest are the seven-sided blockhouse, with its interpretive exhibits, and the small, wooden Orthodox chapel. And be sure to stop at the Fort Ross Visitor Center, a new facility with Russian, Pomo and natural history exhibits.

When you've completed your walk through history, another surprise awaits: a hike out on the lonely, beautiful headlands.

In 1990, the state park tripled in size; the addition was the former Call Ranch, more than 2,000 acres of wooded canyons and dramatic coastline. From the old fort, you can walk two miles north along the coast via old logging roads dipping into Kolmer Gulch, where there's a picnic area, and continuing to a stand of redwood and Douglas fir.

You can also walk two miles (or more) south along the coast, as detailed below. North- or south-bound hikers will enjoy grand views of the fort and up-close looks at the result of earthquake action along the San Andreas Fault.

Directions to trailhead: Fort Ross State Historic Park is located off of Highway 1, some twelve miles north of the hamlet of Jenner.

The walk: Exit the fort's main gate, follow the stockade walls to the left, and join the downhill path. It's a short walk to secluded Fort Ross Cove, one of California's first shipyards. You'll find an interpretive display and picnic tables here.

Cross Fort Ross Creek on a small footbridge. Earthquake action along the mighty San Andreas Fault has altered the course of the creek by more than a half-mile. Follow the path inland along the creek, which is lined with bay laurel, willow, alder and Douglas iris. After a hundred yards of travel, look to your right for an unmarked, narrow path leading south.

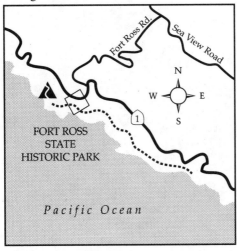

The indistinct path travels onto an open coastal terrace. You'll no doubt see some sheep eating the pastoral vegetation. Follow the undulations of the rye grass- and barley-covered headland, and meander first southeast, then southwest. Continue down-coast until you spot a path descending to a dirt road. (Don't try to climb the sheep fence; use the stile located where the road dead-ends.)

Descend the dirt road to Reef Campground, formerly a private campground, and now a state park facility. It's a good place for a picnic.

Across the road, another stile beckons to the entrance of Sonoma County's "lost coast," so named because high cliffs and high tides keep this seven miles of beach remote from most hikers.

Should you continue, a mile of walking across boulder-strewn beaches brings you to Fort Ross Reef, which discourages further progress.

Salt Point State Park, Kruse Rhododendron State Reserve

Kruse Rhododendron Loop Trail, Salt Point Trail

Terrain: Coastal bluffs, second-growth redwood forest
Highlights: Waterfalls spilling into coves, rhododendron
  blossoms
Distance: Kruse Rhododendron Loop is 2¼ miles, Salt Point
  coastal trail is 2 to 6 miles round trip
Degree of difficulty: Moderate

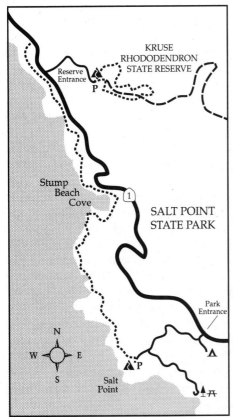

The rhododendron's success depends on its struggle for light in a dark world, dominated by the tanbark oak, Douglas fir, and redwood. A severe forest fire that scorched the slopes in this area was responsible for the sudden emergence of the rhododendrons here. Now, as the tall tree forest regenerates, it restricts the light available to rhododendrons, thereby diminishing their grand display.

The Kruse family established a ranch here in 1880, raised sheep, and extensively logged the coastal slopes. Edward Kruse donated the land to the state in 1933, in memory of his father, who was the founder of San Francisco's German Bank—later, First Western Bank.

The 317-acre Kruse Rhododendron Reserve adjoins 6,000-acre Salt Point State Park. Sheer, sandstone cliffs, and sandy coves highlight the state park's seven miles of coastline.

Directions to trailhead: Salt Point State Park is located about 90 miles north of San Francisco (or 18 miles north of Jenner, seven miles north of Fort Ross) on Highway 1. To reach Kruse Rhododendron State Reserve, turn east off Highway 1 onto steep Kruse Ranch Road and travel a half-mile to the trailhead. To hike Salt Point: From Highway 1, turn west into the state park's campground and follow signs to Marine Terrace Parking Area.

The walk *(Kruse Rhododendron State Reserve):* Since this is a loop trail, you may begin from the leg north of Kruse Ranch Road or from the leg to the south. The trail crosses two gulches—Chinese and Phillips. You'll explore the mouths of these gulches if you take the Salt Point Trail through the state park.

The walk *(Salt Point):* Hike north atop the dramatic bluffs of Salt Point. In a quarter-mile, you'll cross Warren Creek. At the creek mouth is a little cove, one of about a dozen you'll encounter along the state park's coastline.

The path reaches the bluffs above Stump Beach Cove, which is not, as you might suspect, named for the remains of redwoods logged nearby; the name honors Sheriff Stump, one-time law-and-order man for Salt Point township.

An old farm road leads down to the cove, where there's a picnic area. You can sit a while and watch the terns, cormorants, gulls, osprey and brown pelicans.

If you return to the trailhead from Stump Beach Cove, you'll have hiked a total of 2½ miles. To continue this hike, you follow the trail up the north slope above Stump Creek. Rejoining the bluffs, you dip in and out of Phillips Gulch, Chinese Gulch, and other little gullies.

The path is not particularly distinct, and you must devise your own route in places along the edge of the grassy headlands. Photographers will marvel at the spectacle of surf meeting rock. Waterfalls spill into picturesque coves at the mouths of Chinese and Phillips Gulches.

The trail becomes easier to follow, and alternates between open meadowland and wind-sculpted stands of Bishop pine and Douglas fir.

A good destination is the picnic area south of Fisk Mill Cove, which is about three miles from the trailhead. Or you can even continue another two miles north to Horseshoe Cove at the northern end of the state park.

Van Damme State Park

Fern Canyon Trail

> **Terrain:** Lush fern canyon
> **Highlights:** Ferns, Pygmy Forest
> **Distance:** Van Damme State Park Campground to Fern Canyon
> is 5 miles round trip with 200-foot gain; to Pygmy Forest is 7
> miles round trip with 400-foot gain
> **Degree of difficulty:** Moderate

Five-finger and bird's-foot, lady and licorice, stamp, sword and deer—these are some of the colorful names of the ferns growing in well-named Fern Canyon. This lush canyon, the heart of Van Damme State Park, is also rich with young redwoods, red alder, big leaf maple and Douglas fir, as well as a tangled understory of wild cucumber and berry bushes.

Little River meanders through Fern Canyon, as does a lovely trail which crosses the river nine times. Fern Canyon Trail, paved along its lower stretch, follows the route of an old logging skid road. For three decades, beginning in 1864, ox teams hauled timber through the canyon.

A lumber mill once stood at the mouth of Little River. During the late nineteenth century, schooners used for shipping logs and lumber were constructed at a boatworks located at the river mouth. Lumberman/San Francisco businessman Charles F. Van Damme was

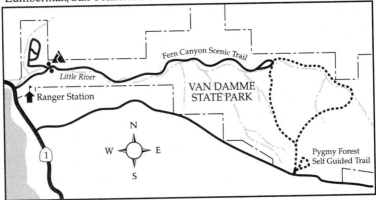

born in the hamlet of Little River. He purchased land on the site of the former sawmill and bequeathed the river mouth and canyon to the state park system.

In Van Damme State Park, another very special environment awaits the walker: the Pygmy Forest. A nutrient-poor, highly acidic topsoil, combined with a dense hardpan located beneath the surface that resists root penetration, has severely restricted the growth of trees in certain areas of the coastal shelf between Salt Point and Fort Bragg.

The Pygmy Forest in Van Damme State Park is truly Lilliputian. Sixty-year-old cypress trees are but a few feet tall and measure a half-inch in diameter. The walker has a choice of two trails that lead to the Pygmy Forest. One route loops 3½ miles through Fern Canyon; another, the one-mile long Logging Road Trail leads more directly to the forest. A self-guided nature trail, built upon an elevated wooden walkway, loops through the Pygmy Forest.

Directions to trailhead: Van Damme State Park is located off Highway 1, three miles south of Mendocino. Turn inland on the main park road, and follow it through the canyon to a parking area at the beginning of signed Fern Canyon Trail.

The walk: The first and second crossings of Little River give you an inkling of what lies ahead. During summer, the river is easily forded; in winter, expect to get your feet wet.

The wide path brings you close to elderberry, salmonberry and a multitude of ferns. Two miles and eight river crossings later, you'll pass the state park's environmental campsites—reserved for walkers and bicyclists.

The road splits into a short loop and the two forks rejoin at the end of the paved road. Both trails lead to Pygmy Forest. To the left, the longer loop continues east through Fern Canyon before joining the old logging road and traveling to Pygmy Forest. For a shorter walk to Pygmy Forest, cross Little River and follow the Old Logging Road Trail a mile.

Mendocino Headlands State Park
Mendocino Headlands Trail

> **Terrain:** Majestic bluffs
> **Highlights:** Ideal town made for walkers, plus blufftop views of sea caves, tidepools, beaches.
> **Distance:** 2 to 5 miles round trip
> **Degree of difficulty:** Easy

Few coastal locales are as photographed as the town of Mendocino and its bold headlands. The town itself, which lies just north of the mouth of Big River, resembles a New England village, no doubt by design of its Yankee founders. Now protected by a state park, the headlands are laced with paths that offer postcard views of wave tunnels and tidepools, beaches and blowholes. Today Mendocino may be familiar to fans of the television series "Murder She Wrote"; it stands in for Cabot Cove, sleuth Jessica Fletcher's hometown.

Like the town, the headlands have a storied past. Booldam—"Big River" is what the Pomo called their village here. Wave tunnels, one

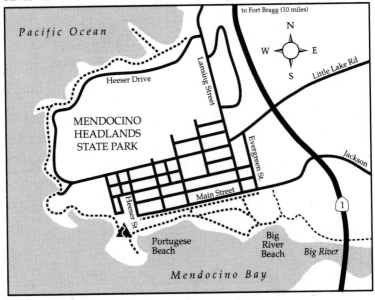

measuring more than 700 feet long, penetrate the Mendocino Bay bluffs. By some fanciful accounts they've been the death of ships—particularly during the days of sail, when a number of vessels were reportedly blown into the tunnels and never seen again.

Despite rough surf conditions, one of California's first "doghole ports" was located here. A railway, built in 1853, carried redwood lumber from a nearby mill to a chute located on the point. It was a tricky loading operation, to say the least.

Once the most cosmopolitan of little ports, Mendocino declined in economic and cultural importance as the logging industry came to a halt in the 1930s. The town revived in the 1950s when a number of San Francisco artists established the Mendocino Art Center. What was bohemian and cheap in the 1950s and 1960s is now upscale and pricey, but the town's Maine village look has been preserved.

Mendocino's citizenry not only preserved the town in a historical district, but succeeded in placing a portion of the majestic bluffs, threatened with a modern subdivision, under the protection of Mendocino Headlands State Park in 1972.

Mendocino is a great town for the walker to explore. Grand Victorian houses and simple New England saltboxes mingle with a downtown that includes several fascinating nineteenth-century buildings. Among the architectural gems are the Masonic Hall, built in 1866 and topped with a redwood sculpture of Father Time, the Mendocino Hotel with its antique decor and the Presbyterian Church, constructed in 1867 and now a state historical landmark.

Be sure to check out the historic Ford House perched above the bay on the south side of town. Inside the house are exhibits interpreting the human and natural history of the Mendocino coast.

A summer or weekend walk onto the headlands allows you to escape the crowds, while a winter walk, perhaps when a storm is brewing offshore, is a special experience indeed. From the end of town you can walk down-coast to Big River or up-coast to a blowhole.

Directions to trailhead: From "downtown" Mendocino, follow Main Street up-coast past the Mendocino Hotel to Heeser Street. Park wherever you can find a space.

The walk: The unsigned trail leads southwest through a fence and soon forks; the route down-coast to Big River Beach is described first.

Heading east, the trail delivers you to some blufftop benches and a coastal accessway leading down to Portuguese Beach, known as Point

Beach by locals. Wooden steps cross a gully and the trail soon forks again—offering both a route along the edge of the bluffs and another heading on a straighter course toward Big River.

Notice the cross-ties, remains of the old oxen-powered railway that hauled lumber to the bluff edge, where it was then sent by chute to waiting ships.

Wildflowers seasonally brightening the grassy headlands include lupine and Mendocino Coast paintbrush. More noticeable are non-native species gone wild—nasturtiums, calla lilies, hedge rose—as well as Scotch broom, an unwelcome pest that thrives along the north coast.

After meandering past some Bishop pine, the path descends moderately to steeply to the beach where Big River empties into Mendocino Bay. The quarter-mile long beach is also part of Mendocino Headlands State Park. Upriver is a marsh, Big River Estuary, a winter stopover for ducks and geese. Salmon and steelhead spawn upriver.

Return the same way or detour through town to admire some of Mendocino's historical buildings.

To the Blowhole and beyond: Bearing right at the first trail junction from the trailhead, leads to the blowhole. While no aqueous Vesuvius, the blowhole can at times be a frothy and picturesque cauldron.

The path continues north along the edge of the headlands for another mile. You'll pass a plaque dedicated by the sister cities of Mendocino and Miasa, Japan "to the peaceful pursuit of the peoples of the Pacific and to the protection of the environment that all living things therein may exist in perpetual harmony."

Russian Gulch State Park
Russian Gulch Trail

> **Terrain:** Dramatic shoreline, lush coastal canyon
> **Highlights:** A waterfall spills into the gulch; waves fill "The Punchbowl"
> **Distance:** Campground to Falls is 6½ miles round trip with 200-foot elevation gain
> **Degree of difficulty:** Easy to moderate

Russian Gulch is a lush coastal range canyon filled with second-generation redwoods, Douglas fir, and California laurel. Beneath the tall trees grows an understory of ferns, berry bushes, azaleas and rhododendrons.

By some accounts, gulch and state park take their name from the Fort Ross-based Russian fur hunters who trapped in this area. Historians speculate that the gulch was one of the places where the hunters cached otter skins.

Russian Gulch offers walkers the chance to experience several distinct biotic communities. The mouth of the canyon is framed, as if in a photograph, by a handsome Coast Highway bridge. A beach offers swimming and sunning; however, the cold waters here are more popular as an entry point for wetsuit-clad divers. Urchins and abalone populate the rich subtidal area.

Above the river mouth, the park headlands offer great north and south coastal views, as well as glimpses of Russian Gulch itself. Out on the headlands, seasonally bedecked with Douglas iris and poppies, is The Punch-

bowl, a collapsed wave tunnel that forms a 100-foot-diameter hole. This blowhole, while too large to blow very much, is nevertheless an inspiring sight when the surf wells up inside the hole.

The trail system through Russian Gulch State Park offers a number of alternatives. You may take a direct or a more roundabout route through the canyon and either a longer or shorter route to the waterfall. It's possible to combine all trail options into a delightful nine-mile tour of the park.

Directions to trailhead: Russian Gulch State Park is located just off Highway 1, two miles north of the town of Mendocino. Fern Canyon Trail, a continuation of the park road closed to vehicle traffic, departs from the east end of the campground.

The walk: The paved trail, suitable for bicycles, is nearly flat for the first mile as it winds along with the stream. Along the bottom of the gulch grow alder, willow and big leaf maple. On higher canyon slopes are western hemlock, Douglas fir and second-growth redwoods. The forest was even thicker before early loggers cleared the canyon.

One and a half miles of travel brings you to a small picnic area, where you'll find a couple of picnic tables beneath the redwoods. A short distance past the picnic area, you'll spot signed North Trail, which leads northwest back to the park campground; consider this path as an alternate return route. Hikers may continue about 100 feet past this trail junction to the signed beginning of the waterfall loop.

Russian Gulch forks here and so does the trail. Take the left, shorter, route and climb by trail, wooden steps and footbridges ¾ mile to the falls. The falls cascade 36 feet into a small grotto.

If you continue on the loop trail (this adds 2.3 more miles to your walk), you'll climb stone steps above the falls, then switchback away from the creek through tan oak forest. After topping a ridge, the trail drops into the south fork of Russian Gulch and returns you to the lower trail junction and the return route to the trailhead.

Jug Handle State Reserve
Jug Handle Ecological Staircase Trail

> **Terrain:** Coastal terraces—an "Ecological Staircase"
> **Highlights:** Eco-journey back in time, pygmy forest
> **Distance:** 5 miles round trip with 300-foot elevation gain
> **Degree of difficulty:** Easy to moderate

The watershed of Jug Handle Creek holds a rare natural phenomenon—an "ecological staircase"—that attracts scientists and nature lovers from all over the world. The staircase is composed of five terraces, each about 100,000 years older and about 100 feet higher than the one below it.

The terraces were sculpted into the sandstone cliffs by wave action. As a result of tectonic action—our North American plate crunching against the offshore Pacific plate—the terraces were uplifted. In fact, today the terraces continue their inexorable uplift at the rate of an inch per century. Wave action is ever-so-slowly forming a sixth terrace at the mouth of Jug Handle Creek.

Terraces, and the forces forming them, are by no means unique to Jug Handle Creek; however, in most California coastal locales, the terraces are eroded and indistinct. Only at the state reserve are the evolutionary sequences so distinguishable, and so well preserved.

Your walk up the staircase will be greatly aided if you pick up (at

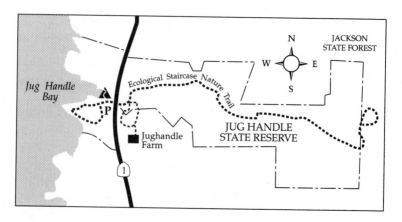

small cost) an interpretive pamphlet from the vending machine at the park office.

Directions to trailhead: Five miles south of Fort Bragg, and just south of Jug Handle Creek, turn west off Highway 1 into the Jug Handle Reserve parking area.

The walk: Head west on the signed trail out onto the grassy blufftops. The trail loops toward the edge of the bluffs, offers a view of Jug Handle Cove, then returns east to dip under the highway bridge.

The first terrace supports native grassland. and wind-sculpted Sitka spruce. Second-growth redwood trees are the most noticeable feature of the second terrace. The upper terraces are the site of the Mendocino Pygmy Forest. Cypress and pine are but five to ten feet tall, and shrubs such as rhododendron, manzanita, and huckleberry are also dwarf-sized.

Adding to the somewhat bizarre natural world of upper Jug Handle Creek, are a couple of sphagnum bogs—layers of peat standing in water—which support mosses and an insectivorous plant called sundew that uses its sticky leaves to capture its victims.

When you reach the end of Jug Handle Ecological Staircase Trail, you can rejoin Gibney Fire Road for a quick return to the main trail leading back to the parking area.

MacKerricher State Park
Ten Mile Beach Trail

Terrain: Sand dunes, wetlands, coastal bluffs
Highlights: One of coast's most extensive dune systems
Distance: From Laguna Point to Ten Mile River is 10 miles round trip; shorter hikes possible
Degree of difficulty: Moderate

Ten Mile Dunes and Inglenook Fen, Laguna Point and Cleone Lake. These are some of the intriguing names on an intriguing land—

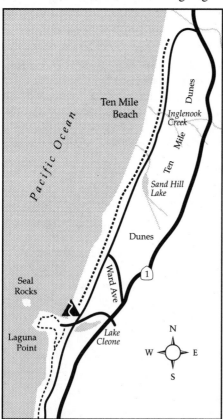

MacKerricher State Park. Extending from just north of the Fort Bragg city limits to Ten Mile River, this park offers the walker a chance to explore headlands and wetlands, sand dunes, forest and meadowland.

The vast redwood forests of the coast range in the areas bordering Ten Mile River were heavily logged. An early coast railroad connected the mills of the town of Cleone with a landing at Laguna Point. Lumber was loaded onto flatcars which rolled by gravity to waiting schooners; horses hauled the cars back to the mill. At the point, anchor pins and other signs of the old landing can be seen.

A more obvious reminder of this coast's logging history is the old haul road that crosses the park. In 1949, the road replaced a railway, which for three decades carried timber from the Ten Mile River Area to the Union Lumber Company in Fort Bragg. A 1982, winter storm washed out sections of the road, closing the five-mile stretch from Cleone Lake to Ten Mile River. The road is closed to motor vehicles and is a superb path for walkers.

The old haul road travels the length of Ten Mile Beach to the mouth of Ten Mile River, so named because it's ten miles north of Noyo River. The beach is backed by one of the California coast's longest dune systems.

Directions to trailhead: From Highway 1, three miles north of Fort Bragg, turn west into the main entrance of MacKerricher State Park. Follow the signs to the Laguna Point Parking area.

The walk: Immediately west of the underpass, a short gravel road leads up to the paved ex-logging road. Walk north on the high embankment. You'll soon observe Cleone Lake, a tidal lagoon cut off from the sea by the road. Many shore and water birds visit the lake.

Soon you'll pass some squat shore pines—a coastal form of the much better-known lodgepole pine. You'll also walk past a side trail leading to the state park campground. A quarter-mile later another side trail beckons; this one leads over the dunes. About 1½ mile north of the trailhead, you'll encounter a washed-out section of road and, a few hundred yards farther, another bad section.

Two miles north of Laguna Point, tucked in the dunes, lies Inglenook Fen; it's a sensitive area and not open to the public. A botanist studying this unique ecosystem gave it the Old English word fen—meaning something like a bog or marsh. Sandhill Lake and the marshy area around it support many rare plants such as marsh pennywort and rein orchid, as well as many endemic varieties of insects.

After walking three miles, you'll pass a couple of small creeks and begin crossing the widest part of the sand dunes, which at this point are about a mile wide and measure more than one hundred feet high. Four and a half miles from the trailhead, the road turns inland with Ten Mile River. You can continue walking north a short distance if you wish down to the mouth of Ten Mile River.

The main route travels inland above the east bank of Ten Mile River. A side trail leads southeast to a parking area beside Highway 1, while the paved road continues under the highway bridge.

Sinkyone Wilderness State Park
Lost Coast Trail

Terrain: Steep coastal mountains
Highlights: Some of wildest shore in California
Distance: To Jones Beach is 2 miles round trip; to Whale Gulch
is 4½ miles round trip
Degree of difficulty: Easy
Precautions: State park road may be impassable in winter

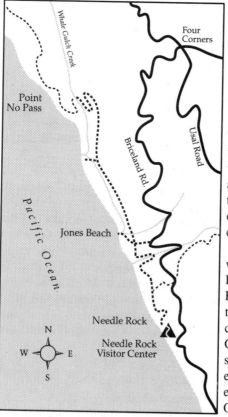

The land we now call Sinkyone Wilderness State Park, located about 225 miles north of San Francisco, has long been recognized as something special. During the late 1960s, the great Catholic theologian, Thomas Merton, felt that the Needle Rock area would be an ideal place for a life of prayer and contemplation, and talked of establishing a monastic community there.

The state park, along with the U.S. Bureau of Land Management's King Range National Conservation Area to the north, comprise California's Lost Coast, 60 miles of wild shoreline located in northern Mendocino and southern Humboldt counties. One reason the coast is "lost" is because no highways cross it. So rugged is this country, highway engineers were forced to route Highway 1 many miles inland from this coast—and the region has remained sparsely settled and unspoiled. It's magnificent vistas and varied terrain—dense forests, prairies, coastal bluffs, beaches—reward the hardy explorer.

Usal Road meanders along the northern boundary of Sinkyone Wilderness State Park. The road, lined with heavy brush and trees, has changed little since Jack London and his wife drove it in a horse-drawn carriage on a trip from San Francisco to Eureka in 1911.

The sea is an overwhelming presence here, and its rhythmic sounds provide a thunderous background for a walk along land's end. The sky is filled with gulls and pelicans, sea lions and harbor seals gather at Little Jackass Cove, and the California gray whale migration passes near shore during winter and early spring.

A herd of Roosevelt elk roams the park. These magnificent creatures were once common here and in the King Range, but were exterminated in the last century. The Roosevelt elk that lucky visitors see today are "extras" relocated from Prairie Creek State Park.

Lost Coast Trail travels the length of Sinkyone State Park north through King Range National Conservation Area. The sixty-mile trail would make an ideal week-long backpacking adventure.

The portion of the Lost Coast Trail detailed here explores the northernmost, and most easily accessible, portion of the state park. It's a relatively easy introduction to a challenging trail.

Directions to trailhead: From Highway 101, take either the Garberville or Redway exit and proceed to "downtown" Redway, located 3 miles north of Garberville on Business 101. Turn west on Briceland Road.

After 12 miles of travel, fork left to Whitethorn. A mile or so past the hamlet of Whitethorn (don't blink or you'll miss it), the pavement ends, and you continue on a potholed dirt/mud road for 3½ miles to a junction called Four Corners. Leftward is Usal Road, rightward is a road climbing into the King Range National Conservation Area. Proceed straight ahead 3½ miles to the Sinkyone Wilderness State Park Visitor Center.

The park road is steep, winding, and only one lane wide.

Maps and information are available at the visitor center.

The walk: Begin at the Needle Rock Visitor Center. During the 1920s, a small settlement and shipping point were established at Needle Rock. The Calvin Cooper Stewart family were the main residents of Needle Rock, and today their ranch house serves as the park visitor center.

Walk up the park road toward the old barn. Notice a trail leading to the bluff edge, then down to the beach. Famed Needle Rock is a short distance up the dark sand beach.

Join Lost Coast Trail, which leads behind the barn and dips in and out of a gully. You'll pass Barn Camp, one of the state park's primitive, or walk-in, campsites. A quarter-mile of travel brings you to Streamside Camp, another of the park's primitive, but superb, camps.

You'll soon reach a junction with a trail climbing to the east. This is Low Gap Trail, which ascends the coastal bluffs and crosses the park road. The trail plunges into the forest, travels along Low Gap Creek, and, after a stiff climb, reaches Usal Road.

Lost Coast Trail, your route, continues along the lovely bluffs to Low Gap Creek, heads inland briefly, then crosses a bridge over the creek. The path heads toward a stand of eucalyptus, which shelters the Jones Beach campsites.

The trail forks. The left fork leads a quarter-mile to Jones Beach. If it's low tide, you can walk back to the trailhead via the beach.

Lost Coast Trail proceeds with the right fork and soon descends into a canyon. You cross two creeks, which drain an area that can be very marshy during the rainy season. You walk near the edge of cattail-lined pond, climb to higher ground, and pass a second pond.

Soon you are treated to a bird's-eye-view of Whale Gulch. A rough, unmaintained path descends to the mouth of Whale Gulch, where there's a small lagoon and piles of driftwood logs. A recently constructed section of the Lost Coast Trail travels inland along the south wall of Whale Gulch. Eventually, this trail crosses the gulch, and heads up Chemise Mountain to join the trail system in King Range National Conservation Area.

After sitting on a driftwood log for a while and contemplating the Lost Coast, return to the trailhead the way you came.

Foot notes: The southern end of the Lost Coast Trail (five miles round trip) from Usal Beach to Anderson Gulch offers some grand coastal vistas. Another favorite stretch of Lost Coast Trail is the short hike from Orchard Creek Camp to Bear Harbor; the four-mile round trip climb to the redwoods of Joseph Smeaton Chase Grove and the nine-mile round trip journey to Jackass Creek and Wheeler Camp are also wonderful adventures on the Lost Coast.

Patrick's Point State Park

Rim Trail

> **Terrain:** Dramatic, spruce- and fir-forested headland perched
> above the Pacific
> **Highlights:** Grand blufftop views; Agate Beach, famous for its
> agates and wave-sculpted driftwood
> **Distance:** From Palmer's Point to Agate Beach Campground is
> 4 miles round trip
> **Degree of difficulty:** Easy
> **Precautions:** Avoid walking too close to the edge of the eroded,
> hazardous bluffs

Though Patrick's Point State Park is positioned in the heart of the
redwoods, other trees—Sitka spruce, Douglas fir, and red alder—predominate on the park's rocky promontories. The state park takes its
name from Patrick Beegan, who homesteaded this headland in 1851.

For hundreds of years the Yurok spent their summers in the Abalone Point area of the headlands. The Yurok gathered shellfish and

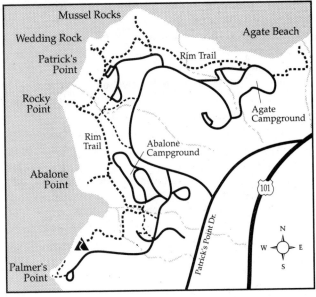

hunted sea lions. Game and a multitude of berries were plentiful in the surrounding forest. The area now called Patrick's Point also had some spiritual significance to the native people. According to the Yurok, Sumig, spirit of the porpoises, retired to Patrick's Point when humans began populating the world.

Rim Trail follows an old Indian pathway over the park's bluffs. Spur trails lead to rocky points that jut into the Pacific and offer views of Trinidad Head to the south and Big Lagoon to the north.

Directions to trailhead: Patrick's Point State Park is located thirty miles north of Eureka and five miles north of Trinidad. Exit Highway 101 on Patrick's Point Drive and follow this road to the park. Once past the park entrance station, follow the signs to Palmer Point.

The walk: The trail plunges into a lush community of ferns. Abalone Point is the first of a half-dozen spur trails that lead from Rim Trail to Rocky Point, Patrick's Point, Wedding Rock, Mussel Rocks, and Agate Beach. Take any or all of them. (These side trails can be confused with Rim Trail; generally speaking, the spurs are much more steep than Rim Trail, which contours along without much elevation change.)

From Patrick's Point and the other promontories, admire the precipitous cliffs and rock-walled inlets. Gaze offshore at the sea stacks, a line of soldiers battered by the surging sea. Seals and sea lions haul out on the offshore rocks, which also double as rookeries for gulls, cormorants and pigeon guillemots.

Rim Trail meanders through a tapestry of trillium and moss, rhododendron and azalea. Rim Trail ends at the north loop of the Agate Beach Campground road.

Hikers wishing to explore Agate Beach should continue a short distance along the road to the signed trailhead for Agate Beach Trail. This short, steep trail switchbacks down to the beach.

In marked contrast to the park's rocky shore that you observed from Rim Trail, Agate Beach is a wide swath of dark sand stretching north to the state parks at Big Lagoon.

Beachcombers prospect for agates in the gravel bars and right at the surf line. The agates found here are a nearly transparent variety of quartz, polished by sand and the restless sea. Jade, jaspar, and other semiprecious stones are sometimes found here. One more noteworthy sight is the huge quantity and quality of the sea-sculpted driftwood on this beach.

Humboldt Lagoons State Park

Big Lagoon Beach Trail

> **Terrain:** Long, sandy, barrier beach
> **Highlights:** Wild, wilderness-like beach, Sitka spruce forests, great bird-watching
> **Distance:** Along sand spit is 6 miles round trip; to Big Lagoon County Park is 8½ miles round trip; to Patrick's Point State Park is 10 miles round trip.
> **Degree of difficulty:** Moderate

Big, Big Lagoon is 3½ miles long, walled off from the power of the Pacific by a 600-foot-wide strip of sand. The lagoon's marshy habitat is an important rest stop for migratory birds on the Pacific flyway.

Long, sandy Big Lagoon Beach, along with Dry Lagoon and portions of Stone Lagoon, comprise Humboldt Lagoons State Park. The park appeals to hikers and fishermen, who enjoy the lonely beauty of the sand spits and wetlands.

The park is much more than marshlands. Sitka spruce thrive on the

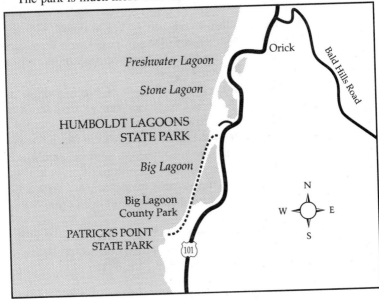

north and southwest shores, and even some wind-blown old-growth redwoods cling tenaciously to life on the east shore.

Gold-seekers swarmed into the area in 1849 when discoveries were made along the Klamath and Trinity rivers. Prospectors attempted to mine the sand spits along Big and Stone lagoons, but managed to extract very little gold despite considerable effort.

Dry Lagoon State Park was established in 1931. The park expanded over the next half-century to more than 1,000 acres, added a couple more lagoons, and in 1981 its name was changed to Humboldt Lagoons State Park. Recent land acquisitions by the Save-the-Redwoods League have further enlarged the park.

Walking Big Lagoon Beach means paying attention to the tides. Several times each winter, Big Lagoon's barrier beach is breached by waves; the beach at these times is impassable. During other seasons, best hiking is at lower tides. Consult a local tide table.

Directions to trailhead: From Highway 101, some 7 miles south of Orick, turn west onto the signed state park road and travel a mile to road's end at a beach parking lot.

The walk: From the parking lot, follow the beach south. Atop the nearby wooded bluffs are some excellent environmental campsites. About a half-mile along, the mixed black-and-white sand beach broadens. You'll reach the north end of Big Lagoon about ¾-mile from the trailhead.

Now you'll walk the crest of the barrier beach, dotted with sea rocket, dune tansy and sand verbena. Two miles out, you'll notice a couple of low spots in the sandspit. During very high tides, waves crest the sandspit, spilling into the lagoon.

Three miles along, you'll get a good view of Big Lagoon at its widest—more than a mile across. On the east side grows a forest of Sitka spruce and some wind-sculpted redwoods.

Rest awhile on the driftwood logs scattered on the beach. Down-coast is a nice view of Agate Beach and the dramatic, wooded bluffs of Patrick's Point State Park; it's another two-mile walk.

Return the same way, or, if you want to extend your walk a bit more, curve around the lagoon to the south shore where you'll find Big Lagoon County Park.

Foot notes: Dry Lagoon offers a mile-long beach hike north of the lagoon, plus a one-mile loop trail around the environmental campsites. You can take a two to three-mile hike along the barrier beach fronting Stone Lagoon.

Walking State Historic Parks

Old Town San Diego State Historic Park, built around a central plaza, offers a chance to stroll through California history, San Diego-style, during the Mexican and early American periods. Walkers (with the help of park pamphlet) can view La Casa de Bandini, once a hotel, now a restaurant, and La Casa de Estudillo, a mansion with a lovely courtyard. Other historic buildings include a schoolhouse, a newspaper office and a stable with a carriage collection.

El Presidio de Santa Barbara State Historic Park, located in downtown Santa Barbara, preserves a bit of the old military fortress built by the Spanish in 1782 to guard the central coast. A walking tour (pamphlet available) tours El Cuartel, the old guardhouse, and Santa Barbara's oldest adobe, and the recently restored Presidio Chapel. Several adobes and historical buildings nearby, as well as the famed Santa Barbara Courthouse, entice the walker to further exploration.

Old Sacramento State Historic Park offers a wonderful, 20-stop-or-so self-guided walking tour, which begins at the visitor center (pick up a map here) on Front Street. Stroll along the balcony-covered boardwalk and relive the early days of California's state capital. Don't miss the California State Railroad Museum, the largest interpreted railroad museum in North America.

San Juan Bautista State Historic Park preserves the original town plaza, the old Plaza Hotel, and the Mexican-era home of leading citizen José Castro. Visit the carriage and coach collection on display at the old stable. Further beckoning the walker is Mission San Juan Bautista with its small history museum located on the north side of the plaza, and the slow-paced modern town with shops and restaurants.

Hearst Castle (Hearst San Simeon State Historical Monument) offers four fabulous walking tours of the palatial estate of the late William Randolph Hearst. More than 1 million visitors a year arrive annually to see the collection of world treasures on display in the 130-room palace. Tour No. 1, recommended for first-time visitors, includes the major rooms of the mansion, swimming pools and gardens.

Monterey State Historic Park beckons California history and enthusiasts, architects and city strollers to spend a day walking

Monterey's "Path of History." Highlights include the Old Custom House, oldest government building on the Pacific Coast, the Robert Louis Stevenson House, Pacific House and many more old adobes. Some guided tours, as well as self-guiding brochures are available.

Sonoma State Historic Park preserves Mission San Francisco Solano, last of the California missions, as well as the Sonoma Barracks which housed Mexican Army troops under the command of General Vallejo. The general's first home, La Casa Grande, is also part of the park. A self-guided walking tour (pick up a map at the park visitor center) winds through the streets surrounding a central plaza and visits more than a dozen buildings (built between 1823 and 1855). There is an excellent museum, plus plenty of shops and restaurants.

Bodie State Historic Park preserves a one-time gold rush boom-town of the 1870s-80s in a state of "arrested decay." A park brochure details a lengthy 69-stop walking tour of Bodie, which has a remarkably diverse collection of buildings in various states of decrepitude. The old Miners' Union Hall is today the park museum for Bodie, considered by many to be the very best ghost town in the West.

Columbia State Historic Park offers an excellent self-guided walk through one of the best preserved towns of the Mother Lode. (It's well preserved because after a couple fires, the business district was rebuilt with fire-proof brick.) Allow an hour and a half (plus some time to dawdle) to stroll Columbia, today a nice blend of historical museums and displays, as well as restaurants, hotels and shops.

Shasta State Historic Park preserves the Shasta County Courthouse and Litsch General Store, now both museums. A self-guided walk (brochure available from the park visitor center) takes in the historic business district, and the ruins of "Brick Row" which, during the prosperous 1850s was once one of California's largest communities. Footpaths lead to a Catholic Cemetery and to various ruins scattered about the park.

Contacting California State Parks

Help From Sacramento

You may purchase a copy of a map that locates all state parks, entitled "Official Guide to California State Parks" by sending $2 to: Publications Section, Department of Parks and Recreation, P.O. Box 942896, Sacramento, CA 94296. For more information about state park publications, call (916) 653-4000.

District Offices

Often, individual state parks are hard to reach by telephone. Field staff are usually out in the field—and thus keep irregular office hours.

One way to go for information is to contact district offices, each of which usually administers several parks in a particular area. Sometimes the first person who answers the phone is quite helpful, sometimes not, but if you're persistent you'll usually get an answer to your questions.

Northern Division

American River District
c/o Folsom Lake SRA
7806 Folsom-Auburn Road
Folsom, CA 95630
(916) 988-0205

Bay Area District
95 Kelly Avenue
Half Moon Bay, CA 94019
(415) 726-0500

Calaveras District
c/o Columbia SHP
P.O. Box 151
Columbia, CA 95310
(209) 532-0150

Four Rivers District
31426 West Highway 152
Santa Nella, CA 95322
(209) 826-1196

Gold Rush District
101 J Street
Sacramento, CA 95814
(916) 445-7373

Marin District
1455-A East Francisco Blvd.
San Rafael, CA 94901
(415) 456-1286

North Coast Redwoods District
600-A West Clark Street
Eureka, CA 95501
(415) 456-1286

Northern Buttes District
400 Glen Drive
Oroville, CA 95966
(916) 538-2200

Russian River District
P.O. Box 123
Duncan Mills, CA 95430
(707) 865-2391

Sierra District
P.O. Box Drawer D
Tahoma, CA 96142
(916) 525-7232

Silverado District
20 East Spain Street
Sonoma, CA 95476
(707) 938-1519

Southern Division
Angeles District
1925 Las Virgenes
Calabasas, CA 91302
(818) 880-0350

Channel Coast District
24 East Main Street
Ventura, CA 93001
(805) 654-4611

Colorado Desert District
200 Palm Canyon Drive
Borrego Springs, CA 92004
(619) 767-5311

Los Lagos District
17801 Lake Perris Drive
Perris, CA 92571
(909) 657-0676

Monterey District
2211 Garden Road
Monterey, CA 93940
(408) 649-2836

Orange Coast District
3030 Avenida del Presidente
San Clemente, CA 92672
(714) 492-0802

San Diego Coast District
3990 Old Town Avenue, #300 C
San Diego, CA 92110
(619) 237-6766

San Joaquin District
P.O. Box 205
5290 Millerton Road
Friant, CA 93626
(209) 822-2332

San Luis Obispo Coast District
3220 S. Higuera Street #311
San Luis Obispo, CA 93401
(805) 549-3312

San Simeon District
Hearst San Simeon SHM
750 Hearst Castle Road
San Simeon, CA 93452
(805) 927-2020

Santa Cruz District
101 Madeline Drive
Aptos, CA 95003
(408) 688-3241

The Parks

Anderson Marsh State Historic Park
5300 Soda Bay Road
Kelseyville, CA 95451
(707) 994-0688, 279-2267

Andrew Molera State Park
Big Sur Station #1
Big Sur, CA 93920
(408) 624-7195

Angel Island State Park
P.O. Box 318
Tiburon, CA 94920
(415) 435-1915

Annadel State Park
6201 Channel Drive
Santa Rosa, CA 95409
(707) 539-3911

Año Nuevo State Reserve
Pescadero, CA 94060
(415) 879-2025

Antelope Valley Poppy Reserve
(805) 942-0662

Anza-Borrego Desert State Park
Box 299
Borrego Springs, CA 92004
(619) 767-4205 (visitor center)
(619) 764-4684 (recording)

Auburn State Recreation Area
P.O. Box 3266
Auburn, CA 95604
(916) 885-4527

Austin Creek State Recreation
    Area/Armstrong Redwoods SR
17000 Armstrong Woods Road
Guerneville, CA 95446
(707) 869-2015

Benbow Lake State Recreation Area
(707) 946-2311

Benicia State Recreation Area
(707) 648-1911

Big Basin Redwoods State Park
21600 Big Basin Way
Boulder Creek, CA 95006
(408) 338-6132

Bodie State Historic Park
P.O. Box 515
Bridgeport, CA 93517
(619) 647-6445

Border Field State Park
c/o San Diego Coast District
3990 Old Town Ave. #300-C
San Diego, CA 92110
(619) 428-3034

Bothe-Napa Valley State Park
3801 St. Helena Hwy. N.
Calistoga, CA 94515
(707) 942-5370

Burton Creek State Park
c/o Sierra District
(916) 525-7232

Butano State Park
1500 Cloverdale Road Box 3
Pescadero, CA 94060
(415) 874-0173

Calaveras Big Trees State Park
P.O. Box 120
Arnold, CA 95223
(209) 795-2334

California Citrus State Historic Park
c/o Los Lagos District
(909) 657-0676

Candlestick Point State Recreation
Area
c/o Bay Area District
(415) 557-4069

Carmel River State Beach
c/o Monterey District
(408) 667-2315

Castle Crags State Park
P.O. Box 80
Castella, CA 96017
(916) 235-2684

Castle Rock State Park
15000 Skyline Blvd.
Los Gatos, CA 95030
(408) 867-2952

Caswell Memorial State Park
28000 S. Austin Road
Ripon, CA 95366
(209) 599-3810

China Camp State Park
RR 1, Box 244
San Rafael, CA 94901
(415) 456-0766

Chino Hills State Park
1879 Jackson Street
Riverside, CA 92504
(909) 780-6222

Clear Lake State Park
5300 Soda Bay Road
Kelseyville, CA 95451
(707) 279-2267

Columbia State Historic Park
P.O. Box 151
Columbia, CA 95310
(209) 532-0150

Colusa-Sacramento River State
Recreation Area
P.O. Box 207
Colusa, CA 95932
(916) 458-4927

Crystal Cove State Park
c/o Orange Coast District
(714) 494-3539, 848-1566

Cuyamaca Rancho State Park
12551 Highway 79
Descanso, CA 91916
(619) 765-3020

D.L. Bliss /Emerald Bay State Parks
P.O. Box 266
Tahoma, CA 96142
(916) 525-7277

Del Norte Coast Redwoods State Park
P.O. Drawer J
Crescent City, CA 95531
(707) 464-9533, 445-6547

Donner Memorial State Park
12593 Donner Pass Rd.
Truckee, CA 96161
(916) 582-7892

El Capitan/Refugio State Beaches
10 Refugio Beach Road
Goleta, CA 93117
(805) 968-1711

El Presidio de Santa Barbara SHP
(805) 965-0093

Empire Mine State Historic Park
10791 E. Empire Street
Grass Valley, CA 95945
(916) 273-8522

Folsom Lake State Recreation Area
7806 Folsom-Auburn Road
Folsom, CA 95630
(916) 988-0205

Forest of Nisene Marks State Park
c/o Sunset State Beach
201 Sunset Beach Road
Watsonville, CA 95076
(408) 724-1266

Fort Ross State Historic Park
19005 Coast Highway 1
Jenner, CA 95450
(707) 847-3286

Fremont Peak State Park
P.O. Box 1110
San Juan Bautista, CA 95045
(408) 623-4255

Garrapata State Park
Big Sur Station #1
Big Sur, CA 93920
(408) 624-7195

Grizzly Creek Redwoods State Park
16949 Highway 36
Carlotta, CA 95528
(707) 777-3683

Hearst San Simeon State Historic
    Monument
P.O. Box 8
San Simeon, CA 94352
MISTIX for tour reservations
(800) 444-7275

Hendy Woods State Park
P.O. Box 440
Mendocino, CA 95466
(707) 937-5804

Henry W. Coe State Park
P.O. Box 846
Morgan Hill, CA 95038
(408) 779-2728

Henry Cowell Redwoods State Park
c/o Santa Cruz Mountains District
(408) 335-4598

Humboldt Lagoons State Park
c/o North Coast Redwoods District
(707) 488-2171

Humboldt Redwoods State Park
P.O. Box 100
Weott, CA 95571
(707) 946-2409

Jack London State Historic Park
2400 London Ranch Road
Glen Ellen, CA 95442
(707) 938-5216

Jedediah Smith Redwoods State Park
1375 Elk Valley Road
Crecent City, CA 95531
(707) 464-9533

Jug Handle State Reserve
(707) 937-5804

Julia Pfeiffer Burns State Park
Big Sur Station #1
Big Sur, CA 93920
(408) 624-7195

La Purísima Mission State Historic
    Park
2295 Purísima Road
Lompoc, CA 93436
(805) 733-3713

Lake Oroville State Recreation Area
400 Glen Drive
Oroville, CA 95966
(916) 538-2200

Lake Perris State Recreation Area
17801 Lake Perris Drive
Perris, CA 92571
(909) 657-0676

Leo Carrillo State Beach
c/o Angeles District
(818) 880-0350

MacKerricher State Park
P.O. Box 440
Mendocino, CA 95460
(707) 937-5804

Malakoff Diggins State Historic Park
23579 North Bloomfield Road
Nevada City, CA 95959
(916) 265-2740

Malibu Creek State Park
28754 Mulholland Highway
Agoura, CA 91301
(818) 880-4089

Malibu Lagoon State Beach
(818) 706-8809

Marshall Gold Discovery State
  Historic Park
P.O. Box 265
Coloma, CA 95613
(916) 622-3470

McArthur-Burney Falls State Park
Rt. 1. Box 1260
Burney, CA 96013
(916) 335-2777

McGrath State Beach
901 So. San Pedro
Ventura, CA 93001
(805) 654-4611

McNee Ranch State Park
c/o Bay Area District District
(415) 726-0500

Mendocino Headlands State Park
P.O. Box 440
Mendocino, CA 95460
(707) 937-5804

Millerton Lake State Recreation Area
P.O. Box 205
Friant, CA 93626
(209) 822-2332

Montaña de Oro State Park
c/o Morro Bay State Park
Morro Bay, CA 93442
(805) 772-7434

Monterey State Historic Park
#20 Custom House Plaza
Monterey, CA 93940
(408) 649-2836

Morro Bay State Park
Morro Bay, CA 93442
(805) 772-2560

Mount San Jacinto State Park
P.O. Box 308
Idyllwild, CA 92549
(909) 659-2607

Mt. Diablo State Park
P.O. Box 250
Diablo, CA 94528
(510) 837-2525

Mt. Tamalpais State Park
801 Panoramic Highway
Mill Valley, CA 94941
(415) 388-2070

Natural Bridges State Beach
c/o Santa Cruz Coast District
(408) 423-4609

Old Sacramento State Historic Park
(916) 445-7373

Old Town San Diego State Historic
  Park
3990 Old Town Avenue #300 C
San Diego, CA 92110
(619) 237-6766

Olompali State Historic Park
P.O. Box 1016
Novato, CA 892-3383
(415) 892-3383

Palomar Mountain State Park
c/o Cuyamaca Rancho State Park
(619) 765-0755

Patrick's Point State Park
4150 Patrick's Point Drive
Trinidad, CA 95570
(707) 677-3570

Pfeiffer Big Sur State Park
Big Sur Station #1
Big Sur, CA 993920
(408) 667-0191

Pismo State Beach
(805) 489-2684

Plumas-Eureka State Park
310 Johnsville Road
Blairsden, CA 96103
(916) 836-2380

Point Lobos State Reserve
Route 1, Box 62
Carmel, CA 93923
(408) 624-4909

Point Mugu State Park
9000 Pacific Coast Highway
Malibu, CA 90265
(805) 488-1827, 488-5223

Point Sur State Historic Park
(408) 625-4419, 667-2316

Portola State Park
Route 2, Box F
La Honda, CA 94020
(415) 948-9098

Prairie Creek Redwoods State Park
Orick, CA 95555
(707) 488-2171

Providence Mountains State
  Recreation Area
P.O. Box 1
Essex, CA 92332

Pt. Sal State Beach
c/o La Purisima Mission State
  Historic Park
(805) 733-3713

Red Rock Canyon State Park
c/o Mojave District Sector
(805) 942-0662

Richardson Grove State Park
1600 U.S. Highway 101, #8
Garberville, CA 95542
(707) 247-3318

Robert Louis Stevenson State Park
c/o Bothe-Napa Valley State Park
(707) 942-4575

Russian Gulch State Park
P.O. Box 440
Mendocino, CA 95460
(707) 937-5804

Saddleback Butte State Park
17102 E. Avenue J
Lancaster, CA 93535
(805) 942-0662

Salt Point State Park
2505 Coast Highway 1
Jenner, CA 95450
(707) 847-3221

Samuel P. Taylor State Park
P.O. Box 251
Lagunitas, CA 94938
(415) 488-9897

San Clemente State Beach
3030 Ave. Del Presidente
San Clemente, CA 92672
(714) 492-3156

San Juan Bautista State Historic Park
P.O. Box 1110
San Juan Bautista, CA 95045
(408) 623-4881

Santa Susana Mountains State Park
c/o Angeles District
(818) 880-0350

Shasta State Historic Park
P.O. Box 2430
Shasta, CA 96087
(916) 243-8194

Silverwood Lake State Recreation
   Area
14651 Cedar Circle
Hesperia, CA 92345
(619) 389-2303

Sinkyone Wilderness State Park
P.O. Box 245
Whitethorn, CA 95589
(707) 986-7711

Sonoma Coast State Beach
3095 Highway1
Bodega Bay, CA 94923
(707) 875-3483

Sonoma State Historic Park
20 E. Spain Street
Sonoma, CA 95476
(707) 938-1578

Standish-Hickey State Recreation
   Area
69350 U.S. Highway 101 #8
Leggett, CA 95585
(707) 925-6482

Sugar Pine Point State Park
P.O. Box 266
Tahoma, CA 96142
(916) 525-7982

Sugarloaf Ridge State Park
2605 Adobe Canyon Road
Kenwood, CA 95452
(707) 833-5712

Tomales Bay State Park
Inverness, CA 94937
(415) 669-1140

Topanga State Park
20829 Entrada Road
Topanga, CA 90290
(310) 455-2465

Torrey Pines State Reserve
12000 N. Torrey Pines Park Road
San Diego, CA 92008
(619) 755-2063

Turlock Lake State Recreation Area
22600 Lake Road—Star Route
La Grange, CA 95329
(209) 874-2008

Van Damme State Park
P.O. Box 440
Mendocino, CA 95466
(707) 937-5804

Washoe Meadows State Park
c/o Sierra District
(916) 525-7232

Wilder Ranch State Historic Park
c/o Santa Cruz District
101 Madeline Drive
Aptos, CA 95003
(408) 688-3241

Will Rogers State Historic Park
1501 Will Rogers State Park Road
Pacific Palisades, CA 90272
(310) 454-8212

Woodson Bridge State Recreation
   Area
25340 South Avenue
Corning, CA 96021
(916) 839-2112

Index